Understanding Religion and Popular Culture

"This volume is a particularly useful and worthwhile addition to the growing literature examining the intersection of religion and popular culture. Accessible for the beginner yet insightful for the veteran, it's a good read to boot!"

Eric Michael Mazur, Virginia Wesleyan College, USA

"As we move further into the new century, it becomes ever more important to understand how religions are changing. This book gives valuable insights into the ways that religions are today remade through popular media."

Stewart M. Hoover, University of Colorado at Boulder, USA

This introductory text provides students with a "toolbox" of approaches for analyzing religion and popular culture. It encourages readers to think critically about the ways in which popular cultural practices and products, especially those considered as forms of entertainment, are laden with religious ideas, themes, and values. The chapters feature lively and contemporary case study material and outline relevant theory and methods for analysis. Among the areas covered are religion and food, violence, music, television and videogames. Each entry is followed by a helpful summary, glossary, bibliography, discussion questions and suggestions for further reading/viewing. *Understanding Religion and Popular Culture* offers a valuable entry point into an exciting and rapidly evolving field of study.

Terry Ray Clark is Assistant Professor of Religion at Georgetown College, USA. He has published multiple articles and essays on the Bible and popular culture.

Dan W. Clanton, Jr. is Assistant Professor of Religious Studies at Doane College, USA. He has written widely on the reception history of biblical literature.

Understanding Religion and Popular Culture

Theories, Themes, Products and Practices

Edited by
Terry Ray Clark and
Dan W. Clanton, Jr.

Routledge
Taylor & Francis Group
LONDON AND NEW YORK

First published in 2012
by Routledge
2 Park Square, Milton Park, Abingdon, Oxon OX14 4RN

Simultaneously published in the USA and Canada
by Routledge
711 Third Avenue, New York, NY 10017

Routledge is an imprint of the Taylor & Francis Group, an informa business

British Library Cataloguing in Publication Data
A catalogue record for this book is available from the British Library

Library of Congress Cataloging in Publication Data
Understanding religion and popular culture / edited by Terry Ray Clark and Dan W. Clanton, Jr.
p. cm.
Includes bibliographical references.
1. Popular culture--Religious aspects. 2. Religion and culture.
I. Clark, Terry Ray. II. Clanton, Dan W.
BL65.C8U53 2012
306.6--dc23
2011045207

ISBN: 978-0-415-78104-6 (hbk)
ISBN: 978-0-415-78106-0 (pbk)
ISBN: 978-0-203-11957-0 (ebk)

Typeset in Galliard
by Taylor & Francis Books

FSC www.fsc.org
MIX
Paper from responsible sources
FSC® C004839

Printed and bound in Great Britain by
TJ International Ltd, Padstow, Cornwall

Contents

Notes on contributors

Eric Bain-Selbo is Department Head of Philosophy and Religion at Western Kentucky University and Co-Director of the WKU Institute for Citizenship and Social Responsibility. He is also Executive Director of the Society for Values in Higher Education. His research spans the disciplines of philosophy and religious studies, focusing primarily on social and political ethics and cultural criticism. He is the author of numerous articles and three books: *Game Day and God: Football, Faith, and Politics in the American South* (Mercer University Press, 2009), *Judge and Be Judged: Moral Reflection in an Age of Relativism and Fundamentalism* (Lexington Books, 2006), and *Mediating the Culture Wars: Dialogical Virtues in Multicultural Education* (Hampton Press, 2003).

Dan W. Clanton, Jr. is Assistant Professor of Religious Studies at Doane College in Crete, NE. He has published two books and numerous articles and chapters on the reception history of biblical literature. He enjoys spending time with his family, reading comic books, listening to jazz, and watching far too much television.

Terry Ray Clark is Assistant Professor of Religion at Georgetown College (KY). He has published multiple articles and essays on the Bible and Popular Culture, including: "Biblical Graphic Novels: Adaptation, Interpretation, and 'Faithful Transfer,'" "A Contract with God? Will Eisner's Seminal Graphic Novel as Anti-theodicy" (both online with the *SBL Forum*) and "Prophetic Voices in Graphic Novels: The 'Comic and Tragic Vision' of Apocalyptic Rhetoric in *Kingdom Come* and *Watchmen*" (in *The Bible in/and Popular Culture: A Creative Encounter*; SBL Semeia Studies 65). He has an essay forthcoming in a Sheffield-Phoenix volume on apocalyptic themes in comic books and graphic novels titled "Apocalypse Then and Now: *Kingdom Come* and the Tradition of Imagining Armageddon."

Douglas E. Cowan is Professor of Religious Studies at Renison University College, the University of Waterloo. Among many other works, he is the author of *Cyberhenge: Modern Pagans on the Internet* (Routledge, 2005), *Sacred Terror: Religion and Horror on the Silver Screen* (Baylor, 2008), and *Sacred Space: The Quest for Transcendence in Science Fiction Film and Television* (Baylor, 2010).

He is currently working on a third volume on religion and film, *Sacred Visions: Film, Television, and the Mythic Imagination*, which will also be published by Baylor University Press. He lives in Waterloo, Ontario, Canada.

Dell deChant is a Senior Instructor and Associate Chair of Religious Studies at the University of South Florida. deChant's specialization is religion and contemporary cultures. His primary foci are religion and popular culture, new religious movements, and religion and ecology. His most recent book is *Religion and Culture in the West: A Primer.*

Mark W. Flory is an Instructor of Philosophy at Metropolitan State College in Denver, CO. His research focuses on spiritual practices, primarily Neoplatonic, Hellenistic, and early Christian. He is married, and has both adult and school-age children.

John C. McDowell has been the Morpeth Professor of Theology and Religious Studies at the University of Newcastle, New South Wales, Australia since 2009, after moving from being the Meldrum Lecturer in Theology at the University of Edinburgh (2000–8). He is the author of *The Gospel According to Star Wars: Faith, Hope and the Force* (Westminster John Knox, 2007) and *Hope in Barth's Eschatology* (Ashgate, 2000), and is the co-editor of *Conversing With Barth* (Ashgate, 2004). He has authored academic articles on numerous topics such as: *Star Wars*, the ideology of the body in Mel Gibson's film *The Passion of the Christ*, hope and the tragic sensibility of George Steiner, theological education, the eschatology of globalization, the ethics of patriotism, Charles Darwin, and the theology of Karl Barth.

Jeremy Rehwaldt is Associate Professor of Religion at Midland Lutheran College in Fremont, Nebraska. He earned an M.T.S. at Harvard University and a Ph.D. at Vanderbilt University. His central teaching emphasis is in ethics, and his current research examines the response of rural Midwestern churches to immigration.

Jonathan Sands Wise is an Assistant Professor of Philosophy at Georgetown College in Georgetown, KY. Along with specializing in Ancient and Medieval Philosophy and Virtue Ethics, his current research interests include the fiction of P.D. James, agrarianism, and the philosophy of food.

Jeffrey Scholes is an Instructor of Religious Studies in the Philosophy Department and Director of the Center for Religion and Public Life at the University of Colorado, Colorado Springs. His research and teaching focus on Religion and the Political Economy and Religion and Popular Culture. He is currently working on a book-length project that explores the political significance of the Protestant concept of vocation.

Rachel Wagner is Associate Professor of Religion at Ithaca College, NY. Her work centers on the study of religion and culture. She serves on the steering committee of the American Academy of Religion's Religion and Popular Culture group, and is co-chair of the Religion, Film, and Visual Arts group. She has chapters in *Halos and Avatars: Playing Games with God* (2010) and *God in the Details* (2010). Her book *Godwired: Religion, Ritual and Virtual Reality* was published in 2011 (Routledge).

Courtney Wilder is Assistant Professor of Religion at Midland Lutheran College in Fremont, Nebraska. She earned an M.A. and Ph.D. at the University of Chicago. Her training is in systematic theology, and her research focuses on Paul Tillich and on contemporary theological movements.

Introduction: What is religion? What is popular culture? How are they related?

Terry Ray Clark

Welcome to the exciting and rapidly evolving field of study known as Religion and Popular Culture! This relatively new academic area is emerging as an important subset of two larger subject areas known as Religious Studies and Cultural Studies, and is represented by a growing number of courses found in institutions of higher education. A cursory glance at colleges, universities, seminaries, theology schools, and other graduate schools reveals a plethora of courses that reflect, to various degrees, the subject matter of this field. These include, but are not limited to, such things as: Religion and Media Studies, Religion/Theology and Film, Religion and Literature, Ethics in Pop Culture and Entertainment, Religion in Contemporary America, Religion and Politics, Communication Studies, and of course, Religion and Popular Culture.

The chief purpose of this book is to provide an entry point for introducing this field of study, providing students, teachers, and researchers with a set of practical and theoretical tools for beginning their own academic investigation of this vast terrain of subject matter. The book is designed to assist readers in beginning to think critically about the ways in which popular cultural practices and products, especially those considered as forms of entertainment, are laden with religious **ideology**, that is, with religious ideas, themes, and values. Some of this ideology is encountered so regularly in everyday life that it goes unnoticed unless one is specifically trying to locate, identify, and study it. Similarly, it is so widespread and common that a vague familiarity often winds up serving as a poor substitute for real recognition and understanding, and therefore the material fails to be critically examined by the very culture that inherits, adapts, produces, or reproduces it. But a culture's popular ideas, products, and practices have much to teach its own members about themselves, including their religious assumptions, their foundational beliefs, and their motivations for certain behaviors. Recognizing this can be the starting point for encouraging people to begin thinking critically about their own society as well as equipping themselves to interact more meaningfully and effectively with those located either inside or outside of their own unique cultural setting.

In addition to these justifications, the academic study of Religion and Popular Culture has the advantage of being, from the outset, less intimidating to new students because much of the subject matter is perceived as being, at least in part, something with which they are already familiar. This is due in large part to the fact that today many of the earth's inhabitants live in an environment of mass communication, a world in which modern technology (e.g. satellite TV, radio, mobile phones, internet, etc.) makes the ideas, products, and practices of others accessible around the globe in the blink of an eye.

The remainder of this chapter attempts to lay a very basic, theoretical foundation for readers to begin exploring some specific ideas, products, and practices in Western popular culture that specifically reflect religious influences, and which therefore contain some amount of religious content. The essays that follow in the remaining chapters provide examples of how some scholars have begun to analyze this seemingly inexhaustible and ever-evolving subject matter. They are not the only legitimate ways to understand the material. Rather, they are intended to provide readers with a starter toolbox, that is, with helpful strategies for beginning their own intellectual journey through this exciting and complex cultural terrain.

Each chapter reflects the same basic format. A popular cultural idea, product, practice or theme is introduced, with emphasis placed upon its religious characteristics or content. Next, a specific theory or method (i.e. tool) for analyzing the cultural data or material is presented, which may be adapted by the reader for analyzing other, similar pop cultural phenomena. The essay then demonstrates the usefulness of the theory or method by applying it to the idea, product, practice, or theme first introduced. Finally, each chapter concludes with a summary, a short glossary of important terms, points for discussion (or further reflection), suggestions for further reading, and a bibliography of cited works.

A practical foundation for studying religion and popular culture

It is often considered helpful when immersing oneself in a new subject of study to define, as clearly as possible, what the boundaries of that subject should be. Therefore, the editors here have chosen to begin this study by providing readers with a set of working definitions of Religion, Culture, and Popular Culture. Working definitions are not necessarily perfect, complete, or universally accepted, but they can provide a practical starting point for further exploration. They can highlight some of the major, foundational problems that scholars must deal with in a particular field without preventing real progress from being made. From our own teaching experience, we have discovered that if too much emphasis is placed on all the challenges, obstacles, or problems of studying Religion and Popular Culture from the outset, new students often become discouraged, disillusioned, and too frustrated to proceed. Hence, this book will provide just enough information to allow the novice to get a foothold in the material, without getting lost in the complexities and difficulties of foundational theory and method. For those who choose to pursue further work in the field, there will be plenty of time to revisit such matters in the future. The theories and methods provided in this book assume that the study of Religion and Popular Culture is a valid and worthwhile endeavor, and each provides its own unique starting point for more in-depth study. Furthermore, each contributor hopes to inspire ongoing conversations with other scholars who likewise recognize the value of pursuing a critical analysis of the religious characteristics of the popular cultural products and practices of our world, in spite of the technical difficulties of defining our subject matter.

From the outset, students should recognize that perfect, universally accepted definitions for Religion, Culture, and Popular Culture have not been produced. However, scholars do agree that religion has been and continues to be one of the most pervasive and important characteristics of human society. Similarly, culture and popular culture are undeniable realities of human existence. They provide real phenomena worthy of academic analysis, and they reflect real ideas, beliefs, and values; they are not merely figments of human imagination. Culture, including popular culture, refers to all the ideas, products, practices, and values of human society. These things emerge from and reflect the hopes, fears, dreams, goals, and struggles of real people. Thus, their study provides an opportunity to better understand human society as a whole, as well as more specific parts of society, including all the groups, sub-groups, and individuals that interact with one another, sometimes cooperatively, and sometimes in the context of conflict.

What is religion?

The problem of defining religion is one of the most difficult, foundational, and pervasive issues plaguing the field of Religious Studies today. Yet, it is usually never even considered outside the realm of academia. Why is this? The answer lies in the simple fact that most people inherit from the beginning of their lives—from their elders, family, religious tradition or larger society—a working concept of what religion is, and what it means to be religious. Most do not need to be taught how to recognize something as religious, at least not within their own tradition. Religion, generally speaking, refers to those practices of any society that are attentive to what is believed to be a sacred, unique, or extraordinary element or quality of human experience. Even societies that do not always clearly delineate what is considered sacred from what is not sacred (i.e. the mundane or ordinary) seem to understand what these terms refer to. Theoretically speaking, they might consider all reality to be sacred, but for all practical purposes they will usually distinguish between certain elements of life that are more sacred than others. How can this be? What is it that makes some things at least appear to be religious or sacred, and other things ordinary? What is the nature of so-called "sacred reality?" Does it really exist, or is it merely a product of human imagination?

There is no lack of scholarly attempts to address these questions. Some definitions assert the existence of a unique substance in the universe that human beings have a special, inexplicable way of sensing. It is believed that this substance can be directly experienced and immediately recognized for what it really is, even though a complete understanding of its nature eludes our grasp. Hence, it remains at least partially **transcendent**. This reality is considered the cause of the human experience and practice of religion. It is assumed that because many, if not most, human beings describe some of their experiences as religious in nature, there must be a separate or unique reality that causes it. Thus, for them, "The Sacred" truly exists as a causal reality, even if this unique substance normally lies hidden from the naked eye (as well as the other four senses of human perception that make up the approach known as scientific observation: sight, sound, smell, taste, and touch). This is because its effects are still believed to be apparent in the observable world.

While this assumption represents a logical fallacy from the perspective of pure, rational analysis (e.g. there could be other reasonable explanations for humanity's religious beliefs and behaviors), believers are undeterred. Of course, no one can really prove or disprove someone else's (or even one's own) claim to have had a genuine encounter with a sacred reality, just as no one can prove or disprove, at least not with scientific evidence, that a sacred reality is or is not the cause. Thus, many scholars will instead direct their attention toward better understanding the other human phenomena that tend to accompany such alleged experiences. This is because human behavior, unlike any theoretically existing sacred reality, does provide a substance or **phenomenon** that can be examined, measured, and described. This approach is referred to as the phenomenological approach to religion. If nothing else, the phenomenon of religion clearly does exist. Many, if not most, people throughout recorded human history have claimed, and continue to claim, to have religious experiences. Such people exhibit behavior that they understand as appropriate responses to what they consider sacred reality. They also believe that at least some aspects of life have, or should have, a sacred quality. Thus, they develop what they consider to be appropriate sacred responses in the form of various religious behaviors or practices. This makes their lives more meaningful, fulfilling, and practical.

So, for pragmatic reasons, many approaches to the study of religion choose to focus exclusively on those beliefs and practices that a particular society understands as their own appropriate response to what is perceived to be a sacred reality. This is the approach to religion adopted by this book. Sacred or Ultimate Reality can refer to whatever a particular person or group considers the most enduring, foundational, and important substance in the universe. It is something that is considered to be deeper, more powerful, and more valuable than the normal, everyday things with which it is often contrasted, although it is also often considered the source of creating and/or sustaining all other reality. It is a reality that deserves appropriate human attention, and for many, this includes all the various forms of human activity known as worship. But it need not be something that is focused upon all the time. For some people, "orientation to ultimate reality takes place by degrees and is restricted to certain times and places, even among 'very religious' people" (Deming 2005: 15). And yet, evidence of one's orientation to "the Sacred" may still be found scattered throughout one's culture, as well as in one's everyday routines, sometimes without one even being aware of it. Religion is not something that is simply relegated to "official" holy days, times, and festivals; it does not merely occur in formal, ritual, or sacred time, in which special religious authorities often conduct formal worship activities. Religion, for many, is something that may occur on any day of the week, at almost any time, and in nearly any place. Sacred reality is something that is believed to permeate most, if not all, reality, and therefore all aspects of human culture.

Granting these general parameters for understanding the concept of sacred reality, what then is a good, working definition of religion? One that is helpful for beginning an academic exploration of the subject matter may be derived from the approach taken by John C. Livingston in his book *Anatomy of the Sacred: An Introduction to Religion* (2008): Religion is a coherent system of beliefs and practices that are "directed toward that which is perceived to be of sacred value and transforming power" (10). The reference here to "power" is an essential aspect of a good definition of religion, because it highlights the practical benefits sought for the religious behaviors of those who perform them. Religious observance is believed to be a source of help for living a more meaningful and fulfilling life, and often this includes the belief that it provides a viable path for life beyond this world. Put succinctly, "whatever powers we believe govern our destiny will elicit a religious response from us and inspire us to wish 'to tie or bind' ourselves to these powers in relations of ritual obligation" (Esposito, Fasching, and Lewis 2009: 7).

This reference to "bind[ing]" is important, because it highlights what many scholars believe is the root meaning of the word "religion." This English word is most likely derived from the Latin prefix *re*, which means "again," combined with the root *lig*, which means "to join" or "connect," thus producing the meaning "to re-connect" or "to join again" (Molloy 2010: 5). This suggests that, at its root, religion refers to any practice that serves to bring back together or to bring back into harmony the sacred and mundane realms of reality that, for various reasons, are often perceived as being disconnected. Religion, then, provides not only an explanation for why human life is in some ways problematic or difficult, but it also seeks to provide a solution to this problem. In the words of Jonathan Z. Smith, "Religion is the quest, within the bounds of the human, historical condition, for the power to manipulate and negotiate one's 'situation' so as to have 'space' in which to meaningfully dwell" (Smith 1993: 291). Religion provides human beings with "a strategy for dealing with a situation," in this case, the human situation (Smith, 299, following Burke 1957: 256); by performing ritual acts of worship, humans hope to "oblige" the powers that be to reward us with a more successful life in the present, and a more rewarding existence in the future.

Thus, for many, if not most, people, religion provides a means of helping us "relate to the unknown universe around us by answering the basic questions of who we are, where we come from, and where we are going" (Molloy: 10). However idealistic it sometimes seems to be, religion provides its practitioners with what are believed to be very rational and practical strategies for coping with the challenges of everyday life. Some of these strategies include **ritual** behaviors that help orient the mind and body toward proper (i.e. religious) ways of thinking and acting. Often, this follows from the belief that a sacred reality represents and/or imposes a value system on the universe that obligates humans to live in accordance with it, and doing so brings more meaning, purpose, and success in life for oneself and for others.

What are culture and popular culture?

Like the phenomenon of religion, which in all its myriad forms falls within the larger domain of human culture, so also popular culture is merely a subset of this larger category of human activity. It is not something that is ever, entirely distinct from the larger context in which it occurs and in which it is defined. But what do these terms really refer to? Like the term religion, scholars have had a difficult time agreeing on what "culture" and "popular culture" really represent. In fact, some scholars treat each of these terms as "an *empty* conceptual category, one that can be filled in a wide variety of often conflicting ways, depending on the context of use" (Storey 2009: 1). However, if the terms are to be worthy of any use at all, they must be clarified in some fashion.

Historically speaking, the term culture has at times been used to designate what some would consider a distinctly higher form of "intellectual, spiritual, and aesthetic development" than that found among the more common masses of society (Williams 1983: 90). In other words, culture here refers to so-called "high culture," or what more privileged or wealthy members of society consider to be most valuable. This use, however, reflects a biased judgment on the part of those individuals who have the power to impose their own value system upon others, and may serve to maintain a distinction in society between people of different economic and political standing. Two other definitions of culture have served as attempts to correct this bias. One considers the term "culture" merely to designate the "particular way of life … of a [particular] people, a period or a group" (Storey 2009: 1), without necessarily evaluating one culture as better than another. This approach includes in the definition practically every idea, product, practice, and value of a society, regardless of the socioeconomic class in which it originates. Finally, a third approach attempts to find a middle ground by using the term culture in a more limited fashion to refer only to those products and practices "whose principle function is to signify, to produce or to be the occasion for the production of meaning" (Storey 2009: 2). In other words, this third use is more specifically geared toward recognizing those products and practices that are purposely designed to communicate ideas in a symbolic way.

Of course, right away, it should be obvious that any product or practice in a society has the power of signifying and/or producing meaning, even if this is not the primary, intended purpose for its existence. Thus, the least biased definition, and the one preferred here, is also the most general and inclusive one. The term "culture" should be used to refer to *all* the potentially signifying products and practices of a society, regardless of the economic, political, religious or social class in which they originate. Immediately, the reader should recognize that our preference here for this particular definition necessarily reflects its own bias in the direction of such values as objectivity and inclusiveness, as opposed to other possible criteria. From an academic perspective, these biases are ones that the authors of this book are willing to take ownership of. However, this does highlight the fact that all definitions contain, to some extent, their own subjectivity, just as all cultural products and practices contain their own subjectivity. They always simultaneously both represent and "present a particular image of the world," including what that image considers to be of greater value (Storey 2009: 4). Every product and practice of every culture reflects its own particular assumptions about "the way the world is or should be," and the definitions put forward in this book are no exception (Storey 2009: 4). One of the foundational goals of the critical study of Religion and Popular Culture should always be to clarify, as much as possible, the particular ideological values reflected in each and every popular cultural practice or product, because often these are never discussed directly or openly by their originators, practitioners, and/or consumers. Usually, these things are communicated implicitly rather than explicitly.

This leads us to another important term (and aspect) of culture that needs to be defined, namely, "ideology." **Ideology**, most literally, refers to "a systematic body of ideas" that, to various degrees, is "articulated by a particular group of people" (Storey 2009: 2). All individuals, and all groups of people, have an ideology, however clearly it is articulated, just as every product and practice of individuals and groups will reflect the ideology of their makers and users. Therefore, the study of culture, including popular culture (the latter of which will be defined in more detail below), necessarily involves the recognition and analysis of competing ideas, beliefs, and values inherent within every cultural product and practice one encounters. Culture must be recognized as a realm of human political activity in which various ideas "are created" and in which various ideas compete with one another (Hall 2009: 122–123). In other words, culture is often a realm of conflict, where different ideas are always being defined, redefined, negotiated, reinforced, and/or rejected. Relations of power, therefore, always lie beneath the surface of cultural activity.

Given these understandings, how should we delineate the realm of popular culture from that of culture in general? John Storey helps to highlight the fact that the term "popular culture" should at least refer to those aspects of culture that are widespread and which may be appreciated by a significant number of people (2009: 5–6). But even this description can be misleading if it fails to acknowledge that products and practices which are widespread and widely appreciated, can achieve this status in a variety of ways. They do not necessarily appear simply by accident, but instead may arise as a result of the conscious efforts by some to influence the values of others. Hence, the issues of opportunity, influence, and power discussed above in relation to the term ideology also apply to the realm of popular culture. This is especially the case in the modern world where advances in technology make the dissemination and proliferation of ideas to a large audience much easier to accomplish. We live in a world of so-called "mass communication," where competing ideas and values clash on a daily basis, where various forms of media often serve as tools of manipulation. This has become far more pronounced since the industrial revolution in the 18th and 19th centuries (cf. Williams 1963; Burke 1994; and Storey 2003). But prior to this, even more basic developments of human society, such as the rise of empires and nations, the growth of international commerce, and the invention of the printing press have all served as important precursors to the modern age of mass communications. Today, most of us recognize that we now live in a global or worldwide society, where a great number of humans around the planet are connected by a variety of satellite-assisted technologies such as radio, television, internet, cell phones, and video games. Thus, many of the planet's residents have multiple ways of communicating with one another, and many of the messages they send, including those with religious content, have the potential to develop a large audience. As a result, this book will use the term "popular culture" to refer to widespread and well-liked products, practices, themes, and values that have achieved their popular status as a result of their dissemination through the vehicles of modern technology, including **mass marketing** strategies.

How do religion and popular culture interact?

Conrad Ostwalt provides an extremely useful model for understanding the ways in which religion and popular culture have related in the past, and continue to relate to one another today. They are not entirely separate things, and never have been. Each finds its meaning in relation to the other. Religion is an element of nearly every human culture, one "strand among many cultural strands that are interrelated in society" (Ostwalt 2003: 23; cf. Geertz 1973: 3). As Oswalt puts it, "Religion ... [is] a cultural form that is directed toward the sacred, and that exists in dialectical relationship with other culture forms that sometimes explore religious content" (2003: 23). "Religion is necessarily entangled with secular culture" (Ostwalt 2003: 23); it is not something that is itself utterly distinct from other cultural forms, nor does it occur in any completely distinct way.

While it is undeniable that something we call religion "happens" quite often throughout the world, whenever something religious occurs, it does so within the confines of other cultural events, that is, within a complex cultural context. This becomes clear when one recognizes that distinct cultures and subcultures regularly define the sacred in their own unique ways. There is no universally agreed upon way that all humans delineate the sacred from the mundane. This varies from people to people, and place to place. In the words of J.Z. Smith, "There is nothing that is inherently sacred or profane. These are not substantive categories, but rather situational or relational categories" (1988: 55). These terms serve as functional "labels" to designate and represent the way humans order their spatial environments and their activities within space (Smith 1988: 54–56; cf. also Smith 1992: 11). This is a way that humans uniquely organize their environments. And the significance of this is that, whenever something religious can be said to have happened, it must be understood as doing so in relationship to other things that are not considered sacred.

This insight represents a revolution in thinking about the role of religion in culture, especially in the Western world. Prior theories typically drew a fine line of separation between that which a society considered sacred and that which it considered non-sacred or secular (Ostwalt 2003: 8–14). Ostwalt, in his own treatment of so-called **secularization theory**, refers to this as a false or artificial dichotomy. His response is to argue for a more nuanced approach that recognizes how sacred and non-sacred elements of society are always interacting because the boundaries between the two are not firmly fixed (2003: 29). In fact, in the current situation, especially in contemporary America, there are two directions or movements of secularization that must always be considered. In the first, traditional sources of religious authority in society (i.e. those that have held sway for some significant amount of time) "are becoming increasingly more attune[d]" to those things that are typically considered non-religious, especially those things that are highly popular (Ostwalt 2003: 29). In some cases these traditional religious authorities (i.e. religious institutions, leaders, texts, etc.) even "seek to emulate [secular practices and products] in the effort to remain relevant" to those audiences that value them (Ostwalt 2003: 29). For example, in the case of sacred texts, this is clearly seen in the way modern readers tend to interpret scriptures in light of their own, modern day concerns, often with little reference to the ancient contexts in which they were originally composed. In the second direction or movement, Ostwalt recognizes that "popular cultural forms, including literature, film, and music, are becoming increasingly more visible vehicles of religious images, symbols, and categories" (2003: 29). In other words, more everyday products, practices, and modes of communication are reflective of (and influential upon) the way people understand religious truth. We should conclude from this insight that there is an ever-present flux, negotiation, or re-negotiation that occurs in any society between those elements or sources that are considered predominantly religious authorities and those considered to be predominantly secular or non-religious authorities. Societies, over time, do not necessarily become more secular or more religious, but differently-secular or differently-religious (Ostwalt 2003: 31). Those things in society that are considered to be either religious or secular are always being defined or redefined, in relation to one another.

How to use this book

In the remainder of this book, the reader will encounter a variety of essays that attempt to clarify certain ways in which religion and popular culture interact in modern society. Popular cultural practices, products, themes, and values that reflect some concept of the sacred will be discussed and examined in order to assist the reader in better understanding and appreciating the validity of Ostwalt's theory as well as the very real complexity of this particular aspect of human culture. By reflecting on these examples and by attending to other available resources for further exploring these and related topics, readers will hopefully begin to acquire a set of introductory tools for analyzing important places in society where religion and popular culture intersect. It is hoped that they will begin to recognize the value of studying their culture through the unique lenses provided by the academic field of Religion and Popular Culture. And it is hoped that they will be inspired to pursue further study beyond the undergraduate classroom, eventually making their own contribution to the development and application of new theories and methods in this rapidly expanding subject area.

Summary

- The field of study known as Religion and Popular Culture is complex, interdisciplinary, and relatively new to the academy, requiring foundational work in defining and delimiting its boundaries and definitions.
- Despite the difficulties and imperfections, working definitions for Religion, Culture, and Popular Culture are available and adequate for further study to proceed.
- "Sacred" and "Mundane" are empty conceptual categories used uniquely in different cultures to order the worldview of their participants.
- Ostwalt's more nuanced theory of secularization better explains the complex, fluctuating relationship between religious and secular authorities in our world.

Points for discussion

- Keep a log for one full day, recording every instance of a religious message found in the various pop cultural products and practices encountered, including everyday language or phrases (e.g. references to biblical material), song lyrics, TV commercials and shows, movies, advertisements, sports events, newspapers, literature, internet material, etc. Discuss how pervasive religion really is in pop culture today.
- What is the nature of these religious messages, and how do they reflect the negotiable boundaries between competing religious voices/authorities in your particular societal context?
- Discuss whether or not you agree with the idea that the concepts of sacred and profane represent empty conceptual categories for ordering human existence, versus realities in and of themselves. How would one go about proving or disproving that a unique, sacred reality truly exists and/or was encountered in some fashion by human experience?
- What are the potential risks or dangers associated with people becoming differently religious over time? Who or what is most at risk, and how?

Glossary terms

Ideology – "A systematic body of ideas" that, to various degrees, is "articulated by a particular group of people" (Storey 2009: 2). (See also the treatment of this term in the glossary at the end of Chapter 7.)

Mass marketing – the attempt to sell some commodity or product to a very large audience, often by utilizing some form of modern technology.

Phenomenon – an experience, event, or reality that is observable by the human senses, and which can be verified by factual data.

Ritual – a sequence of actions performed in a strict, pre-established pattern whose purpose is to reinforce certain beliefs, practices, and values as well as to produce some real benefit for the participant(s). (See also the treatment of this word in Chapter 5, including the glossary term at the end of the chapter.)

Secularization theory – traditionally speaking, the idea that human religious behavior is a primitive holdover from ancient times that will eventually fade away as society evolves. Ostwalt refutes this theory and reconceptualizes it.

Transcendent – something that remains at least partially beyond full human apprehension and/or comprehension. (See also the treatment of this word in Chapter 5, including the glossary term at the end of the chapter.)

Further reading

Paden, William E. (1994) *Religious Worlds: The Comparative Study of Religion*, Boston: Beacon Press.

This is a very readable introduction to the academic study of religion, geared toward undergraduate students, which attempts to simplify the comparative method by focusing on a limited number of universal religious categories such as Myth, Ritual and Time, Gods, and Systems of Purity.

Kessler, Gary E. (2008) *Studying Religion: An Introduction through Cases*, 3rd edn, New York: McGraw-Hill.

This text has the advantage of introducing new students to the phenomena of religion (power, myth, ritual, etc.) while also providing real-life examples of how they occur in various traditions through a case-study approach.

Storey, John (ed.) (2009) *Cultural Theory and Popular Culture: A Reader*, 4th edn, Harlow: Pearson Education.

Designed as a potential supplement to Storey's *Cultural Theory and Popular Culture: An Introduction* (2009), this is a sizable collection of readings on various theoretical approaches to understanding the workings of culture and pop culture. It includes units on Marxism, Feminism, Structuralism, Racism, Postmodernism, and Politics.

Journal of Religion and Popular Culture, University of Saskatchewan, ed. Mary Ann Beavis. Online. Available HTTP: www.usask.ca/relst/jrpc

This free, online, peer-reviewed journal provides relevant, timely articles that explore the "interrelations and interactions between religion … and popular culture."

Lynch, Gordon (2005) *Understanding Theology and Popular Culture*, Malden, MA: Blackwell Publishing.

An introduction to studying popular culture from several different theological perspectives, including text-based, ethnographic, and aesthetic approaches. Lynch also provides a definition of popular culture and discusses the technological and consumer-oriented nature of "everyday life in contemporary Western society."

Mazur, Eric Michael and McCarthy, Kate (eds) (2000) *God in the Details: American Religion in Popular Culture*, New York: Routledge.

A collection of essays on the intersection between religion and popular culture in America, covering a variety of products, practices, and themes including civil religion in popular music, popular morality and the supernatural in television, apocalyptic in film, secular rituals in religious holidays, consumerism and religion, and internet religion.

Forbes, Bruce David and Mahan, Jeffrey H. (eds) (2005) *Religion and Popular Culture in America*, rev. edn, Berkeley, CA: University of California Press.

An updated collection of essays on religion in modern day film, internet, literature, music, sports, television, and other cultural products, practices, and themes.

Culbertson, Philip and Wainwright, Elaine M. (eds) (2010) *The Bible in/and Popular Culture: A Creative Encounter*, Semeia Studies, 65, Atlanta, GA: Society of Biblical Literature.

A collection of essays specifically focusing on the adaptation and interpretation of biblical images, texts, and themes in popular cultural products like literature and music.

Bibliography

Burke, Kenneth (1957) *Philosophy of Literary Form: Studies in Symbolic Action*, rev. and abr. edn, New York: Vintage.

Burke, Peter (1994) *Popular Culture in Early Modern Europe*, Aldershot: Scholars Press.

Deming, Will (2005) *Rethinking Religion: A Concise Introduction*, New York: Oxford University Press.

Esposito, John, Fasching, Darrell J., and Lewis, Todd (2009) *World Religions Today*, 3rd edn, New York: Oxford University Press.

Geertz, Clifford (1973) "Thick Description: Toward an Interpretive Theory of Culture," in *The Interpretation of Cultures: Selected Essays*, New York: Basic Books, 3–30.

Hall, Stuart (2009) "The Rediscovery of Ideology: The Return of the Repressed in Media Studies," in John Storey (ed.) *Cultural Theory and Popular Culture: a Reader*, 4th edn, Harlow: Pearson Education.

Livingston, John C. (2008) *Anatomy of the Sacred: An Introduction to Religion*, 5th edn, Upper Saddle River, NJ: Prentice Hall.

Molloy, Michael (2010) *Experiencing the World's Religions: Tradition, Challenge, and Change*, 5th edn, New York: McGraw-Hill.

Ostwalt, Conrad (2003) *Secular Steeples: Popular Culture and the Religious Imagination*, Harrisburg, PA: Trinity Press International.

Smith, J.Z. (1993) *Map is Not Territory: Studies in the History of Religions*, Chicago: University of Chicago Press.

——(1992) *To Take Place: Toward Theory in Ritual*, Chicago: University of Chicago Press.

——(1988) *Imagining Religion: From Babylon to Jonestown*, Chicago: University of Chicago Press.

Storey, John (2009) *Cultural Theory and Popular Culture: an Introduction*, 5th edn, New York: Pearson Education.

——(2003) *Inventing Popular Culture: From Folklore to Globalisation*, Oxford: Blackwell.

Williams, Raymond (1983) *Keywords*, London: Fontana.

——(1963) *Culture and Society*, Harmondsworth: Penguin.

1 Saved by satire?

Learning to value popular culture's critique of sacred traditions

Terry Ray Clark

Introduction

When I first began teaching Religion and Popular Culture as a college course, I was surprised to find that a significant number of students failed to appreciate religious satire. It seemed that from their perspective, some television programs, movies, and literature, while occasionally humorous, contain highly exaggerated and mean-spirited depictions of religious people and their practices. As a result, students found these cultural products offensive, and failed to appreciate their value as entertainment or as educational tools.

Over time, it seemed that this sort of reaction was more common among students who self-identified as belonging to more conservative religious traditions. In addition, it appeared that such students were, by and large, more offended when their own traditions were satirized than when they encountered satires of someone else's traditions. Did the failure of these students to appreciate religious satire derive from a lack of understanding about what really satire is and how it works? Were they simply insecure about their own traditions? Were certain religious topics strictly off limits for critique or humor?

Although I never performed a scientific study to identify the exact causes, I concluded that many students would benefit from being better educated about the nature of satire as a genre, as a method of communication, and as a contributor to the maintenance of a free and open society that ascribes value to the notion of separation of church and state. This essay is an attempt to make available to students and teachers a useful approach to understanding religious satire when it occurs in the context of popular cultural media.

I would like to begin by briefly reviewing a few of the real life examples that convinced me of the necessity of this endeavor. One day while teaching a college course on Religion and Pop Culture, I made reference to the highly provocative episode of *South Park* titled "Christian Rock Hard" (Season 7). The episode critically examines the degree to which a contemporary Christian may actually have a "personal relationship with Jesus." This was apparently in response to the reality that the language of personal relationship is so common in evangelical Christian circles. To demonstrate their conviction that some Christians take this idea too literally, the creators of the show decided to explore the notion of an intimate relationship with Jesus in an obviously ludicrous and blasphemous way.

In the episode, the character named Cartman, who regularly functions as a stereotype of bigotry and selfishness, creates a Christian rock band in an attempt to win a bet with his friends to see who can be the first to make a platinum album. Cartman chooses the genre of Christian music for his band because he believes Christians are gullible and easily persuaded into buying a product simply because it has a Christian label or Christian lyrics, regardless of how superficially religious the message. After quickly securing a record deal, Cartman's band makes a television commercial in which he sings a few lines from a number of cheesy love songs that treat Jesus as the object of the singer's romantic feelings. In one particular song that parodies the prayer life of the believer, Cartman's lyrics suggest that he would like to have oral sex with Jesus: "I wanna' get down on my knees and start pleasin' Jesus; I wanna' feel his salvation all over my face."

This is one of the most provocative and potentially offensive treatments of Christianity I have ever encountered in a popular culture product, and I cringe whenever I show this episode in the classroom. However, I continue to use it because I consider it very effective for demonstrating several important characteristics of religious satire. One day, after merely referring to (rather than showing) the scene described above, one of my students was so offended that he accused me in a private e-mail of personally making fun of Christianity "as a matter of principle." It seemed that, from the student's perspective, my use of this material in the classroom was equivalent to advocating the disrespectful ideology it was perceived to express. It quickly became apparent to me that I had failed to communicate clearly and convincingly why I considered this material worthy of my students' time, attention, and tuition dollars. I hope this essay does not repeat that mistake.

A second enlightening incident occurred one semester when a particular student asked in advance to be excused altogether from viewing any episodes of *South Park*. The class had been forewarned in the syllabus about the potentially offensive nature of certain course material, but as a concession to the student, I suggested that she view some episodes of *The Simpsons*. I assumed that this material would serve as a less provocative and offensive substitute, but still demonstrate some of the key principles of satire that I wanted my students to learn. The student's reaction, however, was to say in so many words, "I'd rather not. I really don't want to fill my head with that kind of stuff." I was stunned, and temporarily found myself in a rare situation—I was at a complete loss for words. How could I teach the nature of religious satire in a Popular Culture class without actually introducing the student to real life, modern-day examples? What was it about religious satire that made it so offensive that students really didn't care if they understood it or not? How could I impart a deeper understanding and appreciation for this method of communication? This essay is, in part, an attempt to answer these questions.

First, the reason for exposing students to religious satire, and the goal for any other teaching endeavor, should never be simply "to fill a student's head with something," as if education were merely an exercise in indoctrination, rather than the application of critical analysis to various subject matter. Professors should never seek to "make fun of" any religious tradition "as a matter of principle" (whatever that principle might be). While I will admit that all education has its ideological slant, ultimately, good education seeks to develop important skills in the student, including the ability to analyze data in intelligent ways. Education necessarily requires students to be exposed to new ideas, and new ways of viewing old ideas, but it need not require them to agree with everything they hear, read, see, and reflect upon. In the case of teaching Religion and Popular Culture, the goal should be to enlighten students about the nature of popular culture and its religious aspects, particularly the ways in which Western culture typically provides room for religious ideas, themes, and values to be communicated, explored, and evaluated in various forms of so-called "secular" media. Second, and conversely, students should be taught to recognize ways in which religious communities sometimes make use of popular secular ideas, products, and practices to further their own so-called "sacred" goals. Students should never be required to agree or disagree with a particular ideological perspective, and all participants in the academy should be expected to provide supporting evidence for their positions. So, given these clarifying and apologetic comments about the study of religious satire, what is it about the nature of this material that makes it so difficult for some to appreciate or even study without revulsion?

Theory and method

What is satire, and how does it work?

Satire, and more specifically, religious satire, is not a new phenomenon. One of the earliest written examples can be found in the Hebrew canon of scriptures (equivalent in content to the Protestant Christian Old Testament). In the second major section of the prophetic Book of Isaiah (Chs 40–55), probably written sometime in the early post-exilic period (late 6th to early 5th century BCE), one encounters an Israelite **caricature** of the religious practices of non-Israelites. One particular text pokes fun at those who worship their god(s) by constructing images out of wood and/or stone, and bowing down before them (Isa 44:9–20). The depiction is far from flattering. In fact, it is downright inaccurate and unfair, grossly misrepresenting the religious beliefs and practices of many ancient Near Eastern peoples. It suggests that foreign worshipers are delusional because they bow down before what is obviously and only an inanimate object that their own hands have fashioned. It has no real life or saving power within it. Such worshipers are treated as idiots, and so is anyone who behaves like them.

Of course, the purpose of this caricature is **polemical**—that is, it is designed to discourage such a practice among the originally intended ancient Israelite readers of the text. It represents a particular type of religious rhetoric (i.e. argumentation). It does not matter to the author that he exaggerates or misrepresents the foreigner's real intentions and understandings about the way the god(s) might inhabit a divine image in order to be present in some meaningful way to the worshiper. From the author's perspective, this is simply a ridiculous superstition (because it is considered to be false), and therefore it should be harshly criticized. The main point is this: if some belief or practice is considered to be false, it can and should be made fun of, even if it belongs to the sacred beliefs and practices of some other culture. In fact, some believers consider it a sacred task to do this, because such satire holds the potential to improve the world by abolishing what is believed to be a false and foolish tradition.

A number of ancient Greek writers also incorporated satire into their compositions in order to criticize their rivals as well as what they considered the ludicrous beliefs and practices of their own cultures. Aristophanes, a famous Athenian playwright of the late 5th century BCE, provides a famous example in his comedic play *The Frogs* (405 BCE; cf. Aristophanes [1993] *Frogs*, ed. Kenneth Dover, Oxford: Clarendon Press: 2). In this work, Aristophanes implicitly ridicules the religious beliefs and practices surrounding the worship of the sensual god Dionysus. The god is depicted in stereotypically effeminate ways, and is made to look the fool by his own slave. Eventually, Dionysus holds a satiric contest in Hades with two famous, but dead playwrights, Aeschylus and Euripides, whereby the dead poets also use satire to criticize one another's work. The winner of the contest is promised rescue from the underworld and an opportunity to revive Athenian society with his own literally resurrected career.

Other examples throughout human history could be mentioned, but I suppose you have the idea. Humor has been used by numerous individuals for centuries as a helpful tool for critiquing what some consider potentially dangerous, excessive, or just plain silly beliefs and practices. It has served, and continues to serve, an important educational function. The modern era is no exception. Not only is satire regularly utilized by political cartoonists to critique what they consider the failings of governmental leaders, but many standup comics also discuss the subject matter of religion and politics for the chief purpose of entertainment, artfully and effectively tying together education and humor. Here, the subject matter of religion, often in more formal settings considered a topic off-limits to frivolity, is effectively used for entertainment for the very reason that people need an occasional break from too much seriousness about anything, including, and perhaps especially, religion. But how, exactly, does satire work?

One of the most helpful resources for understanding the nature and function of satire is Dustin Griffin's *Satire: A Critical Reintroduction* (1994). Although originally designed to clarify the nature of ancient satirical works, Griffin's theory applies quite readily to modern day manifestations of the genre, such as literature, television, and film. I have adapted here the basic principles of Griffin's approach for the sake of helping others better appreciate what satire is, and how it works.

According to Griffin, while satire is often humorous and entertaining, it is primarily an act of inquiry or exploration into the truth, falsity, or reasonableness of a particular idea or practice. It does not necessarily provide answers for all the questions that it raises and explores, nor does it necessarily prescribe alternative beliefs and practices to replace those that it criticizes. Satire is not simply a straightforward act of rhetoric or argumentation, with a predetermined conclusion that it seeks to persuade its audience to agree with. Instead, its ultimate goal is to create a more reflective, more critical thinking, and therefore wiser audience. Here, Griffin asserts a clear contrast between the purpose of satire, which is primarily exploratory, and that of classical rhetoric, which is argumentative and conclusive. Ultimately, however, at least in practice if not theory, this assertion is somewhat overstated.

In reality, satire often does put forward an argument—an alternative version of the truth—albeit sometimes in rather subtle ways. Even if an argument is not explicit, an implicit truth claim is present in many satirical works. (It should be noted that the vast majority of arguments, always and everywhere, are conducted by means of implicit, rather than explicit, truth claims. In normal everyday language, as opposed to the kind of language one finds in a logic textbook, one rarely tries to persuade with very explicit language.) In other words, satire often *does* intend to move an audience to agree with its own alternative version of reality, and this will become clear later in this essay when we review a few examples of modern day satire.

Aside from his somewhat overreaching claim about the difference between rhetoric and satire, Griffin provides an extremely useful method for analyzing satirical texts, which he sees as made up of the following key components: Inquiry, Provocation, Display, and Play, with the occasional added element of "Unstable Irony" (1994; cf. Booth 1974: 248). Inquiry and provocation belong together, and the latter serves the former. For Griffin, the most important characteristic of satire is that it is designed to explore the validity or truth of a particular idea or practice. It asks the question, "Does this really make sense?" or "Is this really true?" Satire is primarily intended to examine something more critically than it has thus far been examined by a particular audience: "The satirist writes in order to discover, to explore, to survey, to attempt to clarify" (Griffin 1994: 39). Often, according to Griffin, the satirist has no pre-determined plan for what the outcome of the inquiry will be; there is no "predetermined argument," although as I have suggested above, many pop culture satires suggest otherwise (Griffin 1994: 39). But by and large, the purpose of a satire is to provide an opportunity for an audience to begin thinking for itself, to think more critically about a topic than it has done so before, and perhaps reach a new level of insight, especially in the area of self-understanding. I would also argue that sometimes the satirist would like to encourage an audience to respond by changing its behavior as well as its thinking, and this represents a form of **deliberative rhetoric**.

The second, and perhaps most controversial component of satire, is provocation. Provocation seeks to inspire critical thought by raising questions about things previously deemed unquestionable. Figuratively speaking, provocation seeks to "pull the carpet out from under" the audience, leaving it naked and exposed to its own folly. Provocation is, by design, rather abrasive. As Griffin puts it, "If the rhetoric of inquiry is 'positive,' an exploratory attempt to arrive at truth, the rhetoric of provocation is 'negative,' a critique of false understanding" (Griffin 1994: 52). The questions that satire raises are "designed to expose or demolish a foolish certainty" (Griffin 1994: 52). In other words, something that the intended audience simply takes for granted as true is targeted for serious scrutiny, if not outright annihilation! But it should be remembered that satire's purpose is not simply for the satirist and his/her allies to enjoy the (sometimes twisted?) pleasure of unleashing destruction upon something that their enemies smugly assume to be indestructible: "Its function is less to judge people for their follies and vices than to challenge their attitudes and opinions, to taunt and provoke them into doubt, and perhaps into disbelief" (Griffin 1994: 52, citing Elkin 1973: 201).

Provocation may take the form of an intentional obscurity, difficulty, puzzle, or absurdity, not merely to confuse the audience, but to gain attention and encourage concentration (Griffin 1994: 52–53). This could take the form of a paradoxical truth, in the popular sense of combining things that are normally considered opposites. For instance, *South Park* will often depict characters like Jesus or Satan behaving as mere mortals, with very human desires and weaknesses, rather than as superhuman beings. However, there is another, classical and more literal sense in which paradox, "another voice," is used as a means of provocation to present an alternate opinion to the so-called majority view, the latter of which often goes unquestioned (Griffin 1994: 53). The purpose of such paradox is to "rouze and awaken the Reason of Men asleep, into a *Thinking and Philosophical Temper*" (Griffin 1994: 53, citing Dutton 1707: 1, as quoted in Morris 1984: 169).

Provocation sometimes takes the form of holding up for the audience a mirror by which they may more accurately view themselves. This includes revealing to viewers their highly idealized self-images, desires, and goals, demonstrating that they are impossible to obtain, or alternatively, that they might actually disappoint them were they to be achieved (Griffin 1994: 62). The satirist "embod[ies] our highest image of ourselves and show[s] us that we are not it" (Griffin 1994: 62). And what some find even more disappointing about satire is that it sometimes either offers no real solution, or suggests that no solution even exists.

> The ultimate provocation—what Swift calls vexing the world—is to make readers look in the mirror and see that they are not and can never be what they claim to be. Satire cannot mend them; it can only hope to make them *see*.
> (Griffin 1994: 62)

Griffin suggests, therefore, that for some satirists, the only positive contribution of their work is to tell the truth, simply for the sake of revelation itself (Griffin 1994: 63). But I suspect there is also hidden beneath the rough exterior of many satires an ulterior motive of sharing the cold, hard facts of reality with others, if for no other reason than the simple fact that sometimes "misery loves company." However, the danger of such an assumption is that it may unfairly paint the satirist as more of a pessimist or skeptic than is really necessary.

One of the challenges of using provocation effectively is knowing where to draw the line between seizing the attention of one's audience, perhaps with shocking material, and offending them to the point of driving them away. One needs to keep an audience around in order to communicate with them. But as Griffin points out, "An unregulated spirit of ridicule arouses concern, not just for decorum … but for the safety of whatever one holds dear," and this can undermine one's underlying purpose (Griffin 1994: 55). Too strong a defensive reaction from the intended audience can make them deaf to what the satirist ultimately hopes to communicate.

The next two features of satire are display and play, and they are closely related. Both reflect the artistic skill of the satirist, and, like provocation, are ultimately designed to serve the goal of inquiry. Display refers to any satiric feature intended to demonstrate the satirist's gifts and talents for entertaining, for acquiring the audience's admiration and respect, even if it occurs in the context of being highly critical of something the audience holds dear. It builds respect and trust, both of which are useful for keeping an audience's attention, and for softening the abrasiveness of, or building tolerance for, the author's provocation. According to Griffin, "Anybody can call names, but it requires skill to make a malefactor die sweetly" (Griffin 1994: 73).

In *South Park*, while Cartman regularly infuriates the other characters around him (and the audience as well) with his extreme bigotry and racism, the audience celebrates much more enthusiastically when his evil plans (which are often a key plot element) fail miserably. He is the character that every viewer loves to hate, and as such, he is a highly effective negative example that clarifies what are more appropriate attitudes and behaviors for the rest of the world. He helps to highlight any latent, revolting attitudes in the audience, and brings these things out into the open, expressing that which is, under normal circumstances, taboo (i.e. off-limits or unholy). In doing so, he earns a certain amount of embarrassing respect from the audience for his unbridled honesty. But ultimately, he plays the role of the sacred clown, teaching that the opposite of Cartman is really what the creators are advocating. This, in fact, is one of the strategies of satire that immature or unenlightened viewers most often fail to understand.

Play refers to any element of fun and humor, any delightful or "self-delighting activity that has no concern for morality or for any real-world consequences save the applause of the spectators" (Griffin 1994: 84). Play is a "joyous exercise or movement," which not only entertains, but also provides an "arena … marked off from business or serious purpose" (Griffin 1994: 84). As a result, satiric play makes room for the treatment of otherwise serious subject matter in ways not normally allowed. This technique is clearly seen in the amount of religious satire found in standup comedy, as well as in the effective use of caricatures, for some of the most provocative satiric messages. It is no accident that some of the most potentially offensive religious satires occur in cartoon sitcoms. A fictitious character like Cartman, in a cartoon where all the characters are depicted in a very flat, two-dimensional way, can get away with much more provocation than a more realistic, human character. What some criticize as cheap, unrealistic artwork in *South Park* is actually an important and ingenious display of skill for more effective communication through provocation.

The last element of satire to be discussed is unstable **irony**. According to Griffin, satire sometimes "acquires a momentum of its own" and spins out of control (Griffin 1994: 64). The satirist can display an almost devilish attack on anything deemed worthy of destruction, even if this undermines the overarching purpose of inquiry. Here one encounters an "ambivalence" that makes it difficult to "reconstruct that author's precise meaning with any confidence" (Griffin 1994: 67). This kind of satire primarily "takes the form of an evasion, a refusal to commit, a negative rather than an assertion" (Griffin 1994: 69, following Kierkegaard 1968: 263–281). Griffin suggests that sometimes "the process of inquiry is truly open-ended; its exploration has no territory or map, no particular complacency to disturb," and the satirist "fall[s] into a mindless cynicism where everything is subject to" attack (Griffin 1994: 69–70). The danger in this is that "the satire that attacks everybody [and everything] touches nobody. And the satirist who laughs too widely may be, like Lucian, dismissed as a buffoon," or, I would add, simply evil (Griffin 1994: 70). (Lucian of Samosata, ca. 125–180 CE, was a famous 2nd-century satirist. Cf. A.M. Harmon (trans.), *Lucian, Vols. I–V*, Loeb Classical Library, Harvard University Press, 1913–1936.)

Case studies

South Park

South Park episodes often deal with religious topics, addressing both practical ethics for living a meaningful life, and issues related to the afterlife, including farcical depictions of heaven, hell, and their residents. Three of my favorite episodes with religious content are "Christian Rock Hard" (Season 7), mentioned above, "The Passion of the Jew" (Season 8), and "Best Friends Forever" (Season 9), although there are many more. Currently, all episodes may be viewed in their entirety, for free, on the internet at http://southparkstudios.com. Unfortunately, I only have space here to discuss briefly a few of these episodes.

South Park episodes often contain two story lines that are related and woven together in various ways, and "Christian Rock Hard" is no exception. How the two plots are related in a given episode is not always obvious, but this design encourages viewers to reflect upon the structure of each episode, and usually provides a **cipher** for understanding the creators' message. As stated above, in "Christian Rock Hard" the first story line involves Cartman's attempt to use superficial Christian music to create a platinum rock album before his friends, Stan, Kyle, and Kenny, can. This plot explores such things as the real nature and purpose of Christian music, the potential gullibility of Christian consumers, and what it really means to have a "personal" relationship with Jesus. The second story line explores the ethics of Stan, Kyle, and Kenny illegally downloading secular music from the internet in order to inform their developing style of music. It inquires about whether secular artists should produce music purely for the money, or because they love art for art's sake. It asks whether it is unethical for average consumers to steal music if the artists are already filthy rich, or if they can still make a good living on the proceeds from concerts and the sale of memorabilia.

The relationship between these two plots is quite easily grasped with a little bit of reflection. Both inquire about the ethics of exploitation in a pop culture world of mass marketing and mass consumerism. Both inquire about the integrity of consumers and producers. Together, they raise questions about who is the victim and who is the criminal when greed combines with high tech media to compete for the average consumer's hard-earned dollars. Should musicians consider themselves artists, first and foremost, or are they merely greedy business owners and salespeople? Are consumers merely powerless, gullible pawns at the mercy of greater economic forces? Is Christian music any different from secular music? Are Christian consumers significantly different from secular ones?

In light of the fact that "Christian Rock Hard" is primarily focused on dealing with such complex ethical issues, the highly provocative exploration of the topic of a personal relationship with Jesus, while certainly an attention-grabbing and playful display, is treated quite superficially in comparison. It appears to be designed more for fun and for maintaining viewer interest, rather than as a central topic of inquiry. In the end, the episode asks far more questions than it answers. Apparently, it is enough merely to raise the question about how intimately a believer may know an invisible god. It is left to the viewer to decide the ethics of illegally downloading music from the internet, although, as is often the case in *South Park* episodes, the viewer does encounter a closing scene with a typical moralizing moment. Here, it is common for one of the children, after an episode full of craziness, to suggest a more practical or reasonable course of action for the viewer. This is typical of *South Park*, where the star children eventually display more common sense than their parents or adult neighbors.

By way of contrast, a great deal of the episode's message is communicated more implicitly. For instance, in one scene, a police officer takes Stan, Kyle, and Kenny on a tour of famous music artists' homes in order to demonstrate the so-called devastating effects of consumers downloading music for free from the internet. Here, the boys learn that Lars Ulrich, drummer for the rock band *Metallica*, is in a deep state of depression because he will have to wait a few months before he can afford to install a "gold plated shark tank bar" next to his outdoor pool, all because of people downloading his music for free, rather than purchasing it legally. The boys are stunned, and quite sympathetic. Likewise, Britney Spears is depressed because she has to downsize her private jet from a Gulfstream 4 to a Gulfstream 3, the latter which doesn't even have a remote control for its surround sound DVD system. And finally, the tour ends with a visit to the home of rap artist *Master P*, who will likely be unable to buy his son an island in French Polynesia for his birthday this year. The boys are distraught over the thought that this child's wish of owning his own tropical paradise will not be fulfilled.

A second example of a more implicit argument occurs when Cartman loses his temper at a public award ceremony upon learning that his album did not go platinum, but instead earned a uniquely Christian Myrrh award. Cartman begins cursing and smashes his award, complaining that he will never be able to produce a platinum album with Christian music, because they only award Gold, Frankincense, and Myrrh albums. The presenter of the award protests, "But you spread the word of the Lord; you brought faith in Jesus," to which Cartman responds, "Ahh, fuck Jesus!" Butters, one of the other band members, then states, "Eric, I'm pretty sure you shouldn't say the f-word about Jesus." Cartman, however, doesn't care about the well-being of the band, or blasphemy, and his tirade drives away the entire audience. This is when the third band member, named Token, also responds. (Token is the only black child on the show, and in most episodes where he appears, he is specifically designed to undermine racial stereotypes about blacks. He is one of the richest, most articulate, and most intelligent citizens of the nearly all-white mountain town of South Park, Colorado.) Token criticizes Cartman's self-centered behavior, which has now destroyed the band: "Good job dickhead; you lost the entire audience." His words here reflect the perspective of the creators about the risk artists take by being too self-absorbed and greedy to care about the very audience that has made them successful. After having heaped racist verbal abuse on Token throughout the episode, Cartman then refers to Token one last time as a "Black asshole." Token finally loses control and, for lack of better language, kicks Cartman's ass. Stan then tells Kyle and Kenny, "Hmmn, I guess he got what he deserved," and even Butters, one of the show's most timid and gullible characters, tells Cartman off, and walks away.

Here, one encounters not an explicit argument against Cartman's (and the music industry's) greed and hypocrisy. Instead, one learns it implicitly through the reactions of other characters. The creators of the show are not simply anti-religious, anti-Christian, or anti-music industry. They do not advocate Cartman's sacrilegious behavior any more than they support greed among secular musicians. In fact, for the most part, the Christian characters in the episode are treated rather sympathetically. They may be presented as somewhat gullible and naive, but their behavior is well-intentioned. Likewise, everyday consumers of secular music, including those who download songs illegally, are also handled sympathetically. Provocation in the episode is designed more to help Christians in the audience think critically about not just the way they relate to Jesus, but also how they behave as producers and consumers of religious goods. Are they conducting the business of Christian music any differently than that of secular music? Secular musicians are chided here for the hypocrisy of considering themselves artists when many are only in the music industry for the money. Their potential smugness and greed are highlighted by their petty, superficial concerns for outdoor bars, private jets, and private islands.

Griffin's categories of inquiry, provocation, display, play, and unstable irony can greatly assist the viewer's understanding of the real intentions behind an instance of religious satire. While some of my religious students initially react to *South Park* by focusing too much attention on the provocative religious material, critical analysis in light of the true nature of satire can redirect their attention to the most important objects of inquiry. This helps them see that the provocation is normally placed in service of the inquiry, as are the display and play. Those who focus too much on the graphic language, potty humor, and disrespectful treatment of certain characters, beliefs, and practices in *South Park* fail to grasp that these are usually just a means to an end, not the end itself. They are often playful elements or an attempt merely to display the author's creativity. There are moments, of course, when play for play's sake takes center stage, and sometimes irony or an outright attack on something deemed ridiculous temporarily spins out of control. But the moralistic, teaching emphasis of most *South Park* episodes suggests that cultural critique in the form of satire is the chief purpose. Many episodes even include a so-called teaching moment near the conclusion, when a character (usually Stan or Kyle) raises questions, many of which are merely rhetorical, in order to suggest a better course of action for the viewer than what has been displayed thus far.

Sometimes, these moments do not explicitly state what the authors consider the correct response, but merely highlight what are considered incorrect ones. For example, near the end of the "Best Friends Forever" episode, in which Kenny has become brain dead and his situation has been seized upon by both right-to-life and right-to-death advocates to promote their respective causes, Kyle steps forward, as if speaking directly to the viewer, and makes a series of mature and rational statements. "Maybe we let this thing get out of hand. This issue is so complicated, but maybe we should just let Kenny go in peace." Kyle also suggests that people can do the right thing for the wrong reason, and the wrong thing for the right reason. He ends by saying, "C'mon everybody, I think Kenny wants to be left alone."

These statements are intended to sum up the lessons that the viewer should have learned throughout the viewing experience. They are not necessarily profound, or incredibly insightful. They simply reflect common sense. This episode never provides a conclusive answer to the right-to-life debate, but it does suggest some respectful ground rules for all parties involved, primarily focusing on trying to determine what the patient would have wanted. The purpose of this episode is to explore issues surrounding the right to life debate, specifically concerning disabled and potentially brain-dead individuals in the wake of the famous Terri Schiavo case (1998–2005), in which the patient's husband sought to remove her feeding tube, against the wishes of other family members. The incident became a media sensation, and the Schiavo family found themselves at the center of a political battle in which few parties really cared about them. Instead, various groups manipulated the situation to further their own agendas. Unfortunately, simple human decency and dignity were lost in the midst.

But the episode does not end on this note. Instead, irony prevails, because Kenny was initially killed by divine design before being revived in a vegetative state by human hands (i.e. doctors playing God, just because they can). God had chosen Kenny to lead the forces of heaven in an epic battle against the forces of hell, by intending him to control a golden PSP (PlayStation Portable; a handheld video game), which Kenny had mastered before his death. Eventually, and unbeknownst to all those on earth who fought over his right to life, it is only when Kenny is allowed to die for good that he is finally able to lead the forces of heaven to victory. This irony suggests that no one on earth can truly claim to know the will of heaven on certain issues, and it is presumptuous to assume such knowledge in order to manipulate others.

Saved!

Another popular piece of modern day satire can be found in the movie *Saved!*. The plot surrounds the lead character, Mary, a devout Christian entering her senior year at a conservative evangelical Christian school. Initially, her life seems perfect, but it is quickly turned upside down when she accidentally becomes pregnant out of wedlock in a desperate attempt to "cure" her homosexual boyfriend, Dean, by seducing him into having sex with her. She fails, and her boyfriend is sent off to a camp by his parents to be "de-gayified." Mary then begins to question her faith, including her belief in God's providential care and God's supposed hatred of homosexuals. Her superficial friends conclude that she's possessed, and try to exorcise her demons. When they fail to bring her back in line with their own convictions, they abandon her to perdition. However, in the end, most of the surrounding characters abandon the simplistic religious answers they were raised to believe, and acknowledge that they are all less than perfect, even Mary's chief nemesis, Hilary Fay, who prides herself throughout most of the film on being a better Christian than all her peers. The film does not advocate an outright abandonment of faith, not even a conservative faith, but instead endorses a faith with more grace, humility, maturity, and mercy. However, it must be admitted that the film's desire for a happy closure comes at the price of believability, since the conversion of Mary's friends and family occurs a bit too easily to be realistic.

There is no question that the film takes its share of shots at evangelical Christianity. The stereotyped characters are many, and their depiction is sometimes outrageous, and for some, outrageously funny. But some of my evangelical students find themselves initially taking offense at this film, failing to grasp that, overall, the producers are actually quite sympathetic to all of the main characters. There is something pathetic, if not downright likeable, about them. This includes the hypocritical Hilary Fay, as well as the principal of the high school, Pastor Skip, who falls in love with Mary's mother (a single parent), but won't follow through on his feelings because, as a matter of principle, he refuses to divorce the wife that he is already physically separated from, because it just doesn't fit his own "biblical" understanding of God's plan. In the end, however, all these characters prove to be redeemable when they recognize their own faults and stop being so judgmental of others.

The focus of the film's satiric inquiry is whether it is necessary for some committed Christians to be judgmental and condemning of those who believe differently. The question is raised whether striving to be correct or perfect is really what faith should be about. The film concludes more with a question than an answer, as Mary narrates her thoughts about the year's events to the viewer:

> Ok, I'm pretty sure this isn't what Jesus had in mind when he said, "Help Dean." Look, don't be too harsh. I'm not the first person to ever get the message screwed up. Looking at her [Mary's newborn baby], it's like life is too amazing to be this random and meaningless consequence of the universe. There had to be a God, or something out there, something inside, you just

> have to feel it. I mean, really, when you think about it, what *would* Jesus do? I don't know, but in the meantime, we'll be trying to figure it out, together.[1]

Certainly, this ending puts forward what the creators consider a better approach to the religious life. It is, to a great extent, a mystery, but one that is best explored in solidarity with others, rather than in conflict with them. Prior to this, the film also strongly implies its alternative view of Christianity after the climactic revelation at the senior prom that Hilary Fay resorted to lying and vandalism to frame Mary and her friends in an effort to get them expelled. Here, the film's most super (ficial) Christian publicly falls from grace because, in her zeal to see her own version of justice and truth prevail, she embraced evil. The ends and means are seen as inconsistent, and her plot is foiled by Mary's fellow outcasts: Hilary Fay's own handicapped brother, Roland, and Roland's girlfriend, Cassandra, the latter being the school's first and only openly Jewish student. Feeling betrayed by God, Hilary Fay races away from the prom and purposely crashes her van into a giant, lighted billboard Jesus located in the school parking lot, which causes the savior's wooden head to fall upon her windshield. She responds by screaming out "Jesus Christ!" and then stares into the face of Jesus, who seemingly looks down on her in disappointment, if not judgment.

In what is arguably the film's most tender moment, Roland rushes to Hilary Fay's aid, offering his sister the grace she has refused to offer to him, Cassandra, and Mary.

> Hilary Fay: This is not how I wanted to remember my prom. This is not how I wanted to remember my life.
> Roland: [Jokingly, but sympathetically] Well, maybe we could fix it … with some glue or something.
> Hilary Fay: I am so sorry, Roland.
> Roland: I shouldn't have ratted you out in front of everyone.
> Hilary Fay: I would have probably done the same thing … Do you think Jesus still loves me, Roland?
> Roland: [Jokingly at first] Probably not. [Pause] Yeah. Sure.[1]

Conclusion

In conclusion, it should be clear that Griffin's categories may be readily applied to a variety of satiric texts, including television and film. This should be done carefully, with critical reflection. Over against one of Griffin's conclusions, some satires do more than simply point out something that is deemed incorrect or explore important questions. Sometimes, they suggest what is considered a more appropriate position or a solution to certain problems, even if it is presented by more implicit, rather than explicit, means. Nevertheless, Griffin's approach is helpful for better understanding a satiric author's intentions, regardless of which satiric element dominates. It would behoove all students of satire to clarify the chief topics of a satire's inquiry, asking what issues are being explored, what assumed positions are being questioned, and what more appropriate advice or course of action may be advocated. This should lead to a greater appreciation for the genre, and a better understanding of the role of such elements as provocation, display, and play. Ultimately, if one better understands the nature of satire, there is a greater potential for one to learn from it, and therefore become a more critical thinking, self-aware, and wise consumer. And this would fulfill the overall goal of most satires quite nicely.

Summary

- Satire is a complex genre often misunderstood by those who are unfamiliar with its true nature and purposes.
- Griffin's approach provides an important resource for better appreciating satire's component parts and intentions, especially in pop cultural versions.
- The chief purpose of satire is inquiry, but provocation, display, and play are key tools for grabbing an audience's attention, and keeping it.
- Sometimes the abrasiveness of provocation, as well as unstable irony, can undermine the goal of inquiry, and drive an audience away.
- Sometimes satires go beyond mere inquiry, and they function more rhetorically.

Glossary terms

Caricature – a literary or visual depiction of a person that exaggerates or otherwise distorts certain characteristics of his or her image and/or behavior.
Cipher – either a means of encrypting or hiding one's intended message or the interpretive key to revealing or understanding a hidden message.
Deliberative rhetoric – argumentation designed to convince an audience to change their behavior.
Irony – a situation in which the expected outcome or intended effect is subverted, and the opposite occurs. (See also the treatment of this word in Chapter 10, including the glossary term at the end of the chapter.)
Polemic – an argument intended to dispute a position or person that is considered false or heretical.

Points for discussion

- How many examples of modern day religious satire can you think of, and how many different pop culture genres do they represent (e.g. TV, film, music, literature, etc.)?
- Thinking about these examples, are you convinced that their chief purpose is simply creating a more critically informed audience? Who do you think is their intended audience?
- For how many of your examples can you identify a rhetorical (argumentative) message? How would you describe this message?
- How many of your examples do you think are effective for accomplishing their chief purpose? Why or why not?

Note

1 Extract from *Saved!*

Further reading

Arp, Robert (ed.) (2006) *South Park and Philosophy: You Know, I Learned Something Today*, Blackwell Philosophy and Pop Culture Series, Malden, MA: Blackwell Publishing.

A collection of essays on various aspects of the world of *South Park*, some more insightful than others, which address interesting philosophical, political, and religious topics. These are helpful for better appreciating the intellectual depth and educational value of the show.

Wisnewski, J. Jeremy (ed.) (2007) *Family Guy and Philosophy: A Cure for the Petarded*, Blackwell Philosophy and Pop Culture Series, Malden, MA: Wiley-Blackwell Publishing.

A collection of essays on various aspects of the world of *Family Guy*, some more insightful than others, which address interesting philosophical, political, and religious topics. These are helpful for better appreciating the intellectual depth and educational value of the show.

Walls, Neal H. (ed.) (2005) *Cult Image and Divine Representation in the Ancient Near East*, Boston: American Schools of Oriental Research.

An insightful but technical collection of essays about the form and function of divine images in the ancient Near Eastern world.

Aristotle (1926) *The Art of Rhetoric*, trans. J.H. Freese, Loeb Classical Library 193, Cambridge, MA: Harvard University Press.

One of the most ancient and famous works ever written on rhetorical theory. An excellent starting point for studying this methodology.

Perelman, Ch. and Olbrechts-Tyteca, L. (1971) *The New Rhetoric: A Treatise on Argumentation*, trans. John Wilkinson and Purcell Weaver, Notre Dame, IN: University of Notre Dame Press.

The most extensive single volume on argumentative strategies and techniques. This is a very technical, but exhaustive resource on the topic of rhetoric.

Bibliography

Aristophanes (1993), *Frogs*, ed. Kenneth Dover, Oxford: Clarendon Press.

Booth, Wayne (1974) *The Rhetoric of Irony*, Chicago: University of Chicago Press.

Dutton, John (1707) *Athenian Sport: or, Two Thousand Paradoxes Merrily Argued, to Amuse and Divert the Age*, London: Paternoster.

Elkin, P.K. (1973) *The Augustan Defence of Satire*, Oxford: Oxford University Press.

Griffin, Dustin (1994) *Satire: A Critical Reintroduction*, Lexington, KY: University of Kentucky Press.

Kierkegaard, Søren (1968) *The Concept of Irony*, trans. Lee Capel; Bloomington, IN: University of Indiana Press.

Lucian (1913–1936) *Volumes I–V*, trans. A.M. Harmon, Loeb Classical Library, Vols. 14, 54, 130, 162, 302, Cambridge: Harvard University Press.

Morris, David (1984) *Alexander Pope: The Genius of Sense*, Cambridge: Harvard University Press.

2 Religion and ecology in popular culture

Dell deChant

Introduction

Ecological issues regularly confront us in today's world, and popular culture is replete with accounts of these issues, from the BP oilrig disaster in the Gulf of Mexico to the mysterious maladies affecting bees and bats, and from catastrophic weather events such as Hurricane *Katrina* to environmental degradation due to strip-mining. **Ecology** is in the news today, without question, and ecological topics (typically, various ecological calamities) are features of nearly every weekly news cycle. Seldom do more than a few days pass without reports airing of challenges related to ecology—habitat loss for major predators (tigers, polar bears, panthers) and hydraulic fracturing, GMOs and melting glaciers, invasive species and contaminated food supplies, record-breaking heat and devastating floods, and so on. The list is long and lengthening.

Clearly, ecology is one of the more significant interests of contemporary popular culture, and the study of religion and popular culture rightly includes ecology as a major subject area. Curiously, however, despite the widespread interest in ecological issues and questions for both scholars and the general public, there are relatively few academic texts that engage the religious dimensions of the ecology in popular culture. This is not to say there are not important studies of religion and ecology or popular culture and ecology. There certainly are. In fact, these two subject areas represent important new areas of scholarly inquiry. What seems missing, however, are studies giving significant and explicit attention to religion in the context of the intersection of ecology and popular culture.

The purpose of this chapter is, thus, to offer an initial encounter with a largely underexplored and only sketchily mapped subfield within the field of religion and popular culture. Despite its relatively marginalized status at present, religion and ecology in popular culture is an extremely important area of inquiry and one that presents us with a vast array of issues and questions—too many, in fact, to be taken up in a brief introduction such as this. What can be done here is sketch the ways in which religion and ecology intersect in popular culture, and present some theoretic concepts that may help in better understanding that intersection.

To develop this sketch, the theory and method section will first survey the development of the subfield of Religion and Ecology, then specify key terms used in studies of religion and ecology, and conclude with a summary of major theoretic concepts that typically guide studies of religion and ecology. The case study that follows will consider how these concepts might be reconfigured to better engage religion and ecology *in* popular culture, and better analyze and evaluate the religious dimensions of a well-known ecological issue—Climate Change—in popular culture.

Theory and method

Historical context

The field of Religion and Ecology is one of the newest areas of research in Religious Studies. It emerges in the context of both the growth of Religious Studies as a recognized scholarly field and the rise in public awareness of the ecological challenges facing the world. As a distinct subfield of Religious Studies, the origin of Religion and Ecology is typically traced to a series of conferences entitled "Religions of the World and Ecology," hosted by Harvard Divinity School's Center for the Study of World Religions from 1996 to 1998. As noted by one of the major organizers, Mary Evelyn Tucker, the conferences were intended to:

> Provide a broad survey that would help ground a new field of study in religion and ecology .... Recognizing that religions are key shapers of people's worldviews and formulators of their most cherished values, this research project uncovered a wealth of attitudes and practices toward nature sanctioned by religious traditions.
>
> (Tucker 2006: 407)

Most scholars working in this area would agree that the Harvard conferences, and subsequent publication of a ten-volume collection of papers from the conferences, launched Religion and Ecology as a significant subfield within Religious Studies. By the same token, many scholars would also recognize important work prior to the conferences, especially the pioneering efforts of David Barnhill and Eugene Bianchi who established Religion and Ecology as a regular topic area at meetings of the American Academy of Religion (AAR) beginning in 1989 (Taylor 2008: 1373). Of course, long before the Harvard conferences and the appearance of Religion and Ecology at the AAR, a scholar of medieval culture and technology by the name of Lynn Townsend White, Jr. published the seminal article in the field, "The Historical Roots of Our Ecologic Crisis" (White 1967).

White's article was the first to engage issues (in this case, what he identified as a "crisis") in ecology in terms of religion. It was a bold and provocative study, which offered a rather severe critique of the role (and culpability) of religion in bringing about the degradation of the natural world. Following closely the publication of Rachel Carson's *Silent Spring* (1962), which arguably initiated the environmental movement in popular culture, White's article traced the origins of the West's cavalier attitude toward the natural environment and disregard of ecological systems to Christianity and (in White's reading, at least) the sacred sanction it gave to the exploitation of nature. White's "Roots" is still referenced by contemporary scholars, and it is fair to say that few texts have had as great an impact on a field of study as this short article has had on Religion and Ecology.

Today, Religion and Ecology is a vital, dynamic, and very diverse area of scholarly activity. The past decade has seen the publication of numerous academic texts on Religion and Ecology, several substantial reference books, a number of collections, and two scholarly journals dedicated to the topic. Universities have developed specific concentrations in Religion and Ecology, and faculty at many schools of higher education have developed and continue to develop courses in this area.

Religion and ecology today

As a rapidly expanding and still emerging field, it is risky to specify distinct theories and methods unique to Religion and Ecology. Suffice it to say that the general tools of scholarship used in the academic study of religion are also relevant in this area, with some being more important or more frequently encountered here than in other areas. Rather than presenting a wide collection of theories and methods, I will note those that seem of particular importance for general purposes and basic familiarity. In this regard, several preliminary understandings are critical to our encounter with Religion and Ecology in Popular Culture.

First and foremost, as noted previously, despite the important and rapidly expanding work being done in both Religion and Ecology and Ecology and Popular Culture, the area of our particular interest has been largely overlooked—at least as a clearly delineated topic, or subfield. This being the case, inquiries into Religion and Ecology in Popular Culture are best thought of as preliminary and rightly attentive to terms and concepts being used.

As Professor Clark demonstrates in the "Introduction" to this book, the study of religion and popular culture necessarily begins with definitions, and he carefully presents a set of working definitions of key terms; specifically, religion, culture, and popular culture. You will find that this is not uncommon in academic texts in new and still developing areas of inquiry, such as religion and popular culture, religion and gender, religion and sports, religion and ecology, and others. If you happen to explore Religion and Ecology in other courses or on your own, you will find texts in this area usually give careful attention to definitions of key terms—especially religion.

In this regard, we are reminded of Daniel L. Pals' correct observation that: "As we proceed, it will be wise to keep in mind that the matter of defining religion is closely linked to the matter of explaining it" (Pals 2006: 13). In other words, there is a close link between definition of critical terms of a field and theories used to guide critical inquiries into subjects of that field. This is certainly the case in studies of Religion and Ecology.

Key terms

So, as we consider Religion and Ecology in Popular Culture, our first concern is establishing a working vocabulary. For purposes of order and coherence, we will accept Professor Clark's descriptions of *religion*, *culture* and *popular culture*, given in the "Introduction." Clark's description of *religion* will be nuanced a bit in the "Case Study" section with the addition of the concept of the **sacred**, and an explanation of the theoretic relationship between religion and the sacred.

From among the many other terms and concepts relevant to studies in this area, three are especially critical: **nature**, **the environment**, and **ecology**. For scholars of Religion and Ecology, these three terms have importance, and attention to their usage in the literature is necessary.

Most broadly, the term **nature** refers to the physical-material world, and all entities, features, properties, and processes occurring therein. In this broad sense, "nature" necessarily includes humankind. More typically, however, nature has referred to the physical-material world as it exists independent of human modifications or distinct from human control and manipulation.

Today, however, human life has so fundamentally altered the natural world that nature as an independent force no longer exists. In this regard, Bill McKibben's notion of "**the end of nature**" (McKibben 1989) has broad acceptance among scholars of religion and ecology. Further, in popular usage, nature has an antiquated, anachronistic resonance. What once might have been referred to as nature (or natural), today is referred to as "the environment" (or "environmental"). Thus, in this area, nature tends not to be used as frequently as it once might have been, although the first, broader meaning of nature (given above) remains of enormous importance to understanding the planet and the life it sustains.

Increasingly, where nature once might have been used, **the environment** is the preferred technical term. Most broadly, the environment refers to the immediate context in which something exists or is located. It is often used as a synonym for nature (in the second sense), now that the traditional sense of nature has been compromised and begun to decline in popular usage. For example, in popular discourse, we more often hear of calls to "protect the environment," but not so much to "protect nature." The environment is not a synonym for nature, however; for what this usage reveals, subtly perhaps, is that nature, per se, does not exist independently of human contexts. The environment is always contextual, and human beings supply the context—affecting it, being affected by it, and defining it. Where "nature" may at times imply independence from humans, the "environment" seldom has such a connotation.

In a related sense, the derived term, Environmentalism, typically refers to outlooks, beliefs, and sources of action that respect and seek to protect the *natural* environment. Although "the environment" usually is taken to mean the natural environment, it can refer to any number of non-natural settings—e.g. the domestic environment, the economic environment, the political, the urban, the educational, and so on. Notably, however, when used without modification, it is usually understood to refer to the *natural* environment; and the term environmentalism is *always* understood this way.

In the context of the evolving meanings and nuances of the terms previously presented, **ecology** has received broad acceptance as the covering term for academic enterprises concerned with the relationship of human beings to the world of nature (or the environment). Most generally, ecology refers to the study of the interrelationship of organisms and the world around them. Beyond this initial understanding, the term has come to mean the study of the interrelationship of all things in nature (as a whole) and the specific relationship between specific actions and distinct effects. Importantly, in the context of Religion and Ecology, according to a recent textbook, "ecology is a *morally instructive* system of interconnections, a claim about the interrelated character of nature that has instructive lessons to teach all people" (Bauman *et al.* 2011: 230; italics mine). Aside from these more academic meanings, in terms of popular culture, the meanings and implications of ecology are extremely wide-ranging, politically and socially charged, publicly disputed, and economically problematic. It is of critical importance that all inquirers (from elementary school students in science classes to professional scholars) recognize this reality. Most do not.

Theoretic elements to consider and re-consider

It is at this point we can consider three general theoretic elements of relevance to Religion and Ecology and how they might be reconsidered or reconfigured to engage this area in Popular Culture. First, Religion and Ecology is surprisingly normative and "activist"; second it tends to be unusually focused on traditional expressions of religion; and third it generally overlooks the relationship of this area to culture as a whole—in which environmental issues and ecological concerns have come to comprise a much-disputed terrain, and one contested by powerful secular forces such as business, politics, government, and the media. Each of these elements will be briefly considered here in the context of Religion and Ecology, and then reconsidered in light of Religion and Ecology *in* Popular Culture.

First, although it may be a bit surprising to some, Religion and Ecology is recognized by many as a field of inquiry in which scholars are allowed (even expected) to be activists. The passage from the textbook on Religion and Ecology cited earlier is suggestive of this normative character of many studies of Religion and Ecology. Notice how the authors understand ecology to be "morally instructive" and that the "interrelated character of nature has instructive lessons." Implied in these assertions is that there is an intrinsic value and even virtue in ecology. Moreover, they stress:

> Scholars in the field of religion and ecology seek to make a practical difference in the world. This field exists not just to develop theories and ideas, but also to contribute to the activist cause of building a more sustainable world.
>
> (Bauman *et al.* 2011: 8)

Underscoring the normative nature of this field, one of its major theorists, Roger Gottlieb, affirms that the study of religion and ecology emerged in the context of the massive ecological crisis facing the world today, and that one of the major questions that "form the heart of the study of religion and ecology" is "how must beliefs (and actions) change as we face the *environment*" (Gottlieb 2006: 6). Note again the normative character of this approach. The question is not whether beliefs and actions will change or even that they should, but rather *how must* they change.

While the normative approach may seem quite reasonable, and certainly worthy of serious consideration in today's world, some may find it problematic from a scholarly standpoint. Once ecology (however it may be conceived) is deemed morally instructive the neutrality and objectivity of the inquirer may be questioned. Further, if inquiry begins with the presupposition that we are confronted with a massive ecological crisis that requires change in (religious) beliefs and actions, the inquirer's objectivity may again be questioned, with the risk that the findings and conclusions of the inquirer are deemed to be compromised. Yet, such risks are common in this area of study. When considering religion and ecology in popular culture, we may find a more suitable method to be the neutral approach that is typical of Religious Studies.

The second consideration in our reflection on theoretic approaches to religion and ecology in popular culture is the recognition that all too often previous studies have focused their attention quite heavily on major world religions. Elsewhere, I have referred to this method of assessing the value and meaning of religion in contemporary secular culture as the "usual suspects approach" (deChant 2008: 77–79). While there are exceptions to the usual suspects approach, as will be noted below, for the most part the study of religion and ecology is restricted to explorations of beliefs, practices, and current attitudes of well-known and well-established religions. These studies also tend to be developed in the context of Lynn White's original critique of over forty years ago (White 1967). That is, there is often a presumption that *mainstream* religion should be doing something about the "ecological crisis." Attention then is given to what mainstream religion is or is not doing—with accolades extended to activities deemed meritorious and encouragement to do more.

As we study religion and ecology in popular culture, I think we can do better than the usual suspects approach. We can consider what Bron Taylor terms "green religions" and "dark green religion," taking seriously the presence of important religious expressions in marginal movements such as neo-paganism, Native American spirituality, and New Age religions (Taylor 2006: 598–599); and even including the emergence of a non-supernaturalistic "civic earth religion" (Taylor 2006: 604–606). Even more successfully, as I will argue in the case study that follows, we can deploy the thought of Jacques Ellul (with some modifications) and discover the sacred function of seemingly secular cultural systems.

Case study: Finding the sacred in the climate change debate

To introduce this specific case study (the Climate Change Debate), let me begin by noting the third and final theoretic feature of Religion and Ecology that we may reconsider—namely, that studies in this area generally overlook the relationship of Religion and Ecology to culture as a whole. In doing so, they tend to minimize the reality that environmental issues and ecological concerns have come to comprise a much-disputed terrain, and one contested by powerful secular forces such as business, politics, government, and the media. The assertion that there is a massive ecological crisis, as routinely occurs in literature on Religion and Ecology, is far from a generally accepted fact in contemporary American culture. When reading the fine work by important scholars on the various issues and questions pertaining to religion and ecology, folks who are even marginally familiar with the wider world of culture are doubtless quite mindful that much (if not all) of what is being presented in these marvelous studies will be rejected out of hand by a large percentage of the American population and the vast majority of the elected leaders of one of America's two great political parties. For them there is no more an ecological crisis today than there was one when Lynn White wrote his article in 1967. Moreover, for them, not only is there not a crisis, the very idea of one is a pernicious hoax concocted by a political elite.

As Robin Blumner reminds us (citing a Pew Research poll), in October, 2010, "only 34 percent of respondents said global warming is caused by human activity" (Blumner 2011). More strikingly, Senator James Inhofe (Oklahoma) has called global warming "the greatest hoax ever perpetrated on the American people" (Kolbert 2006: 160). Skeptics abound, yet in "legitimate scientific circles it is virtually impossible to find evidence of disagreement over the fundamentals of global warming" (Kolbert 2006: 162).

It is here, in the midst of the furiously disputed terrain of contemporary public opinion about the environment that Religion and Popular Culture may help us better understand and navigate the emerging field of religion and ecology. How this might happen will be presented in the context of an exploration of the heated climate change debate.

The volatility of the climate change debate in popular culture is hard to ignore and easy to observe. Those who are interested are invited to use a simple Google Search and type in "Climate Change." What you will find in the first four or five headings of the optimized list are "climate change facts" and then "climate change hoax." My most recent check (2/7/2011) resulted in over seven million sites under the "facts" heading; and a little over a million sites for the "hoax" heading.

In both instances, we are presented with what is aptly classified as an **availability cascade**, an ever increasing phenomenon in contemporary popular culture (especially cyber culture) and a powerful force in shaping understandings and perceptions of large portions of the population. An availability cascade, which seems virtually inevitable in internet research and communication using social-networking systems, is "a self-reinforcing process of collective belief formation by which an expressed perception triggers a chain reaction that gives the perception of increasing plausibility through its rising availability in public discourse" (Kuran and Sunstein 1999: 683).

In terms of our analysis of the climate-change debate, what this little exercise reveals is that no matter which side of the debate you are on, there is an overwhelming amount of information (facts, data, evidence, authorities) to support your case. The issue is polarized, and the competing availability cascades assure us that the issue will remain polarized. Why change your mind when you can craft a torrent of supporting information for your view? Moreover, why consider a competing position, when the position you have taken seems so obviously correct?

Doubtless many people do indeed form their views and convictions about climate change and numerous other issues due to availability cascades; and there does not seem to be any good reason to change one's mind or consider competing positions if one is captured in one of these cascades. However, students of religion and culture, and every other field of academic study, have a responsibility to get beyond the cascades of self-reinforcing facts and data—no matter how painful and unpleasant that may be. For us, the task at hand is to understand the matter before us; and to do that, we must set aside our personal beliefs and commitments.

What this means is that although one may have a rather profound personal interest in the environment and the relationship between human beings and the natural world, in order to understand and analyze this topic, one must necessarily set aside personal interest and commitment. This is the methodological approach known as **bracketing**, and it is predicated on one of the guiding principles of Religious Studies—neutrality. If I were to allow my personal stand on the issue to guide my scholarship, I would quickly move in the direction of the side that I agreed with, thus limiting my ability to understand the other side and to present that side fairly and honestly.

So, the first methodological step we are encouraged to take moves us away from the way Religion and Ecology is typically approached. In short, we *are not* taking a normative position on the issue; and unlike many scholars working in this area, *in terms of our research here*, we will not "consider nature to be sacred in some way" (Taylor 2006: 598). The status of the debate in popular culture does not allow us to do that. Note, nature may well be sacred (or not) for us, but the point is that *in terms of our research here* we have no commitment one way or another. What we do want to understand is the debate as it appears in popular culture, why it is so fractious, and how religion comes into play.

This brings us to the next methodological consideration; and, again, another departure from the traditional approach taken in Religion and Ecology. Rather than trying to compartmentalize and contextualize our study in terms of major religious traditions, we will take a broader approach.

While we certainly would learn something by using the usual suspects approach, what we would learn would not be all that meaningful or all that helpful to understanding the full fury and rigor of the climate-change debate. What we would find, by the way, is that most mainstream religions concur with scientific findings that climate change is occurring, is caused by humans, and humans must take action to mitigate its impact on future generations. This is notable and helpful, but it skirts the larger issue, which is why this topic is so heated, and why the sides are so polarized.

So, instead of researching specific religious traditions, or resorting to an "explanation by cascade" approach, we might apply a theory that expands the concept of the sacred and broadens the concept of **religion** so as to include cultural elements of a seemingly secular nature. The specific theory proposed here is derived from one introduced and first constructed by Jacques Ellul, namely that in the contemporary world, the sacred may be something more and something quite different from traditional notions of divinity (Ellul 1975). Further, and as a result, our relationship with the sacred is mediated through institutions other than traditional religions. For Ellul, in brief, the Ultimate Power of a culture is the sacred of that culture; and religion is the human institution through which the sacred is mediated within a society (Ellul 1975: Chs 3, 4, and 6).

For Ellul, technology is the sacred of contemporary culture, and politics is the dominant religious expression. In other words, technology is the Ultimate Power, and politics is the institution through which that Power is mediated in society. As I have argued elsewhere, Ellul's theory is extremely helpful; all it needs is a little fine-tuning (deChant 2002: 29–32). Specifically, the content of the two categories requires adjustment. Where Ellul argues for technology as the contemporary sacred, I argue for the economy; and where Ellul argues for politics as the religious institution that mediates the sacred, I suggest it is consumption—i.e. retail spending: shopping and buying products (deChant 2002: 36–40; for a thorough exposition of this theory and its deployment in an analysis of the religious dynamic of contemporary culture, see deChant 2002: 25–50).

Using this modification of Ellul's theory gives us a new vantage point for understanding why the climate-change/global warming debate is so contentious. It is not about science, and the Keeling Curve, the greenhouse effect, or data generated by NOAA (National Oceanic and Atmospheric Administration) and NASA (National Aeronautics and Space Administration) showing conclusively that the earth is warming and human activity generating CO_2 is the cause. Although both sides have their own respective availability cascades with torrents of facts and data, the substance of the debate does not ultimately concern facts and data.

Using the variation of Ellul's theory suggested above, we might better understand the debate in terms of the sacred and religion, in this case, the sacred of economic growth and expansion and the religion of consumption. What the hard science supporting climate change encounters in the world of popular culture are the deep seated religious beliefs of postmodern America, a world constructed on glorious myths of **American Exceptionalism** and unfettered economic growth, fueled by cheap oil, and energized by personal religious rituals of consumption of material goods at ever increasing rates. To reiterate and clarify, using this line of analysis, for contemporary American culture, the sacred (or Ultimate Power) is the economy, and our relationship with this sacred reality is fully experienced through the religion of consumption.

Using Ellul's theory, as modified here, gives us a better idea of why climate change, and various other ecological issues, cause such controversy. What is at stake is a sacred order of existence, and the religion that engages us with that sacred order. If the climate-changers are right, then it is this very order that is to blame for impending (and now appearing) global calamities. If global warming is actually occurring, and the dire consequences it promises are coming to pass, then the sacred world of American Exceptionalism, with its unending economic expansion and rituals of personal consumption, is coming to an end—and, ironically, bringing about its own demise.

It is, thus, for good reason that many leaders in government, commerce, and industry challenge and dismiss the claims of climate change. It is not a scientific debate, although it may assume the rhetorical trapping of such a debate. The science appears pretty well settled. For some it may appear political, and a case can be made for reading it this way.

Following Ellul, however, the challenge to the climate changers is not based on science or even politics. Instead, it is a thoroughgoing rejection of climate change on religious grounds. The opposition rejects climate change arguments because they compromise the sacred reality (of the economic order) of American culture and undermine its religion (of consumption). Critics of climate change are as adamant as they are because they are on a religious mission to eliminate a heretical belief. When analyzed in this way, we may not be in a position to better resolve the climate change debate or any of the other disputed ecological issues that surface in contemporary culture, but we might understand just why they are so contentious and why they are more religious than they might otherwise seem to be.

Summary

- Ecology and ecological issues are popular topics in contemporary culture, and although scholars have given attention to distinct subject areas of (1) Religion and Ecology, and (2) Ecology and Popular Culture, little attention has been given to Religion and Ecology *in* Popular Culture.
- Key concepts relevant to Religion and Ecology are: nature, environment, ecology, religion, and the sacred.
- To better address Religion and Ecology *in* Popular Culture certain theories and methods typically used by scholars of Religion and Ecology need to be reconsidered, specifically: (1) the normative/activist approach; (2) the focus on traditional expressions of religion; and (3) the tendency to overlook the relationship of Religion and Ecology to culture as a whole.
- Reconsideration and reconstruction of these three elements allows better understanding of Religion and Ecology in contemporary culture, and also why the issues in ecology are so contentious.

Glossary terms

American Exceptionalism – mythic narrative affirming the glorious destiny of the United States, predicated on the belief that the United States is unique among all nations in the history of the world. Stress is given to various ideals (self-governance, freedom of association, economic opportunity, and others) as definitive of America's exceptionalism and the sources of its world-historic success.

Availability cascade – process through which a claim becomes accepted by ever increasing numbers of persons due to the frequency of its occurrence in communication networks.

Bracketing – conscious suspension of personal beliefs about a topic of professional inquiry, for the purpose of maintaining greater objectivity.

Ecology – study of the interrelationship of all things in nature (or the environment), and the full spectrum of relationships between specific entities, other entities, and the environment in which they exist. Also, an academic field that studies these interrelationships. In contemporary America, the meanings and implications of ecology are quite broad, complex, politically and socially charged, economically problematic, and much-disputed in popular culture.

"End of nature" – a concept developed by Bill McKibben in a book by this title, identifying the contemporary/postmodern era as a post-nature world; nature as something independent of human beings no longer exists—i.e. there is no physical-material world independent from human modifications or distinct from human control and manipulation.

Environment – the immediate context in which something exists or is located. Often used as a synonym for nature, now that the traditional sense of nature has been compromised and begun to decline in popular usage. For example, in popular discourse, we more often hear of calls to "protect the environment," but not so much to "protect nature." In this regard, a derived term, Environmentalism, typically refers to outlooks, beliefs, and sources of action that respect and seek to protect the *natural* environment.

Nature – most broadly, the physical-material world, inclusive of all entities, features, properties, and processes occurring therein. Although humans are part of nature by definition, typically, nature has referred to the physical-material world as it exists apart from human modifications or distinct from human control and manipulation. In popular usage, nature has an antiquated, anachronistic resonance. What once might have been referred to as nature (or natural), today is referred to as "the environment" (or "environmental").

Religion – see Professor Clark's definition in the Introduction, but note the nuance given here, with religion being understood as the social institution that mediates a relationship between human beings and what they hold as sacred.

Sacred – following the usage of Jacques Ellul and others, sacred is that which serves as the Ultimate Power or Principle of a culture. It is the ground of being and source of meaning and purpose. In this understanding, it functions as the supreme power/principle that is mediated by the social institution of religion.

Points for discussion

- In your own experience, does nature have a religious significance? If so, can you articulate its significance?
- In your estimation, why has so little work been done on religion and ecology in popular culture?

- Do you think that scholars of religion should take public stands on issues related to the "ecological crisis" (e.g. global warming, species extinctions, deforestation, and so on)?
- In your estimation, what is the best course of action for traditional religions to take in response to the "ecological crisis?"
- For anyone seeking "the truth" on a given topic, what are the advantages and disadvantages of living in a digital age of mass information-sharing?
- Have you ever experienced an "availability cascade" regarding a particular subject of study or research? How might you guard against being influenced by such a cascade?

Further reading

Gottlieb, Roger S. (2006) *A Greener Faith: Religious Environmentalism and Our Planet's Future*, New York: Oxford University Press.

Thorough study of religious environmentalism by one of the major scholars of Religion and Ecology. Attention is given to major themes, leaders, and initiatives. Gottlieb contextualizes the religious dimension of environmentalism relative to topics such as secularization, politics, and consumerism.

Hay, Peter (2002) *Main Currents in Western Environmental Thought*, Bloomington: Indiana University Press.

Substantial survey of major intellectual and cultural forces behind and within the contemporary environmental movement. Attention is given to "Ecophilosophy," "Ecofeminism," "Green Political Thought," "Religion, Spirituality, and the Green Movement," and several other critical features of today's environmental movement.

Sturgeon, Noel (2009) *Environmentalism in Popular Culture*, Tucson: University of Arizona Press.

Detailed examination of environmentalism in Popular Culture through the critical lens of cultural studies. Using "intersectional analysis," Sturgeon offers a critical study of the ways in which environmental issues and themes relate to large social concerns, especially problems in equality and social justice.

Taylor, Bron (2010) *Dark Green Religion: Nature Spirituality and the Planetary Future*, Berkeley: University of California Press.

Most recent book by pioneer in the study of the religious dimensions of ecology. Taylor argues for an inner religious dynamic at work in a variety of environmental organizations, helping us understand how seemingly secular causes are better understood as functionally religious in orientation.

Bibliography

Bauman, Whitney A., Bohannon, Richard R., II, and O'Brien, Kevin J. (2011) *Grounding Religion: A Field Guide to the Study of Religion and Ecology*, New York: Routledge.

Blumner, Robin (2011) "Enough of us, already, let's think smaller," *St. Petersburg Times* (30 January): 5P.

Carson, Rachel (1962) *Silent Spring*, Boston: Houghton Mifflin.

deChant, Dell (2008) *Religion and Culture in the West: A Primer*, rev. printing, Dubuque, Iowa: Kendall/Hunt.

——(2002) *The Sacred Santa: Religious Dimensions of Consumer Culture*, Cleveland: The Pilgrim Press.

Ellul, Jacques (1975) *The New Demons*, trans. C. Edward Hopkin, New York: Seabury Press.

Gottlieb, Roger S. (2006) "Religion and Ecology—What Is the Connection and Why Does It Matter?" in Roger S. Gottlieb (ed.) *Oxford Handbook of Religion and Ecology*, New York: Oxford University Press.

Kolbert, Elizabeth (2006) *Field Notes from a Catastrophe: Man, Nature, and Climate Change*, New York: Bloomsbury.

Kuran, Timur and Sunstein, Cass R. (1999) "Availability Cascades and Risk Regulation," *Stanford Law Review* 51 (April): 683–768.

McKibben, Bill (1989) *The End of Nature*, New York: Random House.

Pals, Daniel L. (2006) *Eight Theories of Religion*, 2nd edn, New York: Oxford University Press.

Taylor, Bron (ed.) (2008) *Encyclopedia of Religion and Nature*, London: Continuum.

——(2006) "Religion and Environmentalism in America and Beyond," in Roger S. Gottlieb (ed.) *Oxford Handbook of Religion and Ecology*, New York: Oxford University Press.

Tucker, Mary Evelyn (2006) "Religion and Ecology: Survey of the Field," in Roger S. Gottlieb (ed.) *Oxford Handbook of Religion and Ecology*, New York: Oxford University Press.

White, Lynn Townsend, Jr. (1967) "The Historical Roots of Our Ecologic Crisis," in *Science* 155: 3767 (10 March): 1203–1207.

3 Religion in science fiction film and television

Douglas E. Cowan

Introduction

Outtake: two prophetic voices

Scene One: Thirty thousand light years from home, the aging warship continues its journey into the vast expanse of the galaxy's Delta Quadrant, crewed by the great-grandchildren of those who set out more than a century before. Convinced that "the Empire [has] lost its way," a small sect of Klingon warriors follows the prophecies contained in a set of sacred scrolls and continues their quest for the *kuvah'magh*, the savior who will lead them to a new Empire, a restored and purified time of Klingon honor and glory. Their leader, Kohlar, believes that they have at last found this savior—in the unborn child of B'Ellana Torres, the Federation starship *Voyager*'s half-Klingon chief engineer. As much as anything else, *Star Trek: Voyager*'s seventh season episode, "Prophecy," turns on the various interpretations of these Klingon sacred texts. "The scrolls," Kohlar tells his fellow warriors, "say that 'You will find me after two warring houses make peace.'" Since the Klingon Empire and the Federation have been at peace for more than three generations now, to Kohlar the fulfillment of the prophecy seems obvious and imminent. "The other signs are present," he continues, quoting the scrolls: "'You will know me before I know the world.'" "The child is unborn," responds another Klingon, wide-eyed in amazement. "It does not know the world." "You interpret the scrolls well," nods Kohlar.

Scene Two: Deep in the outback of a post-apocalyptic Australia, prophecy continues to serve a vision of hope for the future. In *Mad Max: Beyond Thunderdome*,[1] the redoubtable Max has been betrayed in Bartertown by Aunty Entity and exiled to the unforgiving heat and dust of the post-nuclear wasteland. Given up for dead, he is found by a tribe of children—the "Waiting Ones"—who claim to recognize in him their promised savior, Walker. Using a rudimentary icon of a television screen to frame her narrative, a young woman named Savannah Nix "takes the Tell" and recounts their sacred story in an effort to convince Max that "they ain't been slack," that they are worthy of the salvation they believe he brings. It's an astonishing sequence in the film. As the other members of the tribe provide sound effects and antiphons—actively participating in what amounts to the ritual retelling of a creation myth—Savannah recalls first the "Pox-Eclipse, full of pain," from which "were birthed cracklin' dust and fearsome time," with "Mr. Dead chasin' them all." Shortly after the nuclear holocaust, a small group of survivors tried to flee the destruction in an aircraft, but crashed—perhaps because of what the Tell remembers as "a gang called Turbulence." Eventually, survivors led by the pilot, Captain Walker, left the larger group to seek help—"the Great Leaving"—but promised that one day "one of us would come." "And somebody did come," Savannah tells the assembled tribe, finishing the story for the first time in the history of the Tell. A reed screen is drawn aside, revealing a crude painting of Max, who stares at it in wonder as what is left of the captain's hat is placed reverently upon his head. "We's ready now," says First Tracker. "Take us home."

Wonder, amazement, and the fulfillment of prophecy. Little different from the ways that religious believers construe prophecy in the off-screen world, these on-screen believers both place themselves at the center of great salvation dramas and interpret their sacred texts in light of current events. For the Waiting Ones and the Klingons, the promise of a savior—whether Captain Walker or the *kuvah'magh*—bolsters a vision of hope for the future.

As so often happens in religious life off-screen, however, these on-screen movements are also complicated by alternative, often countervailing interpretations of the prophetic message. B'Ellana, for example, refuses to believe that her unborn daughter could be the promised savior of a revived Klingon Empire, while T'Greth, Kohlar's second-in-command, questions whether the true *kuvah'magh* could ever be born of mixed Klingon–Human parentage. Needing their guiding prophecies to be true, on the other hand, Kohlar urges B'Ellana to tell him about herself, to see what else in her life might be made to fit the sacred story of the *kuvah'magh*.

Similarly, once Savannah Nix finishes the Tell and First Tracker crowns Max with Walker's cap, the road warrior simply rises and walks away. "That ain't me," he says. "You got the wrong guy." "Quit joshing, Captain," replies one of the lost tribe, advising him instead to "catch the wind." When Max throws the hat away, though, a rogue updraft in their little valley does catch it, carrying it over the crest of the hill and out of sight, a clear sign to the Waiting Ones. Max may not believe, but they know: Walker has returned.

Numerous other examples of prophetic failure and fulfillment could easily be gathered from programs ranging from Ronald Moore's reimagined *Battlestar Galactica* to Gene Roddenberry's *Star Trek: Deep Space Nine* and *Andromeda*, and from the miles-long space station of *Babylon 5* to the post-apocalyptic pilgrimage of *The Book of Eli*. Indeed, decades of science fiction film and television yield myriad examples of religious quest and conflict, hope and disappointment, apocalypse and millennium.

Unfortunately, it is easy for critics to take episodes and story arcs such as these and use them simply to dismiss the place of religious belief in science fiction film and television. They become, as it were, the cinematic version of the old canard that warns, "You can make the Bible say anything you want." Indeed, in much of science fiction (and science fiction commentary), religion is ridiculed and reduced to a cultural holdover, a survival from less enlightened times. Although there are certainly story lines to support that kind of reading, leaving the issue invites us off the interpretive train, as it were, rather than inviting us on. It ignores the richness of what these stories can teach us about the quest for transcendence—the search for something beyond ourselves, something that can give our lives meaning, something that we claim as sacred.

After all, what is the sacred? Is it the so-called "word of God," the divine edict contained in story and scroll? There are myriad sacred texts, but few religious groups agree which are holy. Even those that do agree offer contested interpretations of their meaning. Any number of sacred places dot the landscape, but no one place is considered holy by everyone. Is the sacred a personal experience of God, an inner certainty that one has been touched by the holy? Perhaps, but if so, why doesn't everyone either experience this in the same way or even acknowledge that the experience exists? Rather, as every first-year religious studies student learns, nothing is sacred, in and of itself. Rather, it is a socially constructed reality in which we participate.

Put simply, the reality of the sacred resides in *agreement*, in the consensus that groups of believers share—or come to share—about the nature of reality and their place within it. This is the "Amen" that concludes the Christian or Jewish prayer, the "Inshallah" of the devout Muslim, the "So say we all" of the remnant humanity following signs and portents aboard the battlestar *Galactica*. Put thus, in terms of both on-screen entertainment and off-screen reality, the question is not whether a prophecy is correct or not, fulfilled or no—and to think that it is misses the point entirely. Indeed, to judge it on that basis alone highlights how narrow our religious thinking can be, how small are the gods we claim to worship, and how limited is our willingness to imagine a world beyond the confines of our own shadowy cave. The real question is how we come to that agreement, how we maintain our sense of the sacred in the face of doubt and fear, how we reinforce it when others challenge its veracity and criticize its worth. About these things, science fiction film and television has much more to teach us than we might think.

In this chapter, we will first explore two of the main critiques commentators have offered about the relationship between religion and science fiction—dismissing religion as irrational, and rejecting on-screen religion because it does not sufficiently resemble religious belief and practice off-screen. Then, using two extended examples, one each from episodes of *Star Trek: Deep Space Nine* and *Babylon 5*, we will see that closer analysis reveals far more about the resilience of religion in popular culture than many critics have been prepared to admit.

Theory and method

Roads too often travelled: diss(miss)ing religion in science fiction

Often, science fiction film and television present religion as little more than a showcase for the quaint and the outmoded, portraying religious believers as anything from simple-minded and gullible to conniving and duplicitous. Numerous episodes from the various *Star Trek* franchises, for example, depict religion less as an active force in human (and non-human) affairs than as a relic of cultures less enlightened than those in the Federation, (e.g. "The Apple"; "Who Mourns for Adonais?" [*Star Trek*]). Others expose those who claim to be gods (or demons) as little more than pretenders to the divine throne (e.g. "Devil's Due" [*Star Trek: The Next Generation*]; "False Profits" [*Star Trek: Voyager*]). Not surprisingly, then, burdened by the ongoing cultural conflicts between science and religion—a **technophilic** conceit that not infrequently rivals religious arrogance—many critics write off religious content in science fiction, rejecting it as extraneous or absurd.

Commenting on the death of Pastor Matthew Collins, for example, one of the central characters in George Pal's overtly religious 1953 version of *The War of the Worlds*, Joe Dante points out that when Collins is killed, "it is very polite of the Martians to let him finish the prayer" before vaporizing him with their death ray (2005). Indeed, Dana Polan writes that, "in many '50s monster films, there is a character, often a priest, whose attitude toward the monsters is, 'Let us try to reason with them.' Several seconds later that character will be a smoldering pile of ashes" (1996: 202). In *Monsters and Mad Scientists*, Andrew Tudor is arguably the most dismissive of religion in the 1950s sci-fi/horror hybrid. Referring both to *The War of the Worlds* and *The Day of the Triffids*, he contends, "a religious gloss is given to the fact of humanity's final relief, though … that gloss seems so extraneous as to be laughably implausible to any audience" (Tudor 1989: 54; for a very different interpretation, see "Further reading" and "Bibliography" for details of Cowan 2010: 105–38). More than a generation after *The War of the Worlds* came to the screen, critics are still trying to explain away the presence of religion in sci-fi. Proposing off-screen analogies for on-screen characters in *Star Trek: Deep Space Nine*, for instance, *New York Times* critic Jon Pareles dismisses the Bajoran religion that lies at the heart of the series with a barely concealed racism. "With their religious rituals, caste system, pierced ears, and newly won freedom from the Cardassian Empire," he writes, "[the Bajorans] might be Indians or Palestinians" (1996). As I point out in *Sacred Space*, though, "By reducing *Deep Space Nine*'s various nonhuman species to a series of cultural or political stereotypes … Pareles relieves himself—and, by implication, his readers—of any responsibility to ask deeper questions, to understand the series in anything but the most banal terms" (Cowan 2010: 144).

Underpinning much of this style of criticism is the concept of secularization, the debatable late modern belief that religion is vestigial in human culture—and if it isn't, it should be. It is a part of our history that may have served us well in the past, but it has little place in the present and even less in the future. For those who accept this premise, in the past religious belief and practice allowed us to explain the unexplainable, to understand why floods inundated the land or earthquakes shattered the mountains above us. Now, since we know about rainfall patterns, soil erosion, and plate tectonics, divine intervention in the physical world seems quaint and outmoded. Once upon a time, religious myth and story placed us at the center of a great cosmic drama, teaching us how we should live in relation both to each other and to the universe. Since **terracentricity** has given way to **heliocentricity**, however, and astronomy teaches us each day how infinitesimal is our planet's place in the galaxy, the notion of a "god" who not only created but controls the entire cosmos seems outmoded indeed.

When we look with eyes less clouded by scientistic and sociological prejudice, however, it becomes clear that religion is as much a part of science fiction as it is of ongoing human (and, as it happens in the multitude of sci-fi universes, non-human) experience. Religion may have figured variously in the other *Star Trek* franchises, for example, but *Deep Space Nine* is religious from beginning to end, its assorted story arcs anchored in the contested interpretation and fulfillment of religious prophecy. *Stargate SG-1*, one of the most popular science fiction series in North American television history, is founded on what I have called "the von Däniken paradox": the gods, as it turns out—at least most of them—*are* from outer space (see Cowan 2010: 171–96). Although *Babylon 5*'s creator, J. Michael Straczynski, identifies himself as an atheist, he recognizes the central role religion plays in society—both human and non-human—and established that as a central element in the series. However much they may disagree on its content, few of the tens of millions of fans who tuned in to Ronald D. Moore's reimagined *Battlestar Galactica* could have missed its essentially religious message (see Cowan 2010: 225–60). Finally, even science fiction videogames bring religion to the center of the universe. When all the firefights are done and the Covenant driven back, Bungie's wildly popular *Halo* series finds a back story that is profoundly religious. That is, especially in *Halo 2*, led by the Prophets of Truth, Mercy, and Regret, the alien Covenant is on a religious mission to purge the galaxy of heretics and non-believers, to reinstate the worship of what they regard as holy artifacts—the Halo rings.

Even when this religious content is recognized, however, it all too often leads to the second criticism: that these must be false gods or counterfeit faith because they don't look like "real religion." That is, on-screen religions do not sufficiently resemble their off-screen counterparts and, because of this, interpreters dismiss them as artificial and their practitioners as gullible or misguided. Much of the action in *Deep Space Nine* orbits around the planet Bajor, which has recently won its freedom from a brutal occupation by an alien race, the Cardassians. During the many decades of the occupation, it was the Bajoran religion, their faith in what they know as the Prophets, that held them together and helped them survive. Despite the destruction wrought by the Cardassians, the Bajorans never lost sight of the fact that they mattered, that they were connected to something greater than themselves, and that this connection gave their lives meaning and purpose. To others, however, the Bajoran prophets are a race of utterly alien beings who inhabit the nether regions of a stable wormhole between the Alpha and Gamma Quadrants of the galaxy. They exist outside of normal space and beyond linear time. To non-believers they are not gods but "wormhole aliens." Unfortunately, this is a dichotomy to which many commentators fall prey. These mysterious beings are either gods or aliens, but they can't be both. One problem with this is that it ignores precisely how religion functions off-screen. Indeed, the religious debate throughout *Deep Space Nine* mirrors discussions in the real world about how we understand the religions of others, how we hold in tension our nonbelief with their belief. Too often, unfortunately, our inability to appreciate the beliefs of others leads us simply to dismiss them as false.

Similarly, in the *Stargate* universe, if the alien races of the Goa'uld and the Ori are demonstrated to be false gods—and this is *SG-1*'s most basic premise—then the religions that have evolved around them must be false as well. For critics such as these, the issue is not proving religion obsolete, but demonstrating that it is portrayed in science fiction incorrectly. Peter Linford points out, for example, that "we should not fall into the trap of discussing [the Bajoran religion of *Deep Space Nine*] as though it were real," (1999: 77). That is, "we ought not forget that this is fiction and that its characters—and their various religions—are the products of human imagination" (Cowan 2010: 150). Although this point seems obvious, it bears repeating because fans often become so caught up in their love for a show that they do begin to discuss the characters as though they are real. This, however, is exactly what Linford does, criticizing the Bajoran religion because it does not appear to be a "personal" faith or because "facets that we might expect to see in a religion are more clearly absent" (1999: 78). "There is," he continues, "no creativity attributed to the Prophets. Nor is there any **soteriology** … [and] the prophecies do not seem to offer moral teachings, myths, or eschatology" (1998: 78).

Although he denies doing so, in one breath Linford cautions us not to treat religion on *Deep Space Nine* (or, by extension, in any science fiction story) as though it were real and in the next criticizes the Bajoran faith for not living up to what he considers the standards of "real" religion. Much of the criticism of Moore's *Battlestar Galactica* fell into the same trap. Commenting on the utilitarian ends to which both humans and Cylons put their respective religions, Bryan McHenry asks, "Is manipulation of religious beliefs ever justifiable?" (2008: 221), while Taneli Kukkonen (2008: 170) wonders whether "the Cylons and Colonials [are] justified in their respective faiths."

While these may be interesting intellectual exercises, given that religious beliefs off-screen are regularly manipulated in the service of a wide variety of goals and that the notion of rational justification implies some empirical standard of measurement, questions such as these ring naïve in the extreme. They define religion in their own narrow terms, and then fault religion as it is portrayed in science fiction film and television for not living up to those standards. Indeed, this is precisely the problem Carl Sagan identified in his 1985 Gifford Lectures, which were later published as *The Varieties of Scientific Experience*—a play on *The Varieties of Religious Experience* by William James, his Gifford Lectures from 1902 and one of the foundational texts in the field of Religious Studies. Toward the end of his first lecture, Sagan remarked that "a general problem with much of Western theology in my view is that the God portrayed is too small. It is a god of a tiny world and not a god of a galaxy, much less of a universe" (2006: 30).

Putting aside questions of irrelevance and falsity—questions that all but inevitably lead us down blind alleys, given that for the vast majority of humankind religion is neither irrelevant nor false—what can science fiction tell us about religious belief and behavior? Quite a bit, actually. Indeed, science fiction film and television are significant cultural texts that both reflect and reflect on problems of religious diversity, questions of theological struggle, and ethical and moral dilemmas. That is, science fiction narratives often reflect or embody prevalent social or cultural concerns. They propose solutions and explore their potential for success or failure. They follow various paths of social development to their logical—and not infrequently devastating—conclusions. For example, sci-fi films of the 1950s were often consumed with the prospects of nuclear war (*Them!*; *Godzilla*); in the 1970s and 1980s, fear of computers and robots run amok (*Westworld*; *Colossus: The Forbin Project*; *The Terminator*); in the early twenty-first century, the perils and prospects of advanced biotechnology (*The Island*; *Gattaca*).

Perhaps more than any other genre, science fiction allows us to ask—and to answer—some of the most significant "What if?" questions. What if the machines we create develop self-awareness and when does that present the potential for a spirit or a soul (*Battlestar Galactica*; *I, Robot*; *Short Circuit*)? What if the extraterrestrial intelligences we encounter have religious traditions vastly different than our own—or eerily similar (*Babylon 5*; *Star Trek: Deep Space Nine*)? What if we discover that our gods are, indeed, from outer space (*Stargate SG-1*)?

In the context of religion and science fiction, consider the two following examples: Weyoun and Mollari.

Case studies

Weyoun: "Isn't that what gods do?"

Much of the narrative arc in *Star Trek: Deep Space Nine* tells the story of an epic battle for control of the Alpha Quadrant of the galaxy. There are myriad players, but the principal antagonists are the Federation and the Dominion. The Dominion is ruled by a race called the Founders, a liquid life form whose individuals exist only as temporary excerpts of a larger whole known as the Great Link. A reclusive and xenophobic species, the Founders prosecute their various affairs through two subordinate races—the Jem'Hadar and the Vorta. While the warrior Jem'Hadar serve as the Founders' military arm, the Vorta administer the vast bureaucracy of the Dominion. Both races, however, have been genetically engineered to revere the Founders as gods. Since both are aware of their genetic programming, it is tempting to dismiss the Founders as false gods and either belittle their followers as dupes or pity them as victims. This implies, however, that there are "true gods" against which the false may be measured, and that we are in a position to make that kind of determination. Doing so ignores not only the deeper meaning of the story, but also the reality of religious life off-screen.

Throughout history, for example, numerous cultures have revered their leaders as divine or semi-divine. Egyptians, Romans, Chinese, Tibetans, Japanese—all at one time or another have believed their rulers were not only appointed by, but descended from, the gods. Like our sacred texts, our gods are who we agree they are and those who follow in our religious footsteps not only inherit the decisions we made about the gods, but both modify and rationalize them to suit their own situations. Thus, when textual scholars in the late nineteenth century argued persuasively that Moses did not, in fact, write the first five books of the Old Testament, but that there were at least four voices involved in their production over many generations, this did not bring about the end of Christian faith. Rather, this new information was integrated into the evolution of that faith. It was not that God did not act in the inspiration of scripture, but that our understanding of how that action occurred is also evolving. Although our relationships with them may change, the gods remain the gods. This may not entirely satisfy believers (or non-believers), but we need to remember that all religions adapt in order to survive. As cultures evolve, as religious traditions are transmitted across cultures, as other faiths compete for space in the marketplace of religious ideas, systems of belief and practice struggle in the attempt to remain both faithful and relevant.

Complicating matters in the *Star Trek* universe, however, is the fact that Odo, the stalwart Chief of Security aboard Deep Space Nine, is a member of the Founder race, though he has never lived as part of the Great Link and is completely loyal to the Federation. As the war progresses, some of the Dominion combatants begin to question what they are fighting for. In the episode "Treachery, Faith, and the Great River," one of the Vorta, Weyoun, has defected from the Dominion because he no longer believes in the rightness of their cause. Luring Odo to a lonely moon, he requests asylum. He is, as it were, rejecting the larger pantheon of the Founders for the uncertain favor of one reluctant deity. As they hide from Dominion forces, Odo angrily rejects any implication that he might be a god. But from Weyoun's perspective, Odo is as much a Founder as those who began the war, whose crusade he has now abandoned.

"Has it ever occurred to you," Odo asks the Vorta contemptuously, "that the reason you believe the Founders are gods is because that's what they want you to believe, that they built it into your genetic code?" "Of course they did," Weyoun answers, a bit surprised. "That's what gods do. After all, why be a god if there's no one to worship you?" Weyoun neither disputes nor dismisses the reality that his devotion has been genetically engineered. He simply accepts this as the natural action of divinity. It is what gods do. In this, he is not unlike millions of Christians who claim the truth of such biblical passages as Revelation 4:11—"You created all things, and by Your will they existed"—as patent evidence that humankind was created for the purpose of worshipping God.

The Dominion, however, will not allow Weyoun to escape, and rather than risk Odo's life further this particular Vorta chooses suicide. As he lies dying on the floor of the small Federation runabout, he looks into the face of his (only remaining) god.

> "Give me your blessing," he pleads, his voice choked with pain.
> "I—I—I can't—," Odo stammers.

"Please, Odo, tell me I haven't failed, that I've served you well."
"You have, and for that you have my gratitude ... and my blessing."

As I point out in *Sacred Space* (Cowan 2010: 168–169), within the restricted confines of the tiny spacecraft, Odo has tried to distance himself physically, psychologically, and theologically from Weyoun. To Odo, the Vorta is nothing more than a prisoner; to Weyoun, however, Odo was never anything but a god. As Weyoun dies, though, the space between them evaporates as Odo holds him gently, their faces only inches apart. It's important to note here that five full seconds elapse between Odo's gratitude and his blessing, an eternity for the Vorta, his eyes filled with pain and uncertainty. In the last moments of his life, fear and hope—what I have called the double helix of religious DNA—are fused. If the Founder cannot offer him benediction and the Vorta dies staring into the face of denial, then for Weyoun all hope is lost. Everything he has believed, everything that has structured his very being vanishes into the void with his last breath. If, on the other hand, that benediction is extended—whether Odo believes in it or not, whether we believe in it or not—then there is something Weyoun can grasp as he makes the great transcendence. He dies knowing that his gods still live and that in some way he is known by them. To Odo, that one small act is an unpleasant acquiescence to the engineered devotion of the Vorta; to Weyoun, it is an affirmation that his faith has not been misplaced. Even in the grand sweep of the universe, he matters. And, after all, isn't that what gods do?

Mollari: "Gods by the bushel, gods by the pound!"

Like *Star Trek: Deep Space Nine*, the story of *Babylon 5* is set aboard a massive space station in the twenty-third century. Portrayed as a kind of Dodge City in space, the Babylon 5 station is an interstellar and interspecies crossroads administered by a military governorship from Earth. As I noted earlier, although *Babylon 5* creator J. Michael Straczynski counts himself an atheist he is equally convinced that religion will continue to be a fundamental component of human—and, for him, non-human—civilization. While a number of episodes concern the religious lives of the station's inhabitants and visitors, the first season's "Parliament of Dreams" explicitly imagines the galactic equivalent of a World Parliament of Religions. All the races that live on or visit the station have been invited to send delegates from their various religious traditions, to demonstrate their practices, explain their beliefs, and hopefully encourage the kind of interspecies tolerance that is the founding principle of the Babylon project. In one part of the station, for example, the Minbari ambassador Delenn, a member of her species' religious caste and a series regular, celebrates their version of a communion service. To the gentle tinkling of small bells, she recalls the creation myth of her people as acolytes reverently offer the gathered congregation small pieces of fruit. Elsewhere, however, the grace and dignity of the Minbari ceremony are rudely offset by the rude **bacchanal** that is the Centauri Festival of Life.

Rather than a ritual meal, Ambassador Londo Mollari leads the Centauri revelers in a magnificent feast commemorating their people's victory over a rival species on their home world. This is their creation myth, their moment of blessing by the Centauri gods. As I point out in *Sacred Space*, laughter fills the air and lively baroque music plays in the background as beautiful Centauri women circulate among the tables, some dancing sensuously, others passing by with braziers of incense or trays laden with food and drink. It is the annual celebration of life and joy, the religious backdrop to the basically hedonistic Centauri lifestyle (Cowan 2010: 199). In the midst of the revelry, one of the station officers asks Mollari about the statues scattered on the tables among the food and drink.

"Ah," answers Mollari delightedly, "our household gods!" Raising his goblet in a toast, he continues, "In a world where every day is a struggle for survival you need all the gods you can get!" Climbing drunkenly on the table, he grabs one of the statues. "Here is Venzann, god of food, and Li, goddess of passion," cradling the golden statue of a nude Centauri female and reverently kissing her buttocks. Scattering food and drink as he moves down the table, Mollari lifts a small gargoyle-like figure. It is "Mogath, god of the underworld ... and protector of front doors!" Overcome by emotion and alcohol, he proclaims happily, "Gods by the bushel, gods by the pound! Gods for all occasions!" As he passes out, his assistant announces exultantly, "He has become one with his inner self!"

As it is off-screen, religion aboard Babylon 5 is not one thing—and to think that it either is or must be misses the point entirely. Indeed, when Sinclair, the station's human commander, introduces Earth religion, he does not recall myths of creation or pantheons of gods and goddesses. He introduces the delegates to a long line of people standing in a cargo bay:

> This is Mr. Harris, he's an atheist. Father Cresanti, a Roman Catholic. Mr. Hayakawa, a Zen Buddhist. Mr. Rashid, a Muslim. Mr. Rosenthal, an Orthodox Jew. Running Elk, of the Oglala Sioux faith. Father Papapoulos, a Greek Orthodox. Ogigi-ko, of the Ibo tribe.

The closing shot fades to black as Sinclair continues to introduce the myriad faiths of Earth.

At its core, religion is not the beliefs by which it is informed, the rituals by which it is framed and enacted, or the ethics and moral vision it imparts or requires. These are important, of course, but they tell us relatively little about religious faith as lived practice, about how believers go about their lives in the midst of sacred texts, religious rituals, and ethical commandments—most of which are framed, administered, and adjudicated by cultural elites. From text, ritual, and commandment, we learn only a fraction of what it means to be a devotee of Venzann, for example, or a follower of the Narn prophet, G'Lan. How these texts inform one's daily life, which rituals brings practitioners a greater sense of religious fulfillment, which commandments are followed more rigorously than others—these are the questions we must ask if we want to know what it means to be religious. Religion—both on-screen and off-screen—is most concretely realized in the everyday actions of believers and the interactions between different believers.

From the magnificent opening sequence of Robert Zemeckis' *Contact* to the polymorphous visions of alien religion in *Babylon 5* and *Star Trek: Deep Space Nine*, from the almost complete rewriting of H.G. Wells' *The War of the Worlds* in order to bring it to the screen in 1953 to the covert Christianization of Robert Wise's *The Day The Earth Stood Still* in the decades that followed its 1951 release (Cowan 2009), science fiction film and television have presented a number of significant challenges to popular understandings of religion. Science fiction film and television demonstrate that religion need be neither irrelevant nor **parochial**. We are not becoming less religious as we learn about the universe, but our concepts of the divine, of faith and belief, and of the quest for transcendence are evolving with us. Imagining, for example, how an alien species might react to our religious beliefs—and how we might respond to theirs—offers important insights into the nature of interreligious dialogue as we encounter it in the off-screen world today. What challenges to religion does the prospect of first contact with an extraterrestrial intelligence present? When we finally learn that we are not alone in the universe, how will that affect our sense of meaning and purpose, or our understanding of humanity as a single species rather than a disparate collection of tribal and racial associations? If we succeed in creating life, whether robotic, cybernetic, or artificially human, what are the ethical, moral, and religious implications of these accomplishments? As Professor Lanning says in the film version of Isaac Asimov's *I, Robot*, "When does a perceptual schematic become consciousness? When does a difference engine become the search for truth? When does a personality simulation become the bitter mote of a soul?"

Unlike many other genres, science fiction film and television provide unparalleled imaginative spaces in which to explore these ideas and more. They invite us to consider on-screen alternative concepts of belief and behavior that both reflect and refract the contentious religious landscape that exists off-screen. Encouraging viewers to see more than the limited theological perspective offered by so many religious traditions, especially as these are understood in the West, science fiction challenges us to see the possibility of an unseen order in ways other than simply the divine-human relationship, to look beyond the narrow vision of terracentric human exceptionalism or superiority, and to appreciate what the possibility of alien life and faith can teach us about our own religious beliefs and practices.

Summary

- Religion is and always has been an important, if unacknowledged part of science fiction literature, film, and television.
- Religion in science fiction is often dismissed as a cultural holdover and religious believers derided as backward or gullible.
- Science fiction can show us important aspects of religion as it has evolved (and is evolving), as well as encourage us to consider ways in which it might continue to develop.

- Science fiction allows us to ask religious questions that are either not considered or not permitted by other genres: Do robots have souls? Will aliens worship God? Will religious prophecy guide us among the stars as it has on Earth?

Glossary terms

Bacchanal – originally a Roman festival celebrating Bacchus, the god of ecstasy and wine. Now used to describe a wild party with drinking, dancing, song, and sexual (mis)adventure.

Heliocentricity – the astronomical principle that the planets in a solar system orbit their sun or suns, not the reverse. Historically, this discovery is attributed to the Polish astronomer Nicolaus Copernicus.

Parochial – an idea or worldview that is narrow and limited in scope.

Scientistic – an exaggerated faith in either the scientific method or the abilities of scientists to solve complex social and cultural problems.

Soteriology – the salvation doctrine or narrative of a particular religion.

Technophilic – a person who is devoted to or enthusiastic about technology and technological progress.

Terracentricity – a worldview that places Earth at the center of mythology, activity, and importance. Terracentric human exceptionalists believe that God created Earth as the only inhabited planet in the universe and that humanity is unique in the cosmos.

Vestigial – a survival or remnant from previous times, often considered unimportant or out of date.

Points for discussion

- In small groups, talk about your emotional, intellectual, and religious reactions to different science fiction films or television programs you have seen. Why do you think you react the way you do? How do you account for the reactions of others?
- Watch one (or more) of the television episodes from the introduction to this chapter and discuss the various ways in which religious prophecies are interpreted by certain characters to fit the needs of their own religious faith, or that of others. How is this similar to the ways in which religious prophecy is used off-screen (i.e. in real life by real religious practitioners past and present)?
- Despite the fact that many science fiction films and television shows are filled with (if not based on) religious belief and practice, why do so many commentators insist on either disregarding or dismissing these elements? That is, why do so many commentators insist on scorning religious belief and practice as archaic and irrelevant, as something that will eventually be abandoned as humans evolve? What does this say about the place of religion in late modern society?
- I have suggested that the "sacred" is a function of agreement between members of a particular group. Although there are a variety of social processes

involved, the group determines and maintains what is sacred to them. Using examples from popular science fiction films and television, discuss how this agreement is established and reinforced. How does this help us understand the process of religious belief off-screen? To answer this, you may need to watch several episodes.

Note

1 A complete list of bibliographic references for films mentioned in this essay may be found in the filmography at the end of this chapter.

Further reading

Cowan, D.E. (2008) *Sacred Terror: Religion and Horror on the Silver Screen*, Waco, TX: Baylor University Press.

One of the few in-depth discussions of religion and horror cinema, which includes the popular horror-science fiction hybrid. Cowan uses the principle of sociophobics—the concept that what and how we fear is socially constructed—to consider why so much of cinema horror relies on religion.

——(2010) *Sacred Space: The Quest for Transcendence in Science Fiction Film and Television*, Waco, TX: Baylor University Press.

Considers science fiction film and television as one of the main cultural sites for the social construction of hope and the quest for transcendence. In addition to popular films, Cowan also discusses some of the most popular television series of the past few decades.

Eberl, J.T. (ed.) (2008) *"Battlestar Galactica" and Philosophy: Knowledge Here Begins Out There*, Oxford: Blackwell.

One of several essay collections that appeared during the run of Moore's reimagined *Battlestar Galactica*. Includes chapters on such topics as religious belief and atheism, the pragmatics of hope, the nature of (non-)humanity, and alienation and evil.

McKee, G. (2007) *The Gospel According to Science Fiction: From the Twilight Zone to the Final Frontier*, Louisville, KY: Westminster John Knox.

A good consideration of science fiction film and television from a Christian perspective.

Porter, J.E., and McLaren, D.L. (eds) (1999) *"Star Trek" and Sacred Ground: Explorations of "Star Trek," Religion, and American Culture*, Albany, NY: State University of New York Press.

One of the first essay collections to discuss the relationship between religion and *Star Trek*, includes essays on such topics as *Star Trek* fandom, *Star Trek* and the death of God, New Age spirituality, and biblical imagery in the various *Star Trek* franchises.

Nygard, R. (dir.) (1999) *Trekkies* (motion picture) Hollywood, CA: Paramount Pictures.

A wonderful look at the world of *Star Trek* fandom and the wide variety of people for whom the science fiction visions of Gene Roddenberry provide not only entertainment but a profound sense of meaning.

Warren, Bill (1982) *Keep Watching the Skies! American Science Fiction Movies of the Fifties, Volume I: 1950–1957*, Jefferson, NC: McFarland.

——(1986) *Keep Watching the Skies! American Science Fiction Movies of the Fifties, Volume II: 1958–1962*, Jefferson, NC: McFarland.

Warren's massive two-volume survey is the bible of science fiction films of the 1950s and early 1960s. Indispensable for anyone who wants to understand one of the most important periods in science fiction cinema history.

Yeffeth, G. (ed.) (2003) *Taking the Red Pill: Science, Philosophy, and Religion in "The Matrix,"* Dallas, TX: BenBella Books.

One of several collections of essays discussing the massively popular *Matrix* series of films. Includes chapters on such topics as Buddhism in *The Matrix*, artificial intelligence, the nature of reality, and the question of whether we are already living in something like the Matrix.

Bibliography

Cowan, D.E. (2009) "Seeing the Saviour in the Stars: Religion, Conformity, and *The Day the Earth Stood Still*," *Journal of Religion and Popular Culture* 21/1. Online. Available HTTP: www.usask.ca/relst/jrpc/art21%281%29-EarthStoodStill.html (8 March 2011).

——(2010) *Sacred Space: The Quest for Transcendence in Science Fiction Film and Television*, Waco, TX: Baylor University Press.

Dante, J. (2005) "Commentary," in *The War of the Worlds* (1953), Collector's Edition DVD, Hollywood, CA: Paramount Pictures.

Kukkonen, T. (2008) "God against the Gods: Faith and the Exodus of the Twelve Colonies," in J.T. Eberl (ed.) *"Battlestar Galactica" and Philosophy: Knowledge Here Begins Out There*, 169–80, Oxford: Blackwell.

Linford, P. (1999) "Deeds of Power: Respect for Religion in *Star Trek: Deep Space Nine*," in J.E. Porter and D.L. McLaren (eds) *"Star Trek" and Sacred Ground: Explorations of "Star Trek," Religion, and American Culture*, Albany, NY: State University of New York Press, 77–100.

McHenry, B. (2008) "Weapons of Mass Salvation," in J. Steiff and T.D. Tamplin (eds) *"Battlestar Galactica" and Philosophy: Mission Accomplished or Mission Frakked Up?* Chicago, IL: Open Court, 221–231.

Pareles, J. (1996) "When Aliens Start to Look a Lot Like Us," *New York Times* (29 May): H26.

Polan, D. (1996) "Eros and Syphilization: The Contemporary Horror Film," in B.K. Grant (ed.) *Planks of Reason: Essays on the Horror Film*, Lanham, MD: Scarecrow, 201–211.

Sagan, C. (2006) *The Varieties of Scientific Experience: A Personal View of the Search for God*, A. Druyan (ed.), New York: Penguin.

Tudor, A. (1989) *Monsters and Mad Scientists: A Cultural History of the Horror Movie*, Cambridge, MA: Basil Blackwell.

Filmography

Andromeda, Gene Roddenberry (2000–2005)

Babylon 5, J. Michael Straczynski (1994–1998)

"Parliament of Dreams, The", *Babylon 5*, Jim Johnston, dir. (1994)

Battlestar Galactica, Ronald D. Moore (2004–2009)

Book of Eli, The, Albert Hughes / Allan Hughes, dir. (2010)

Colossus: The Forbin Project, Joseph Sargent, dir. (1970)

Contact, Robert Zemeckis, dir. (1997)
Day of the Triffids, The, Steve Sekely, dir. (1962)
Day the Earth Stood Still, The, Robert Wise, dir. (1951)
Gattaca, Andrew Niccol, dir. (1997)
Godzilla, Ishiro Hondâ, dir. (1954)
Halo: Combat Evolved, Bungie Studios (2001) [videogame]
Halo 2, Bungie Studios (2004) [videogame]
I, Robot, Alex Proyas, dir. (2004)
Island, The, Michael Bay, dir. (2005)
Mad Max Beyond Thunderdome, George Miller, dir. (1985)
Short Circuit, John Badham, dir. (1986)
Stargate SG-1, Brad Wright / Jonathan Glassner (1997–2007)
Star Trek, Gene Roddenberry (1966–1969)
"Apple, The", *Star Trek*, Joseph Pevney, dir. (1967)
"Who Mourns for Adonais?", *Star Trek*, Marc Daniels, dir. (1967)
Star Trek: Deep Space Nine, Rick Berman / Michael Piller (1993–1999)
"Treachery, Faith, and the Great River", *Star Trek: Deep Space Nine*, Stephen L. Posey, dir. (1998)
Star Trek: The Next Generation, Gene Roddenberry (1987–1994)
"Devil's Due", *Star Trek: The Next Generation*, Tom Benko, dir. (1991)
Star Trek: Voyager, Rick Berman / Michael Piller (1995–2001)
"False Profits", *Star Trek: Voyager*, Cliff Bole, dir. (1996)
"Prophecy", *Star Trek: Voyager*, Terry Windell, dir. (2001)
Terminator, The, James Cameron, dir. (1984)
Them!, Gordon Douglas, dir. (1954)
War of the Worlds, The, Byron Haskin, dir. (1953)
Westworld, Michael Crichton, dir. (1973)

4 Religion and cinema horror

Douglas E. Cowan

Introduction

Outtakes: two brief, horrific memories

When I think of the first time I saw *The Exorcist* (dir. William Friedkin, Warner Bros. 1973), it is the smell that I recall most clearly: musty, close, with a cloying sweetness that hangs on the edge like mist. Even now, decades later, whenever I screen this classic film for a course, my sense-memory kicks in and I am back in the E.W. Bickle Theatre in the small town on Vancouver Island where I grew up. Despite the escalating mayhem on the screen, the various horrific images from the film—Regan vomiting pea soup, her head slowly spinning around, the violent levitation of the bed as the exorcists battle the demon Pazuzu—it is the smell of the old theater, the odor of stale popcorn and over-sweetened orange drink in the fountain cooler that returns to haunt me. Indeed, every time I see those images and remember those smells a part of me is fifteen again—and terrified. Back then I know I'd have left the theater if it hadn't meant walking home—in the dark, vulnerable, alone. As it was, weeks passed before I could sleep untroubled by nightmares. It is safe to say that I was not much of a cinema horror fan after that.

Cue the Scooby-Doo special effects and fast-forward thirty years. A sudden bout of the flu keeps me on the couch. I am no longer the frightened fifteen year-old, but a sociologist of religion, specializing among other things in the intricate relationship between religion and popular culture. It is Halloween weekend and a local television station is running a *Hellraiser* marathon. I had, of course, seen the covers in the video store and recognized Doug Bradley's iconic character, Pinhead, from the movie art. While Pinhead's cassock-like leather outfit, the constant references to souls in torment, and an explicit, ongoing concern with the battle between good and evil occasionally caught my attention, I had not seen any of the films. So, when Channel Seven announced the *Hellraiser* marathon that weekend I thought, what do I have to lose? I can always change the channel.

As I watched, though, I grew increasingly fascinated with the religious mythology that underpinned and evolved over the course of the franchise. In the first installment, *Hellraiser* (dir. Clive Barker, New World Pictures 1987), which is based on Clive Barker's novella *The Hellbound Heart* (1986), an intricate puzzle box opens a portal between our world and a dimension inhabited by creatures known as Cenobites—humans horribly mutated, trapped in eternity by their own desires, and living in an **ersatz** community defined only by their shared suffering. Indeed, though many *Hellraiser* fans may not be aware of it, "cenobite" is an explicitly religious term and means a professed religious person—a monk or a nun—who lives as part of a community, rather than as a hermit. Traditional religious icons, though, in this case holy cards, crosses, and statues of the Virgin Mary and Michelangelo's *Pietà*, lie discarded outside the grim, foreboding house in which the central action takes place. There is religion here, there is the reality of an unseen order that impinges on our own, just not the kind with which we are perhaps familiar.

The marathon continued and the *Hellraiser* mythology expanded. In the second installment, *Hellbound: Hellraiser II* (dir. Tony Randel, New World Pictures 1988), we catch a glimpse of what Hell might actually look like. Rather than hellfire, brimstone, and hordes of cackling demons, Hell is a bleak, gray labyrinth through which we wander alone, chased forever by the memories, fears, and desires that brought us there in the first place. In *Hellraiser III: Hell on Earth* (dir. Anthony Hickox, Miramax Films 1992), Pinhead explicitly challenges one of the dominant religions in North America, performing a blasphemous mockery of the Eucharist from behind the altar of a Catholic church. When an outraged priest attacks him for his sacrilege, shouting, "You'll burn in hell for this!" the Cenobite responds gravely, "Burn? Oh, such a limited imagination." Indeed, theologically implicit lines such as these are hallmarks of the first several entries into the franchise. In *Hellraiser*, for instance, when the terrified Kirsty wants to know what the Cenobites are, Pinhead tells her, "We are explorers in the further regions of experience. Angels to some, demons to others." To another character in *Hellraiser III*, he explains, "There is no good, Monroe, there is no evil. There is only flesh." And to Joey, the female lead in that film, he pledges, "Down the dark decades of your pain, this will seem like a memory of heaven." Heaven and hell, angels and demons, souls cast in the balance between good and evil, the hope of eternal salvation and the prospect of eternal suffering—these are all explicitly religious concepts that, although they have become a generalized part of our cultural lexicon, make no real sense apart from the theological traditions in which they are embedded.

For me, though, the principal moment of clarity in the development of the *Hellraiser* mythology comes in *Hellraiser: Bloodline* (dir. Kevin Yagher and Joe Chappelle, Miramax Films 1996), the fourth entry in the series and by far the most ambitious. Although this installment is also the most heavily criticized by the legions of *Hellraiser* fans, I admit that it remains my favorite, not so much for what it does, but for what it implies. Filling in the backstory on the origins of the puzzle box, the **liminal** Cenobite realm, and the future of the doorway between the worlds, the narrative moves uneasily between eighteenth-century France, the late modern period, and some indeterminate time in a science fiction future. In our day, Pinhead tries to coerce a New York architect into building a permanent portal between the dimensions, one through which the Cenobite legions could pass in force and at will. When the architect meets his "employer" for the first time, however, the young man can only exclaim, weakly, "Oh, my God." To which, in his imitable, sepulchral voice, Pinhead responds: "Do I look like someone who cares what God thinks?"

After seven hours of watching the *Hellraiser* mythology unfold, I thought, No, you don't (care what God thinks). Not really. And, in many ways this line both defines the *Hellraiser* series and explains/highlights one of the reasons religion and horror are often tied so closely together. Why don't you care what God thinks? What has happened to the God in which so many hundreds of millions have placed their trust? Has he been banished by science, as an earlier sequence in the *Hellraiser: Bloodline* suggests? Does the presence of the Cenobites—angels to some, demons to others—render him irrelevant? Or, while many still profess belief, does Pinhead in some way reflect a paradox of the late modern world: we may still believe in God, but we don't seem to care what he thinks.

Theory and method

Religion and the problem of cinema horror

Put broadly, we advance knowledge in two distinct but often-interrelated ways: we fill gaps and we correct mistakes. Both of these are on ample display when we consider the problem of religion and cinema horror. For some, horror films do not seem to have much to do with religion, or at least with religion as we commonly recognize it. One seems out of place with the other. Reviewing Rupert Wainwright's 1999 film *Stigmata* (MGM Studios), for example, one critic writes, "You do not expect to find religion and spirituality in a horror film" (Burke 1999). While this writer seems to have missed completely such milestone movies as *Rosemary's Baby* (dir. Roman Polanski, William Castle Productions 1968), *The Exorcist*, and *The Omen* (dir. Richard Donner, 20th Century Fox 1976), critics such as these are often bound by a definition of religion so narrow that they may not recognize its on-screen variations when confronted by them. Indeed, these three films brought Satan into the mainstream cinema (see Cowan 2008: 167–199), and *The Exorcist* has been added to the National Film Registry by the National Film Preservation Board of the U.S. Library of Congress. As I point out in *Sacred Terror*, however,

> Cinema horror is replete with religion and always has been. From a secretive Egyptian priesthood using its occult power to ensure the return of *The Mummy's Ghost* [dir. Reginald Le Borg, Universal Pictures, 1944] to Amanda Donohoe's biting devotion to a pre-Christian snake god in Ken Russell's *The Lair of the White Worm* [dir. Ken Russell, Vestron 1988], from the cross-and-holy-water combination that ultimately defeats the vampire baron in *The Brides of Dracula* [dir. Terence Fisher, Universal Pictures, 1960] to Steve Beck's nervy reinterpretation of the **Charon** myth in *Ghost Ship* [dir. Steve

Beck, Warner Bros. Pictures 2002], religion has proven a staple of cinematic horror since Georges Méliès brought **Mephistopheles** to the screen in 1896 and Frankenstein's creation first lurched in front of Thomas Edison's kinetoscope fifteen years later.

(Cowan 2008: 8)

Other critics, however, simply reject the possibility that cinema horror can function as a useful vehicle for presenting different often challenging visions of religion, faith, and spirituality. This is a more vexing problem since it speaks directly to our oft-displayed inability to imagine or appreciate metaphysical realities other than those to which we are committed. Writing in the *Journal of Religion and Film*, for example, Bryan Stone opines that since "it offends, disgusts, frightens, and features the profane, often in gruesome and ghastly proportions," "other than pornography, horror is the film genre least amenable to religious sensibilities" (2001). Like many who dismiss any meaningful connection between religion and horror, he concludes that "the mere fact that horror films rely heavily on symbols and stories as mere conventions to scare the hell out of us does not make a case for religious vitality in our culture; in fact, their persistence eviscerated of any deeper connection to our lived question may be a good example of the decline of the religious in our culture" (Stone 2001).

In this case, rather than a gap to be filled, this is a mistake that needs to be corrected. For one thing, Stone assumes that religion—which often implies a critic's notion of "real religion" or "my religion"—is not on occasion offensive, disgusting, frightening, or gruesome. History demonstrates clearly, however, that it has been all of these—and a good deal more. For another, by invoking the notion of "religious sensibilities" Stone falls neatly into what I call the good, moral, and decent fallacy, "the popular misconception that religion is always (or should always be) a force for good in society, and that negative social effects somehow indicate false or inauthentic religious practices" (Cowan 2008: 15–16). Similarly, there is neither sociological nor historical evidence to support this. Indeed, as historian of religion Jonathan Z. Smith writes, "Religion is not nice; it has been responsible for more death and suffering than any other human activity" (1982: 110). Human sacrifice to the gods in a variety of cultures, religiously motivated genocide in the Hebrew scriptures, wars of religion between competing sects in mediaeval Europe, the hideous history of witch hunts and heresy trials in a variety of traditions—all of these point to the historical reality that we are never quite so savage as when we visit our savagery upon others in the name of our gods and in the service of what we consider true belief.

At this point, some critics contend that those who commit what seem to us as horrific acts do not really understand religion. They do not "get it right," as it were, and their interpretation of the human/divine relationship is not sophisticated enough to see beyond such mundane human realities as greed, anger, temptation, and cruelty. The problem, though, is that once again this defines religion in terms that are far too narrow. For the Aztecs, human sacrifice to the god Huitzilopochtli *was* traditional religion. For the Roman Catholic hierarchy in fifteenth-century Spain, the requirement to root out heresy was not based on a misunderstanding of Christian theology but on their commitment to what they believed was the *only correct understanding* of it. To suggest now that "they just didn't get it" is altogether too easy, too parochial, too slick. It limits our ability to see the myriad ways in which religion is reflected and refracted—shown to us and changed for us—throughout history and, now, in such popular culture products as cinema horror.

In order to avoid such pitfalls as the good, moral, and decent fallacy, our research requires what phenomenologists call ***epoche***, the willingness to bracket one's assumptions in the quest for **eidetic vision**, a glimpse of what is really there. This does not mean that we eliminate our biases. That is impossible. But, in the interest of understanding something more deeply, we can do our best to set them aside. For example, if my faith commitment compels me to believe that all other religions than my own are false at best and satanic at worst—a position held by tens of millions of fundamentalist Christians around the world—and I am not willing to bracket those assumptions, this may very well prevent me from interpreting my data in a way that is at least fair, if not necessarily objective. What some may regard as a deeply held belief—for example, that the ability to function in the world depends on **propitiating** this or that god—I may simply dismiss as demonic activity, or even possession. But in doing so I impose my own theological views in a way that obscures and distorts the lived reality of another religious believer.

When I began working on *Sacred Terror*, two simple questions drove my research: what fears and why religion? That is, if we accept the premise that religion and spirituality are and always have been integral to the horror genre, and if we reject the notion that cinema horror has nothing to teach us about these things, then what can we learn about what we fear, why we fear, and how we manage our fear? And how do those relate to our ages old quest for meaning and purpose?

The method is simple as well: we have to watch a lot of movies! We cannot simply see a few films and expect to say anything significant about the genre. As science fiction legend (and sometimes horror writer) Ray Bradbury advises, "See every film ever made. Fill up on the medium" (in Witkin 1994: 31). The methodological moral here is that we cannot make any kind of useful generalizations from one or two installments of *Hellraiser*, or by cherry-picking a few examples from the recent spate of so-called **torture porn** films, or by considering only the latest crop of "tween" vampire films without knowing the history of the undead on-screen. We also have to watch them critically. While they may be entertaining, we seek to understand more than their value as entertainment. As we watch, as we immerse ourselves in our subject, we begin to see patterns, meaningful relationships between on-screen action and off-screen reality. It is then that we realize, for example, that, although they both concern species of the undead, vampire films are fundamentally different from mummy movies. Vampire films are predominantly(?) erotica, while mummy movies are typically(?) love stories. Beyond the concern with survival after death, not all zombie movies are even marginally related to religion, while others are religious from beginning to end. Whatever patterns emerge from studies such as these, there will always be anomalies and outliers, but we can only know this through a deep and thorough familiarity with the genre.

This brings us to a second important methodological point. In *Le surrealism au cinema*, Greek filmmaker Ado Kyrou told his readers to "learn to look at 'bad' films, they are sometimes sublime" (1963: 276). Sad or not, the reality is that very few films are very good. Even so-called "blockbusters" are often marred by clumsy direction, artless writing delivered by actors unequal to the task, and special effects that highlight the film's shortcomings rather than add to its achievement. This is true for horror films at least as much as for any other genre. That said, cinema horror is one of the most durable genres in cinema history and no major period in North American or European cinema has been without its scary movies. Cinema horror maintains a devoted, often sophisticated fan base. While most modern horror movies do not see theatrical release but go straight to DVD, even franchises such as *Hellraiser*, which is now in its eighth installment, continue to produce new entries that are eagerly awaited and debated by enthusiasts. Moreover, it appears that no other genre attracts the amateur filmmaker like horror. From backyard zombie movies to class-project vampire films, we remain as enamored of scary movies now as we have been of scary stories for centuries. There is much to see, then, but what can it tell us?

For more than twenty years now, anthropologists, sociologists, and cultural studies scholars have used a concept known as **sociophobics** to help understand the nature of fear in society. Put simply, sociophobics means that what we fear, why we fear it, and how we manage our fears are socially constructed behaviors (see Scruton 1986). We may all share similar physiological responses to fear—increased heart rate, a dump of adrenaline into our bloodstream, sweating and shaking—but what causes these reactions is at least in part a product of socialization. Bollywood is one of the largest film industries in the world that makes movies in every conceivable genre. Zombie films, however, simply don't play well in India. Since cremation is the most common method of corpse disposal in India, there is no body to reanimate and, thus, no cultural history of the walking dead. In Haiti, on the other hand, although zombiism plays only a minor role in **Vodun**, it has a long history and strong cultural resonance among the Haitian people. In short, it makes sense as a fear in one place, but not in another.

Religion and cinema horror reveal a number of different, though often interrelated sociophobics. In no particular order, these include: fear of sacred places; fear of death and of dying badly; fear of supernatural evil; fear of religious fanaticism; fear of the flesh and of religion's inadequacy. Let us consider each of these briefly, then one in more detail.

We fear sacred places. In *To Take Place*, Jonathan Z. Smith points out that "when one enters a temple, one enters marked-off space" (1987: 104), that is, space specifically set apart for interaction between the seen and the unseen orders. They can be places in which we meet our own god or gods. As we saw in *Hellraiser III*, though, this invokes the potential for God's absence, for the inability of the sacred place to provide an accustomed sanctuary. They can be places set aside for other gods—the site of worship for one group but the locus of terror for another—or places abandoned by one faith and taken over by a competing tradition. There are places where many cultures believe that the worlds of the living and the dead most intimately connect: graveyards, cemeteries, cremation grounds, tombs and mausolea. From *The Mummy* to *Poltergeist*, and from *White Zombie* to *Raiders of the Lost Ark*, when we disturb the sacred resting places of the dead we often invite horrific retribution (see Cowan 2008: 93–122).

Our fear of death, however, frequently has less to do with the brute fact of dying than with the potential for dying badly and, perhaps more important, not remaining dead. Ghost stories, vampire lore, mummy movies, zombie films, and the kind of reanimation horror epitomized in Mary Shelley's *Frankenstein* have been staples of cinema horror since the turn of the twentieth century. Although there is no a priori reason to assume that the spirits of those who loved us in life should wish to harm us once they have passed over, cultures throughout the world have exhibited/included elaborate rituals regulating the relationship between the living and the dead. Whether we carelessly fail to honor these rituals or deliberately ignore the requirements of the relationship, the ghostly soul in torment has animated films as diverse as John Carpenter's *The Fog* (ignore the Rupert Wainwright remake) and Takashi Shimizu's *Ju-On* (which he remade for Western audiences as *The Grudge*), and as wide-ranging in theological implications as Tim Burton's *Beetlejuice* and *Corpse Bride*, Steve Beck's *Ghost Ship*, and *13 Ghosts* (see Cowan 2008: 123–166).

Fear of ghosts, however, is only one species of our fear of supernatural evil, especially when this evil is internalized (as in a possession film) or externalized (as in the threat of metaphysical mayhem visited upon our world). Fearsome demonic entities and shadowy satanic groups have figured in films such as *To the Devil A Daughter*, *The Devil Rides Out*, and Val Lewton's 1943 classic, *The Seventh Victim*, all three now-iconic films that brought Satan to the mainstream cinema (the first two in the late 1960s and early 1970s). *Rosemary's Baby*, *The Exorcist*, and *The Omen*, respectively, blended fear of the satanic cult, the dark side of Roman Catholicism, and, in what one critic calls "*The Exorcist* for Protestants" (Jones 2002: 189, in reference to *The Omen*), fundamentalist Christian fascination with the end-times and the identity of the Antichrist with A-list stars and major studio production values. Anyone familiar with Christian predictions of the Antichrist, which show up in dozens of novels beginning at the turn of the twentieth century, will find Richard Donner's *The Omen* somewhat plodding and predictable. Because it appeared at the height of renewed interested in Christian prophecies of the end-times, however, it was a huge financial success for 20th Century Fox. Indeed, the money realized by *The Omen* allowed the studio to finish a little space opera George Lucas was making called *Star Wars* (Zacky 2001; see also Cowan 2008: 167–200).

For decades, on-screen fear of the devil has been accompanied by fear of those who worship him and who seek to prosecute his designs in the world. In *Rosemary's Baby*, since the entire story is told from one young woman's point of view, are the meddling neighbors, Minnie and Roman Castavet, merely annoying or are they truly part of a satanic cult dedicated to the devil's progeny? Are the Palladists in *The Seventh Victim* really just a Greenwich Village social club, or is something more sinister afoot? One of the most important aspects of this particular sociophobic is the on-screen conflation of witchcraft and Satanism. Although modern Pagans have worked diligently for decades to distinguish their religious practices from those of **theistic Satanists**, films ranging from *Horror Hotel* to *The Craft* have either implicitly or explicitly reinforced a cultural fear of witches and devils that is several centuries old. Cults and covens on-screen highlight off-screen fears of religious fanaticism, the willingness of people to carry out unspeakable acts in the name of their god (see Cowan 2008: 236).

The sociophobic converse of religious fanaticism is our fear that, like the hapless priest in *Hellraiser III*, our religious faith will prove inadequate when challenged and we will find our god absent in the moment of crisis. Among others, these are temptation films, the Edenic apples in cinema horror's garden of earthly delights. Power corrupts, certainly, but when the devil appears in these films he most often comes in the flesh. Sexuality, barely suppressed or overtly displayed, has marked vampire cinema since Dracula's wives first tried to make a meal of the young Jonathan Harker in Tod Browning's 1931 classic, *Dracula*. From the 1920s to the 1950s, countless scantily clad women were offered on sacrificial altars in both pulp fiction and cinema horror. The tag lines for Hammer's 1966 film, *The Witches*, read salaciously, "What does it have to do with sex? Why does it attract women? What does it do to the unsuspecting and why won't they talk about it? What do the witches do after dark?" Cue the ominous tympani music. On the other hand, there is "nunsploitation," an entire subgenre of horror that fetishizes the female Catholic religious in films ranging from Bruno Mattei's *The Other Hell* to Lucio Fulci's *Demonia*, and from *Convent of Sinners* to *The Sinful Nuns of St. Valentine*.

Finally, there is what I call the "**metataxis** of horror," our fear that everything we know—or think we know—about the sacred order could be turned upside down in a matter of moments. If in his famous 1841 poem "Pippa Passes" Robert Browning writes, "God's in his Heaven / All's right with the world," horrific metataxis in cinema horror asks us to consider, "What if God's not there? What if heaven has turned to hell?"

Case studies in horrific metataxis

Invasion, inversion, irrelevance

In his classic work *The Sacred Canopy*, sociologist Peter Berger writes that "all socially constructed worlds are inherently precarious" (1967: 29), religious worlds, arguably, most of all. Because they are concerned with the relationship between the seen and the unseen, the empirical and the metaphysical, religious worlds are open to challenge on a variety of fronts and require ongoing reinforcement among believers. Berger also points out that "the sacred has another opposed category, that of chaos. The sacred emerges out of chaos and continues to confront the latter as its terrible contrary" (1967: 26; cf. Beal 2002). That is, whatever we consider sacred is constantly threatened by the potential for chaos, although "chaos" is often a matter of perspective. When the Israelites tore down the sacred poles of the Canaanite peoples, when Christians demolished or appropriated sacred sites across Europe and the Americas, when the Taliban shelled Buddhist statues in Afghanistan, what seems to one group as chaos was to the other the righteous establishment of cosmic order. By proposing a change in the sacred order, cinema horror not only challenges our assumptions about that order but also questions our commitment to it. Although they appear in many different forms, cinema horrors challenge the dominance of the sacred order in three basic ways: inversion, invasion, and irrelevance.

First, horrific metataxis *inverts* popular categories of religious interpretation and expectation. Churches become centers of evil rather than sanctuaries, clergy work for the forces of darkness rather than the common good, and supernatural beings we believe are on our side turn out to be anything but. According to a 2000 survey, for example, 77 percent of Americans believe that "angels, that is, some kind of heavenly beings who visit Earth in fact exist," a belief that "cuts across almost all ranges of education, income, and lifestyle" (Shermer 2000: 244). Five years later, another study found that more than 80 percent of Americans believe either "absolutely" or "probably" in the existence of angels (Baylor Religion Survey 2006). This almost certainly accounts for the enduring popularity of films such as *It's a Wonderful Life* and television series such as *Highway to Heaven* and *Touched by an Angel.* In all of these, angels are inevitably helpful, compassionate, beautiful, and devoted to the betterment of the human condition.

But, as I write in *Sacred Terror*, what if they're wrong? "What if angels are unlike anything we might think or imagine? If the message of these pop-cultural representations is 'Be not afraid,'" what if "the angelic proclamation in [cinema horror] is 'Be afraid. Be very afraid'" (Cowan 2008: 69).

In Gregory Widen's 1995 film *The Prophecy*, the archangel Gabriel has staged a second war in heaven. Bitterly resentful of the divine love lavished upon humans, whom he considers little more than "talking monkeys," Gabriel leads a rebellion designed to return the legions of angelic beings to what he considers their rightful place in the heavens. This film focuses the concept of horrific inversion in two separate ways. Obviously, the war in heaven threatens the entire sacred order. What becomes of angels and demons—a fairly simple, stable cosmic order—when those closest to God choose to follow the path trod first by those who rebelled against him? More interesting, though, especially in the context of popular belief in angels and their inherent goodness, is the second focus: what the Bible actually says about angelic beings. In the film, one of the principal characters is a young homicide detective, Thomas Daggett, who is trying to solve a series of puzzling murders and finds himself on the front lines of Gabriel's insurrection. A lapsed Catholic who almost entered the priesthood as a young man, Daggett is presented as an authority on angels and serves as our chorus throughout the film, explaining how the current popular conception of these beings is distinctly at odds with their representation in the sacred texts.

> **Daggett:** You ever read the Bible, Katherine? You ever notice how, in the Bible, when God needed to punish someone, make an example, or whenever God needed a killing, he sent an angel? Did you ever wonder what a creature like that must be like? Your whole existence spent praising your God, always with one wing dipped in blood? Would you ever really want to see an angel?

The point here is that this is not a fanciful reading of scripture, nor an unreasonable interpretation of the biblical stories in which angels appear. The Hebrew people may have benefited from the angel of death's grisly night's work in Exodus 12, but how horrifying must that have been for everyone else? To the Egyptians at the time, the angel of Yahweh must have seemed like some terrible invading force.

Indeed, *invasion* is the second level of horrific metataxis. Rather than insurrection and inversion, we fear that the sacred order of things may be displaced through incursion and occupation. Off-screen, this is demonstrated clearly when dominant religions try to limit or prevent the activities of newcomer faiths. On-screen, we see this in films such as *The Dunwich Horror*, which is based on the famous H.P. Lovecraft short story ([1929] 2001), *Hellboy*, Guillermo del Toro's effects-driven homage to Lovecraft, and most obviously in Stuart Gordon's *Dagon*, which is adapted from Lovecraft's story, "The Shadow over Innsmouth" ([1936] 1999).

The film *Dagon* is set in the squalid town of Imboca on the Atlantic coast of Spain, where survivors of a shipwreck find themselves in a town overtaken by inhabitants deformed in one way or another. Some have tentacles where arms should be while another has piscine teeth and speaks in guttural grunts. The survivors seek shelter in what appears to be a Catholic church, but discover that it has been re-consecrated as "The Esoteric Order of Dagon." In this film, our chorus is Ezequiel, an elderly man who has lived in the village since childhood, but who has somehow escaped the horrific transformation. Many years ago, Imboca was a prosperous fishing village, but one day the fish disappeared and the town began to suffer. Being pious Catholics, they prayed for the return of their livelihood, but still the fish did not come.

One day a fishing captain named Cambarro tells the people that he knows a god that can bring back the fish, that can bring prosperity home to Imboca. On the rocky shore, Cambarro throws a small golden pyramid carved with the Dagon symbol into the sea. "I hear first time new prayer," mutters Ezequiel sadly. "I wish I never hear. I wish I never see. Soon, Imboca rich … people go against God. No worship Cristo. All worship Dagon, or die." As he speaks, we are shown flashbacks of the villagers smashing the furniture and religious statuary in the Catholic church and murdering the parish priest. The crucifix is replaced by the symbol of Dagon and Cambarro leads the villagers in prayer to their new god. "All worship Dagon or die," says Ezequiel quietly.

Compounding this particular fear is the possibility that the cosmic order will not return to what we consider "normal." That is, there will be no happy ending, no resolution, no ultimate step back from the abyss. In most films, at least in the case of North American cinema horror, the world does return to normal. Good triumphs as evil is defeated—or at least deflected. In *The Dunwich Horror*, Wilbur Whateley's attempts to bring back the Old Ones—elder gods who ruled aeons before the arrival of the religions with which we are now familiar—are defeated in a battle of magical wits by the scholar of all things esoteric, Professor Armitage. The sacred order has been threatened, but the Old Ones are beaten back once again. Similarly, in *Hellboy*, Rasputin's efforts to open the portal for the elder gods are thwarted by agents of the Bureau of Paranormal Research. However refracted through the events of the film, this return to normalcy is a hallmark of North American horror. If nothing else, it opens the way for the invasion of seemingly innumerable sequels.

Ado Kryou's advice about bad movies notwithstanding, some sequels are simply better left unmade. Friedkin's *The Exorcist* is a cinema horror classic, but the two sequels that followed it—even given the star power of Richard Burton in *Exorcist II* and George C. Scott in *Exorcist III*—were dismal by comparison. Fifteen years after *Exorcist III*, however, and more than three decades after Friedkin's original film, directors Renny Harlin (*Exorcist: The Beginning*) and Paul Schrader (*Dominion: Prequel to The Exorcist*) made prequels to fill in the backstory on Father Lankster Merrin, the exorcist played originally by Max von Sydow. In Merrin's story, we encounter elements of the third sociophobic, *insignificance*, that is, the fear that God may not be there when we need him, or if he is his presence simply doesn't matter.

For Merrin, the encounter with unthinkable evil begins in 1944 in a small town in Nazi-occupied Holland. Partisans have killed a German SS soldier and his commander seeks the guilty party. Father Merrin, the parish priest, pleads with him, assuring him that no one in the village could have done this thing. Gathering everyone in the square before the village church, the officer demands that Father Merrin choose ten townspeople for summary execution. Horrified, he cannot and the officer shoots a young woman in the head—in Schrader's version, for making the German wait. If Merrin does not comply, the entire population will be massacred. The priest begs the officer to shoot him instead. In Harlin's version, the German holds his pistol to a young boy's head, demanding again that the priest choose. Merrin's lips move in prayer and the soldier sneers. Merrin begs to take the boy's place. The German soldier looks at him for a moment, then shoots the child. As he walks away he tells Merrin that God is not in the village that day.

A small scene, given different weight in each version of the film, but it embodies one of the singular fears of religious people: what if God is either not there or powerless to act? This is the fear that lies at the heart of **theodicy**, the justification of God in the face of suffering. Here in the small village square is the classic problem of evil that has plagued believers for millennia and provided anti-theists with their most powerful argument against the existence of God. If God is all good and all-powerful, how can such atrocities occur? Arguments ranging from God's tears in the face of human free will to God's willing self-limitation have sought an answer to this question, but cinema horror raises the dilemma for us again and again. Where is God? From *Hellraiser III* to *Dagon*, *Dominion*, and numerous other films, prayers prove ineffective against monstrous evil. Rather than simply movie set pieces for the establishment of a particular horror narrative, these are sociophobic artifacts that reveal significant aspects of our relationship with the divine.

In the late modern West the problem for many people is not secularization but ambivalence, not a decline in the importance of religion, but a deep-seated uncertainty about the power of the unseen order to affect our lives, either positively or negatively. Rather than dismiss cinema horror as unworthy of discussion—after all, it is arguably the most durable of all cinema genres—these films function as significant cultural artifacts of this ambivalence, especially where they challenge accepted (and often naïve) understandings of the Christian Church. From *Hellraiser*'s Pinhead to *The Exorcist*'s Pazuzu to the myriad demons, devils, and sundry dark forces that challenge the sacred order, what many of these films say, in no uncertain terms, is "Your god is too weak"—a prospect that is more frightening to believers than the possibility that God does not exist.

Summary

- Many critics have overlooked the presence of religion in cinema horror or have dismissed its importance as a cultural indicator of religious belief. Both problems require correction.
- These corrections require that we bracket our assumptions about the relationship between religion and cinema horror in order to see more clearly what these important cultural products reveal.
- Cinema horror reveals a number of specific sociophobics—culturally constructed and conditioned fears—including: fear of sacred places; fear of death, of dying badly, and of not remaining dead; fear of supernatural evil; fear of religious fanaticism; fear of the flesh and of religion's inadequacy; and fear of a change in the sacred order.
- Cinema horror can teach us significant things about the way we view religion. Despite continued suggestions that we live in an increasingly secularized world, these films disclose that we maintain a strong, often ambiguous relationship with the unseen order.

Glossary terms

Charon – in Greek mythology, the boatman who ferries the spirits of the dead across the River Styx in return for a gold coin.

Eidetic vision – from the phenomenology of Edmund Husserl, this means to see what is in front of one, rather than what one expects to see. Presumes *epoche*, (see below).

Epoche – from the phenomenology of Edmund Husserl, this means to bracket one's assumptions, biases, and prejudices in order to understand phenomena on their own terms.

Ersatz – false or imitation.

Liminal – based on the work of anthropologist Victor Turner, *liminal* has come to mean an in-between space, somewhere that is not one place or another, but somehow both and neither.

Mephistopheles – a devil usually associated with Goethe's *Faust*, although its origin is obscure. Used now as a cultural synonym for Satan.

Metataxis – a change in the accepted order of life, a disruption in the way we view the world and accept it as viewed.

Propitiate – to satisfy the demands of something or someone.

Sociophobics – the social construction of fear. The sociological position that what we fear, the ways we express fear, and how we resolve our fear are all culturally conditioned.

Theistic Satanists – those who worship Satan as a religious practice, not to be confused with satanic dabblers, who use Satanic worship as a means of social rebellion.

Theodicy – literally, the justification of God, that is the arguments made to justify the existence of God in the face of suffering and evil.

Torture porn – a subgenre of horror films that emphasizes torture, mutilation, and sadism, often with sexual overtones, that began to appear in the early 2000s. Many critics consider these films a resurgence of the splatter, slasher, and Italian *giallo* films of the 1970s and 1980s.

Vodun – the correct way of spelling the Afro-Caribbean religion popularly (and incorrectly) known as voodoo.

Points for discussion

- In small groups, talk about your emotional and intellectual reactions to different horror films that you have seen. Why do you think you react the way you do? Is there a particular type of horror film that frightens you more than others? Why do you suppose that is?
- Watch a series of franchise films and plot the emerging worlds these films create and recreate. How do they reflect and refract off-screen examples of religion?
- How do horror films re-imagine accepted cultural references? Watch a series such as *Wishmaster*, for example, and discuss how these re-present the image and idea of the genie. Research the *djinn* and ask which popular representation is more faithful to the legendary sources. If there are changes, why do you think that is so?
- Using the concept of sociophobics described in this chapter, analyze some of your favorite horror films. What are the kinds of fears represented and why do you think they are presented in the ways they are?

Further reading

Beal, T. (2002) *Religion and Its Monsters*, New York: Routledge.

One of the first academic analyses of the ways in which the monstrous informs our understanding of religion. A scholar of biblical literature, Beal looks at the dark side of religion revealed in sacred texts ranging from the Hebrew scriptures to the *Ramayana*.

Carroll, N. (1990) *The Philosophy of Horror, or Paradoxes of the Heart*, New York: Routledge.

An excellent discussion of the horror genre in its literary, artistic, and cinematic forms. Carroll's work is particularly useful for his "third way" approach to horror, walking a path between metaphysical acceptance and psychological dismissal.

Cowan, D.E. (2008) *Sacred Terror: Religion and Horror on the Silver Screen*, Waco, TX: Baylor University Press.

One of the few in-depth discussions of religion and horror cinema, which includes the popular horror-science fiction hybrid. Cowan uses the principle of sociophobics—the concept that what and how we fear is socially constructed—to consider why so much of cinema horror relies on religion.

——(2010) *Sacred Space: The Quest for Transcendence in Science Fiction Film and Television*, Waco, TX: Baylor University Press.

Considers science fiction film and television as one of the main cultural sites for the social construction of hope and the quest for transcendence. In addition to popular films, Cowan also discusses some of the most popular television series of the past few decades.

Jancovich, M. (1996) *Rational Fears: American Horror in the 1950s*, Manchester, UK: Manchester University Press.

Although generally dismissive of the relationship between religion and horror, Jancovich's book is useful for the ways in which it demonstrates the relationship between off-screen life and on-screen representation, in this case the various sociophobics associated with the Cold War period.

Leggett, P. (2002) *Terence Fisher: Horror, Myth and Religion*, Jefferson, NC: McFarland.

In this book a conservative pastor indulges his fondness for the classic horror films of Britain's Hammer Studios, particularly director Terence Fisher, and reinterprets them as an exercise in Christian evangelism.

Paffenroth, K. (2006) *Gospel of the Living Dead: George Romero's Visions of Hell on Earth*, Waco, TX: Baylor University Press.

Like Leggett, Paffenroth reads the zombie films of George Romero—the classics of the subgenre—both as an interpretation of social conditions and behaviors in late modern North America and as an implicitly theological commentary on the basic issues of human nature, purpose, and meaning.

Scruton, D.L. (ed.) (1986) *Sociophobics: The Anthropology of Fear*, Boulder, CO: Westview.

The classic text on the exploration of fear and fearing as culturally conditioned experiences.

Bibliography

Barker, C. (1986) *The Hellbound Heart*, New York: Harper.

Baylor Religion Survey (2006) *American Piety in the 21st Century*, Waco, TX: Baylor Institute for Studies of Religion.

Beal, T. (2002) *Religion and Its Monsters*, New York: Routledge.

Berger, P.L. (1967) *The Sacred Canopy: Elements of a Sociological Theory of Religion*, New York: Anchor Books.

Burke, R. (1999) "Review of *Stigmata*," *Journal of Religion and Film*, 3/2. Online. Available HTTP: www.unomaha.edu/~jrf/stigmata.htm (21 February 2011).

Cowan, D.E. (2008) *Sacred Terror: Religion and Horror on the Silver Screen*, Waco, TX: Baylor University Press.

Jones, D. (2002) *Horror: A Thematic History in Fiction and Film*, London: Arnold.

Kyrou, A. (1963) *Le surréalism au cinéma*, Paris: Le terrain vague.

Lovecraft, H.P. (1929; 2001) "The Dunwich Horror," in S.T. Joshi (ed.) *The Thing on the Doorstep and Other Weird Stories*, 206–245, New York: Penguin Books.

——(1936; 1999) "The Shadow over Innsmouth," in S.T. Joshi (ed.) *The Call of Cthulhu and Other Weird Stories*, 268–335, New York: Penguin Books.

Shermer, M. (2000) *How We Believe: Science, Skepticism, and the Search for God*, 2nd edn, New York: Owl Books.

Smith, J.Z. (1982) *Imagining Religion: From Jonestown to Babylon*, Chicago: University of Chicago Press.

——(1987) *To Take Place: Toward Theory in Ritual*, Chicago: University of Chicago Press.

Stone, B. (2001) "The Sanctification of Fear: Images of the Religious in Horror Films," *Journal of Religion and Film* 5/2. Online. Available HTTP: www.unomaha.edu/~jrf/sanctifi.htm (21 February 2011).

Witkin, M. (1994) "A Defense of Using Pop Media in the Middle-school Classroom," *The English Journal* 81/1, 30–33.

Zacky, B. (dir.) (2001) *The Omen Legacy*, DVD, Hollywood, CA: Prometheus Entertainment.

Filmography

13 Ghosts, William Castle, dir. (1960)
Beetlejuice, Tim Burton, dir. (1988)
Brides of Dracula, The, Terence Fisher, dir. (1960)
Convent of Sinners, Joe D'Amato, dir. (1986)
Corpse Bride, The, Tim Burton, dir. (2005)
Craft, The, Andrew Fleming, dir. (1996)
Dagon, Stuart Gordon, dir. (2001)
Demonia, Lucio Fulci, dir. (1990)
Devil Rides Out, The, Terence Fisher, dir. (1968)
Dominion, Paul Shrader, dir. (2005)
Dracula, Tod Browning, dir. (1931)
Dunwich Horror, The, Daniel Haller, dir. (1970)
Exorcist, The, William Friedkin, dir. (1973)
Exorcist: The Beginning, Renny Harlin, dir. (2004)
Exorcist II: The Heretic, John Boorman, dir. (1977)
Exorcist III, The, William Peter Blatty, dir. (1990)
Fog, The, John Carpenter, dir. (1979)
Ghost Ship, Steve Beck, dir. (2002)
Grudge, The, Takashi Shimizu, dir. (2004)
Hellbound: Hellraiser II, Tony Randel, dir. (1988)
Hellboy, Guillermo del Toro, dir. (2004)

Hellraiser, Clive Barker, dir. (1987)
Hellraiser: Bloodline, Kevin Yagher (as Alan Smithee), dir. (1996)
Hellraiser III: Hell on Earth, Anthony Hickox, dir. (1992)
Highway to Heaven, Michael Landon (1984-1989)
Horror Hotel, John Llewellyn Moxey, dir. (1960)
It's a Wonderful Life, Frank Capra, dir. (1946)
Ju-on, Takashi Shimizu, dir. (2000)
Lair of the White Worm, The, Ken Russell, dir. (1988)
Mummy, The, Karl Freund, dir. (1932)
Mummy's Ghost, The, Reginald Le Borg, dir. (1944)
Omen, The, Richard Donner, dir. (1976)
Other Hell, The, Bruno Mattei, dir. (1980)
Poltergeist, Tobe Hooper, dir. (1982)
Prophecy, The, Gregory Widen, dir. (1995)
Raiders of the Lost Ark, Steven Spielberg, dir. (1981)
Rosemary's Baby, Roman Polanski, dir. (1968)
Seventh Victim, The, Mark Robson, dir. (1943)
Sinful Nuns of St. Valentine, The, Sergio Grieco, dir. (1974)
Star Wars, George Lucas, dir. (1977)
Stigmata, Rupert Wainwright, dir. (1999)
To the Devil A Daughter, Peter Sykes, dir. (1976)
Touched by an Angel, John Masius (1994-2003)
White Zombie, Victor Halperin, dir. (1932)
Witches, The, Cyril Frankel, dir. (1966)

5 On the sacred power of violence in popular culture

Eric Bain-Selbo

Introduction to violence in religion and popular culture

Contemporary theorists of religion and violence have not looked so much at how religions or religious people can engage in violence in spite of religious beliefs and attitudes. There is no doubt that they can and have for millennia. Instead, contemporary theorists have focused on the *violence that is constitutive of religion*. In other words, religions are not institutions that may or may not engage in violence. They are institutions that are inherently violent. Religion and violence are intertwined. While all violence is not religious, much of it is or at least has religious overtones or dimensions. In this chapter, we will review some approaches to religion and violence and utilize them to interpret violence in popular culture, particularly in the films of Quentin Tarantino and in the sport of football.

Theory and method

Violence by people in religious communities on the basis, and in the service, of religious beliefs or institutions has often been seen as something that happened only in "primitive" or tribal religions and cultures. But even the major religious traditions in more "civilized" areas of the world have been bound with violence. Krishna encourages the warrior Arjuna to engage in warfare in the Hindu ***Bhagavad Gita***. Krishna argues it is Arjuna's sacred duty. The Abrahamic traditions are punctuated with acts of violence, often by God. Whether it is Yahweh's wrath against the Egyptians (the story of the Exodus) or his own people (Exodus 32:25–35 describes the plague that the Lord inflicts on his people, even after his servants—the Levites—had slaughtered about 3,000 of them), God's brutal sacrifice of his own son in the Christian New Testament (not to mention the apocalyptic violence in the book of Revelation), or Allah's legitimation of military force and conquest against unbelievers (see surah 9:73 in the Qur'an), violence is central to the histories and narratives of the Abrahamic traditions. Today, religious adherents often turn to violence as a means of protecting or forwarding explicitly or implicitly religious objectives. In the following sections I explain three functions of violence in religious contexts. All three are interrelated. We then will see how these perspectives or functions can be used to interpret violence in seemingly secular contexts.

Cosmological function: the holy and the damned

Central to understanding religious violence perpetrated between groups is to understand the dichotomy of "us versus them" in religious thinking. This dichotomy is part of a larger dualistic worldview in which there is good and evil. In such a **Manichean** worldview, "we" are good and "they" are evil. Regina Schwartz brilliantly illustrates the "us versus them" dichotomy that is central to the Biblical traditions. Central to her argument are the ideas of identity and scarcity (Schwartz 1997: 3–6).

All groups, by definition, go through a process of identity formation. There has to be some process by which those included in the group are conceptually and physically separated from those outside the group. But identity formation is not something that simply happens at the initial formation of a group. It must continue for as long as the group exists. The parameters and rules of the group must be affirmed continuously to distinguish the group from others. For example, the ancient Israelites formed a group characterized by physical marking (circumcision for the men), particular religious beliefs (e.g. belief in one God), and dietary restrictions (e.g. prohibitions against eating pork). This process of identity formation means that religion by definition *is* violent. It is not just that religion, through identity formation, *can* lead to violence. It is that religion, as a form of identity formation, always already is violent—if nothing else symbolically, in that it *cuts* one group off from another (in this case, the cutting literally of the male foreskin).

Schwartz also draws our attention to the fact that the physical world and human social structures are characterized by a scarcity of resources. Scarcity is a fundamental condition of group life, and it dramatically shapes relations among groups. There is only so much land or food or other resources to go around. Each group is in competition with other groups for limited resources. But there also are psychological or theological scarcities. God or the gods only can provide for some groups, not all. Only some groups will receive divine blessings. We see this most starkly in the identification of Jews as God's "chosen people." But the idea persists in Christianity and Islam. What complicates the matter even more is when the psychological or theological blessings are intertwined with tangible goods like land or food or other resources. So, for example, God's blessing on his people (Jews) entails their possession of the Holy Land (Israel).

When the "us versus them" conflict over scarce resources is understood in the context of a greater, **transcendent** battle between the forces of good and the forces of evil, then we have the makings for a cosmic war. Reza Aslan identifies a cosmic war as "a conflict in which God is believed to be directly engaged on one side over the other … a cosmic war is like a ritual drama in which participants act out on earth a battle they believe is actually taking place in the heavens" (Aslan 2009: 5).

An important aspect of cosmic war is the demonizing of the other—the opponent or combatant. Mark Juergensmeyer describes this as satanization. "The process of satanization is aimed at reducing the power of one's opponents and discrediting them," he writes. "By belittling and humiliating them—by making them subhuman—one is asserting one's own superior moral power" (Juergensmeyer 2003: 186). Satanization is part of the Manichean dualism that is central to cosmic war. In a cosmic war there is no room for compromise. As Bruce Lincoln notes, in cosmic war "Sons of Light confront Sons of Darkness, and all must enlist on one side or another, without possibility of neutrality, hesitation, or middle ground" (Lincoln 2006: 20). Thus, "the stage is set for prolonged, ferocious, and enormously destructive combat" (Lincoln 2006: 95). Even someone who suggests a compromise then is considered an enemy by his own side (Juergensmeyer 2003: 157). Ultimately, this mindset results in apocalyptic thinking—the final confrontation of good versus evil, with good prevailing in the end (Selengut 2008: 88).

Juergensmeyer notes that putting conflicts into a religious context ultimately is about meaning. Opposing the chaos and violence of the world (even with violence) is the *raison d'etre* of religion—and through religion that chaos and violence is given meaning.

Ethical function: justice, order, and vengeance

Combating the chaos and evil that the other represents is not just about restoring order for the sake of restoring order. The restoration of order is a matter of justice—divine justice to be exact. The universe is characterized by a moral order established by God—an order that occasionally can get "out of whack" and that requires the righteous actions of God's soldiers to restore it.

Individuals act justly or righteously when they use violence to establish or re-establish divine order. Such violence often is in response to previous violence, the latter being the source of the creation of disorder. Thus, the use of righteous violence to combat evil violence frequently is a matter of revenge—the revenge of the good (us) against the evil (them). It is an effort to strike back upon those who do harm to others and who disrupt the harmony of the divine order. So the violence is not simply a matter of retaliating against those who perpetrate evil (though such revenge can be sweet), it is a matter of serving a greater divine purpose. Ultimately, that divine purpose makes the use of violence a moral (because commanded—implicitly or explicitly—by God) action. In fact, we can take it a step further and insist that one is obligated morally to perform acts of violence in the service of a greater purpose or order. For example, Christian radicals who blow up abortion clinics or kill abortion providers frequently feel it is their moral and religious duty to engage in such acts. While this perspective is best represented in the Abrahamic traditions (i.e. Judaism, Christianity, and Islam), it also can be found in those major traditions from India (Hinduism and Buddhism) that are based on the **karmic** system. In the *Bhagavad Gita* the impending violence of the warrior Arjuna is justified both in terms of restoring divine order and by the fact that those who will die in battle are paying their karmic debt.

Social-psychological function: sacrifice

Violence in religion is more than simply the acts of God or divinely ordained warfare. It includes that violence that we do to ourselves—self-imposed privations or sacrifices done for religious reasons. Emile Durkheim, the early twentieth-century sociologist, provides good examples of the role of sacrifice in his analysis of aboriginal **totemic** religions in Australia (Durkheim 1995: 84–95). According to Durkheim, the totem, ancestor, or god for whom sacrifices are made ultimately is an expression of the collectivity. Thus, the sacrifices made symbolically for the totem, ancestor, or god reflect the real sacrifices that must be made by the individual for the good of the collectivity. We sacrifice something of ourselves (our freedom, our selfishness) and/or something that is good for us (an animal given for slaughter on the altar or part of our harvest burned to the gods) to forward the aims of the group.

Sacrifices raise us toward something that transcends our individual ego, but that transcendent thing is the collective itself. In this light, the sacrifices made by "primitives" may not seem so strange to us when we consider our own sacrifices (for example, in war) that we are willing to make for the good of the collectivity. In this sense, the fundamental nature of sacrifice has not changed for millennia (Durkheim 1995: 330–354).

A more contemporary scholar like René Girard also tries to make connections between the violence we find in religion (particularly ancient) and events and structures in the world today. Girard is interested especially in the sacrifice of the other, whether that be of animal or human. His hypothesis is that "society is seeking to deflect upon a relatively indifferent victim, a 'sacrificeable' victim, the violence that would otherwise be vented on its own members, the people it most desires to protect" (Girard 1977: 4). How does sacrifice do this? "The sacrifice serves to protect the entire community from *its own* violence," Girard writes, "it prompts the entire community to choose victims outside itself. The elements of dissension scattered throughout the community are drawn to the person of the sacrificial victim and eliminated, at least temporarily, by its sacrifice" (Girard 1977: 8). Any community necessarily will have tensions as individuals vie with one another for a limited amount of goods. By directing negative emotions and energy onto the shoulders of the sacrificial victim, the "**scapegoat**," members of the community are able to overcome those negative emotions and energy through the **ritualized** killing of the victim.

What Girard is getting at clearly has roots in religious life. Indeed, for Girard violence and the sacred are "inseparable" (Girard 1977: 19). Put more strongly, "the operations of violence and the sacred are ultimately the same process" (Girard 1977: 258). The purpose of religion is to prevent "reciprocal violence" (Girard 1977: 55). This continuous retaliation or revenge—fueled by the frustration of the necessary curbing of our egoism or selfishness and our competition for scarce resources—is the never-ending cycle of violence that eventually will destroy a society. Thus, instead of providing an unending cycle of revenge that produces real victims of violence, societies develop religions with sacrificial rituals in which surrogate victims suffer the violence of the community. As Girard concludes, there is no society without religion because without religion society cannot exist (Girard 1977: 221).

The function of ritual is "to 'purify' violence; that is, to 'trick' violence into spending itself on victims whose death will provoke no reprisals" (Girard 1977: 36)—"that is, to keep violence *outside* the community" (Girard 1977: 92). Girard looks across time and cultures to find ritualized behavior that supports his thesis. One of the most common rituals in which the surrogate-victim mechanism is operative is the festival (Girard 1977: 119). The festival will include a variety of behaviors that affirm the social norms via the ritualized practice of breaking those norms. In other words, by permitting *only through ritual practice* what is otherwise prohibited (e.g. sexual promiscuity), the norms of the society during everyday or profane times are affirmed for the members of the community. Festivals also are the events in which the surrogate-victim mechanism is operative. While killing is normally prohibited, during the festival it is permitted—either literally or symbolically.

While most of the examples that Girard uses are from more ancient times, he nevertheless affirms the role of sacrificial rituals in the formation of all societies and the continuing need for them. Girard believes that we more often than not are in a state of "sacrificial crisis" (Girard 1977: 39–67). This crisis is a consequence of the disappearance of sacrificial rituals, preventing the society's ability to find or create a surrogate-victim and perpetrate its violence against that victim. Girard argues that "the disappearance of the sacrificial rites, coincides with the disappearance of the difference between impure violence and purifying violence. When this difference has been effaced, purification is no longer possible and impure, contagious, reciprocal violence spreads throughout the community" (Girard 1977: 49). When all violence is condemned, then we are incapable of ritually affirming violence through the surrogate-victim mechanism. The consequence, ironically, is an increase in non-ritualized violence (including vendetta) throughout the society. This is why Girard writes:

> Sacrifice is the boon worthy above all others of being preserved, celebrated and memorialized, reiterated and reenacted in a thousand different forms, for it alone can prevent transcendental violence from turning back into reciprocal violence, the violence that really hurts, setting man against man and threatening the total destruction of the community.
>
> (Girard 1977: 124–125)

Sacrificial rituals are an effective way to prevent sacrificial crises and thus guard societies against excessive violence.

While sacrifice and promiscuity may be stereotypical aspects of festivals, so too is play. Durkheim argues that games originated in a religious context (Durkheim 1995: 385). Games or play also give rise to collective effervescence—the ecstatic bonding of individuals into a collectivity (Durkheim 1995: 385). Play, for Girard, is an expression of the sacred. It is another means by which genuine violence is avoided by virtue of the ritualized nature of the play itself.

> [W]e must subordinate play to religion, and in particular to the sacrificial crisis. Play has a religious origin, to be sure, insofar as it reproduces certain aspects of the sacrificial crisis. The arbitrary nature of the prize makes it clear that the contest has no other objective than itself, but this contest is regulated in such a manner that, in principle at least, it can never degenerate into a brutal fight to the finish.
>
> (Girard 1977: 154)

The play may be rough and even violent at times. There even is a victim in the form of the loser. But play never gives itself over to unwarranted violence or reciprocal violence. The rules of the ritual prohibit this possibility.

Case studies

Play, ritual, and violence in American football

American football is an exemplary intersection of religion, play, and violence. Michael Oriard, one of the most insightful scholars writing on the cultural history of American football, recognizes the integral role that violence plays in the sport:

> [Football is] the dramatic confrontation of artistry with violence, both equally necessary. The receiver's balletic moves and catch would not impress us nearly as much if the possibility of annihilation were not real; the violence of the collision would be gratuitous, pointless, if it did not threaten something valuable and important. The violence, in fact, partially creates the artistry: the simple act of catching a thrown ball becomes a marvelous achievement only in defiance of the brutal blow. Football becomes contact ballet.
>
> (Oriard 1993: 1–2)

Violence is central to the beauty and power of the game. American football is ritualized violence—it is composed of prescribed and proscribed acts that serve a collective purpose and provide shared meaning. In this way it is religious in character.

In many locales, particularly university campuses, the ritual of American football is performed in the context of a festival, one characterized by the violation of norms that in turn affirms those norms for more profane times. For example, while many people on game day drink alcoholic beverages (sometimes to great excess) on the grounds of the university, they would be escorted off campus or even arrested if they consumed alcohol in the same place at other times. In this case, the exception (being allowed to drink publicly on campus) affirms the rule (no public consumption of alcohol on campus). The festival context sets the stage for the ritual violence.

Football certainly entails violent confrontations between players, but it is controlled violence nonetheless. Michael Novak argues that the controlled conflict "ventilates" our rage (Novak 1994: 84). "The human animal suffers enormous daily violence," he adds, echoing both Durkheim and Girard. "Football is an attempt to harness violence, to formalize it, to confine it within certain canonical limits, and then to release it in order to wrest from it a measure of wit, beauty, and redemption" (Novak 1994: 94).

Sacrifice is a necessary element in football. This sacrifice is not only the "surrogate" or loser of the contest, but all the players. As Novak notes:

> Once an athlete accepts the uniform, he is in effect donning priestly vestments. It is the function of priests to offer sacrifices … Often the sacrifice is literal: smashed knees, torn muscles, injury-abbreviated careers. Always the sacrifice is ritual: the athlete bears the burden of identification. He is no longer living his own life only.
>
> (Novak 1994: 141)

Examples of sacrifices abound. Whether it is broken bones or concussions or even death, American football players sacrifice themselves in the performance of the ritual. Novak concludes "football dramatizes the sacrifice, discipline, and inner rage of collective behavior" (Novak 1994: 207)—sacrifice, discipline, and rage that Durkheim and Girard would find to be fundamentally religious.

Football is a "revelatory liturgy," Novak explains. "It externalizes the warfare in our hearts and offers us a means of knowing ourselves and wresting some grace from our true natures" (Novak 1994: 96). We might not always want to know of our violent and aggressive selves, but at least some cultural creations can turn that violence and aggression into something that has some merit and beauty. American football perhaps is such a thing. It is, as Oriard describes it, "contact ballet."

"Since the earliest times," Michael Mandelbaum writes, "from gladiatorial contests in ancient Rome to public hangings in early modern England to boxing in the nineteenth and twentieth centuries—not to mention Hollywood movies of the twenty-first—staged events with violence at their core have commanded public attention" (Mandelbaum 2004: 176–177). Several questions emerge in our recognition of this historical fact of life. What does it tell us about sport? Is the "staged violence" of sports like American football what gives them their vast appeal? And what is it precisely that the spectator gets from witnessing such a violent spectacle?

Everyone seems to be in agreement that the catharsis theory of sports violence is not sufficient. The catharsis theory suggests that the violence we engage in or watch in sports relieves us of our excessive violent urges and thus allows us to function better psychologically and certainly socially. Robert J. Higgs argues that explanations like the catharsis theory may help to explain the "ubiquity" of sports, but they do not explain "the reverence paid to them" (Higgs 1995: 97). Michael Oriard insists that the catharsis theory may not be wrong, but it at least is "oversimplified" (Oriard 1993: 6). Higgs and Oriard are not social scientists, nor psychologists, but their conclusions are supported by such researchers. Daniel L. Wann and his collaborators note that "there is virtually no empirical evidence validating the existence of catharsis in sport ... The 'blowing off steam' theory of sport spectating may be attractive, but it is quite inaccurate" (Wann 2001: 198). John H. Kerr likewise is suspicious of a catharsis theory of sports violence, insisting that there is little experimental evidence to support it (Kerr 2005: 124).

These perspectives (especially those from Wann *et al.* and Kerr) would seem to contradict Girard and the application of his theory to sport. Girard's work seems to rely upon some notion of a catharsis theory—the sacrificial victim relieving us of the violence that we otherwise would commit against one another. But note that the catharsis theory is not completely and conclusively discredited.

Kerr argues for a more comprehensive psychological understanding of sports violence than simply a catharsis theory. He notes that contemporary life (at least in Europe and the United States) is not very exciting. The range of emotions, especially at the highest or most pleasant end, is fairly narrow (little wonder then that many Western cultures seem fixated on sex, particularly orgasms). Consequently, "people have to actively seek out thrills and vicarious risk-taking through, for example, watching sports" (Kerr 2005: 118). Anyone watching a crowd at a major sporting event can witness the intensity of the emotions that many fans experience. Fans attain high levels of arousal (akin to Durkheim's notion of collective effervescence), and this intense experience is a "pleasant excitement" (Kerr 2005: 98). This experience is particularly prevalent with violent sports like American football and ice hockey. Kerr concludes that "watching violent sports produces increases in levels of arousal, and ... people deliberately watch to achieve elevated arousal" (Kerr 2005: 118). Here then we might have an explanation not only of the psychological appeal of violent sports, but of certain stereotypical religious rituals (e.g. sacrifices) as well.

Is such arousal good or bad for us? The flip-side of the catharsis theory is that participating in or watching violent sports spurs people to act violently in other contexts. This argument is similar to ones made about violence on television or in the movies—that such violence encourages others (especially children) to act violently. Higgs, for example, tries to connect violence in sports with aggression or violence towards women in America (Higgs 1995: 320–322). Along with Michael C. Braswell, they argue that sports initiate a cycle of violence or aggression. "[I]nstead of ventilating aggression," they claim, sports "refuel it so that a loss or setback in sports as in war is a call for stronger retaliation. In the Church of Sports, there is no answer to this that we can see, only rivalry, revenge, and redemption from season to season" (Higgs and Braswell 2004: 107). We then have exactly the kind of violence that Girard claims religion helps to avoid. While such retaliatory violence usually is contained within the context of the rules of the game, there are instances in which the violence of a sport spills into the stands—leading to physical confrontations between players and fans or between rival fans. Kerr's work recounts many of these instances, including some (such as soccer hooliganism in Europe) that led to the deaths of non-participants.

Kerr notes that the research is split on the issue of the connection between violence in various forms of popular culture and among those who participate in or view them. He concludes that the "popular wisdom which suggests media violence and media sports violence has harmful effects on people, especially where those viewers are young children, may not be correct" (Kerr 2005: 130). So if sports violence perhaps does us no harm, does it do any good? The answer, for Kerr, is affirmative. The "pleasant excitement" of violent sports can be an important part of our overall psychological health. He concludes: "[T]here are situations where certain types of aggressive and violent acts are central to people's enjoyment of activities. These activities range from athletic contests to viewing violent sports as a spectator, or watching violent sports movies. Being a part of these activities does no psychological harm to the vast majority of those who participate and may actually benefit their psychological health" (Kerr 2005: 148). The argument that participating in or watching violence produces a psychological good may go a long way to explaining why violence has been such an integral part of our games and sports and religion through the centuries—perhaps redeeming (in some way) Girard's theory as well. The argument, in short, helps explain the pervasiveness of violence in popular culture and why we seem to like it so much (despite our occasional protestations to the contrary).

In addition to the social-psychological function, sports also facilitate "us versus them" thinking. "Our" team is better than "yours." Rivalries run across the athletic landscape—and perhaps none are more heated than those between college football teams and fans in the American South. The South is divided up into "us" and "them," Rebels and Tigers, Gators and Bulldogs.

In a college football game, only one team can win (college football's adoption of an overtime system in 1996 eliminated the possibility of ties). Even more, only one team can earn the honor and adulation that comes with victory. Only one team can have "bragging rights" after the game. In other words, there is a scarcity of goods to go around. This situation undoubtedly contributes to the fervor and even violence of the game. Not surprisingly, violence breaks out occasionally among fans. It is not unusual then to have stories like the one where the University of South Carolina fan shot his friend, a Clemson University fan, when they argued about a $20 bet on the game (the game having been won by South Carolina). One would imagine that it was not so much the sum of money that was in dispute, but what the money signified—victory, honor, superiority, etc. In short, college football in the American South is an exemplary model of how sports reflect a "cosmic war" perspective in which no compromise is possible and it is "winner takes all."

From its sacrifice and play to its "cosmic war" framework, it is little wonder why sports are such an important part of popular culture. The example of football shows how sports not only function religiously, but how violence is part of why that is the case.

Violence in film (Quentin Tarantino, of course)

With American football and many other sports, violence is ritualized in ways similar to religion. In both cases, the ritualizing of violence may be a way of coping with the inherent aggression and violence of individuals in society. The contesting of American football games and the violence that ensues also replicates a fundamental religious perspective (the Manichean divide between good and evil, "us and them," the prerequisite for a cosmic war). Another place where we see the ritualizing of violence is in film, and perhaps no contemporary filmmaker is as noted for his treatment of violence as Quentin Tarantino. Joshua Mooney describes Tarantino's early films as "ultra-violent crime stories [in which] almost everyone dies ... And they do not, as the poet said, go gently. Usually they have to be shot. Their blood doesn't spill so much as it gushes, spurts, splatters, soaks and coats. Sometimes it takes the stragglers an excruciatingly long time to die, but in the end, they get there too" (Peary 1998: 70).

Tarantino certainly is not afraid to take on religious themes or ideas in his movies. Take the example of *Pulp Fiction* (1994), a film written and directed by Tarantino. Hit man Jules (played by Samuel L. Jackson) not only quotes scripture before blowing away those who have wronged his boss, but also he claims to have experienced a miracle when he narrowly survives a shooting. In *From Dusk Till Dawn* (1996), written by Tarantino and directed by Richard Rodriguez, two dangerous criminals (played by George Clooney and Tarantino) hijack a family and its mobile home in order to escape into Mexico (where they end up at the infamous club The Titty Twister, fighting off vampires in a gory, graphic battle). The father (played by Harvey Keitel) is a preacher who, after his wife's death, has turned his back on God. Tarantino directed and wrote both *Kill Bill* movies (2003, 2004), starring Uma Thurman and David Carradine. The films are extremely violent and contain extensive martial arts sequences. The plot draws on magical and philosophical elements of Eastern religions (we might assume Buddhism and Taoism in particular).

Though films like *Reservoir Dogs* (Tarantino's first film from 1992) and *Inglourious Basterds* (his most recent from 2009) do not deal substantively with religious themes, they nevertheless include his trademark violence. The failed heist in *Reservoir Dogs* not only has ample gunshot violence, it also has a torture scene in which one of the criminals cuts off the ear of a police officer, prancing around his bound-to-a-chair body to the music of the 1972 pop classic "Stuck in the Middle with You" (originally performed by the band Stealers Wheel). The scene has been described as "perhaps the single most cited moment of violence in all of the 1990s American cinema" (Gronstad 2008: 171). *Inglourious Basterds*, on the other hand, features a renegade American military unit (made up mostly of Jews) that tracks down, kills, and scalps Nazis. It also features a young female survivor of a "Jew hunt" who plots the demise (in her Paris movie theatre nonetheless) of top Nazi brass (including, we find out, Hitler).

Thomas S. Hibbs argues that violence in film is both a symptom and cause of the aesthetization of evil (Hibbs 1999: 66). In other words, evil increasingly is becoming "art" or "cool" and violence is both one of the ways in which it is happening as well as a reflection that it is happening. Hibbs' argument is drawn from Hannah Arendt's notion of the "banality of evil"—the idea that evil that becomes ordinary or normal can no longer be fought against effectively (Arendt 1994: 287–288). For Hibbs, movie violence is part of our cultural drift toward the banality of evil.

Hibbs also claims that violence in film is both a symptom and cause of the pervasive nihilism in our culture. In part, we are becoming incapable of articulating ethical values—and thus increasingly incapable of living moral lives. All values and moral systems are relative. The values inherent in the moral system of an organized crime syndicate can be judged no better or worse than the values inherent in the moral system of the Amish. As he concludes, the "new problem is not that the meaning of evil is elusive, but that it is increasingly difficult for us to distinguish between evil and goodness" (Hibbs 1999: 49).

While Hibbs represents a common concern about the impact of media violence on culture, others have a particular concern with the impact on children. Psychiatrist Eugene V. Beresin cites studies that indicate that a typical American child will have viewed more than 200,000 acts of violence (including 16,000 murders) by the age of 18. Most of the viewing would be on television (the typical American child watches approximately 28 hours of television a week), but certainly film should be included as well as (more recently) video games and online gaming. Beresin notes that while the causes of youth violence are varied, the "research literature is quite compelling that children's exposure to media violence plays an important role in the etiology of violent behavior" (Beresin 2009).

Given the concerns of scholars, parents, and professionals, it is little wonder that Tarantino has been denounced for the violence in his films. Johann Hari credits Tarantino for the realism of the violence in *Reservoir Dogs*, but sees the use of violence in subsequent films to be morally dangerous. "I'm not saying it makes people violent," Hari argues. "But it does leave the viewer just a millimeter more morally corroded. Laughing at simulated torture—and even cheering it on, as we are encouraged to through all of Tarantino's later films—leaves a moral muscle just a tiny bit more atrophied" (Hari 2009). Concerns about the gratuitous or "hollow violence" in Tarantino's *Inglourious Basterds* are also at the core of the negative review of the movie by Lee Siegel (Siegel 2009).

But what the critics miss is that the violence in Tarantino's movies is far from gratuitous or "hollow." Aaron Anderson makes a compelling argument that violence in film, at least the kind of violence that Tarantino uses, is critical for creating meaning and developing the narrative and the characters. He argues that personal action "necessarily involves a wide array of inner thoughts, both conscious and unconscious. Actions that affect other people—as violence does—therefore constitute a type of pragmatic ethics in which inner views about how one actually interacts with the world become outwardly embodied" (Anderson 2004).

One of the central meanings or themes of Tarantino's violence is revenge. In this regard, he certainly is not an unusual case in American popular culture. As William D. Romanowski argues, "Violence has a central place in American mythology as a means of justice and retribution" (Romanowski 2007: 209). Romanowski consequently points us in an important direction. Revenge is never without meaning or a connection with the idea of justice. Thus, violence associated with vengeance or revenge—either in Tarantino films or as religious acts—is far from nihilistic (in other words, arbitrary or without meaning).

The problem, as we have seen with Girard, is that acts of violence (whether committed in the name of justice or not) simply give rise to more acts of violence. The cycle of revenge is never ending. While Tarantino's films certainly reflect this idea of never ending violence, that is not the message of the films. As Bence Nanay and Ian Schnee claim, "Tarantino's films are concerned with ways to end violence ... the theme of the cycle of violence, and of breaking out of the cycle of violence, is perhaps strongest in *Pulp Fiction*" (Greene and Mohammad 2007: 185). In this regard, many of Tarantino's films can be read effectively through a Girardian lens. His films, like religious, sacrificial acts, seek ways to overcome the never ending cycle of violence.

In *Pulp Fiction*, many of the occasions for violence involve revenge—the administering of punishment or retribution, the meting out of justice. Hit men Jules and Vincent kill several men who betrayed the boss. The boss likewise seeks revenge on a boxer who double-crossed him—failing to throw a fight as agreed. Later in the movie, the boss prepares for revenge on two rednecks who anally raped him. Early in the movie, there also is a conversation between Jules and Vincent in which they consider the moral dimensions of a story they had heard about the boss throwing an associate off a building because the associate had massaged the boss' wife's feet. In short, almost all the violence in the film involves revenge. In all cases, there is an implicit or explicit understanding of justice, and from that understanding of justice violence is demanded (perhaps even morally demanded). Justice is not treated as simply a human construct, but as a given in the universe. In other words, it has a transcendent or religious dimension. While the characters may disagree about what constitutes justice, they are not nihilists. They talk and act as if justice *does* exist.

An important plot development in the movie is the dramatic religious experience of Jules—an experience that leads to a conversion of sorts. Early in the film, Jules recites a passage from the Bible (the claim is that it is Ezekiel 25:17, though only the last two lines are close to the Biblical verse). The passage he quotes is about the punishments that God will administer to evil men, and the shepherding and protection of others that is characteristic of the righteous man.

Given his murderous ways, the vengeful voice of God from this passage fits well with Jules' lifestyle. But after experiencing the "miracle" (Vincent has doubts about this) of having been shot at but having every bullet miss him, Jules identifies more with the first part of the passage—the part about shepherding "the weak through the valley of darkness." Jules realizes perhaps that his lifestyle simply perpetuates the cycle of violence. In the last scene of the film, Jules does not use violence to end violence, he simply walks away. Vincent, as we already have learned from the temporally disjointed nature of *Pulp Fiction*, does not walk away and is killed.

"At the end of the movie," Tarantino reminds us, "for all the talk about the film being violent and this, that and the other, the guy who actually becomes the lead character ... is a killer who has a religious epiphany! And it's played straight. It's not a big joke. That's supposed to be meaningful—and not in a sanctimonious way" (Peary 1998: 147). It is meaningful (whether or not Tarantino meant it this way) because Jules moves beyond the cycle of violence. But the power of that movement comes from the violent context of the film. The violence was needed for the epiphany to have any force.

David Kyle Johnson argues that "for a clear portrayal of revenge as morally justified, one need look no further than *Kill Bill*" (Greene and Mohammad 2007: 59). Uma Thurman plays Beatrix Kiddo, a member of a company of assassins who decides to leave the business and marry a record store owner. Her boss and former lover Bill, played by David Carradine, feels betrayed upon discovering her plans (he initially thought she was dead). He seeks revenge for his hurt feelings, and his band of assassins kills the wedding party at the rehearsal and mercilessly beats Beatrix. Bill then shoots her in the head. Unbeknownst to Bill, however, Beatrix survives the gunshot and after a lengthy coma seeks her revenge on the assassins and finally on Bill.

In the case of *Kill Bill*, the audience most certainly sides with Beatrix in her rampage of vengeance. She has been wronged terribly, and justice demands retribution. In this regard, her violent acts are a way of restoring order out of chaos—a typical function of religious action and central to creation mythologies. Revenge thus becomes a religious exercise. As Beatrix tells us, "When fortune smiles on something as violent and ugly as revenge, it seems proof like no other that not only does God exist, you're doing his will." Revenge then is a moral duty. It is righteous action, for it restores the divine and just order.

Anderson notes that "the film itself is not simply a revenge drama, but also a story of redemption. The only way that Kiddo can deserve a normal life is to pay penance for her own past life. This penance, however, takes the form of more violent actions, involving both Kiddo's ability to inflict harm upon others as well as her ability to endure pain and injury herself" (Anderson 2004). In other words, she must make certain sacrifices (including sacrificing others) in order to re-enter the collectivity.

By the end of the second film, after coolly killing Bill with the Five Point Palm Exploding Heart Technique, Beatrix ends her rampage of revenge and drives off with her daughter. The hope, of course, is that the cycle of revenge is ended. Maybe. In the first film we watch as Beatrix kills Vernita. When confronted by Vernita's young daughter Nikki, Beatrix says "It was not my intention to do this in front of you. For that I'm sorry. But you can take my word for it, your mother had it comin'. When you grow up, if you still feel raw about it, I'll be waiting." Here we see the prospect of the never ending cycle of violence.

In his review of Tarantino's most recent film, *Inglourious Basterds*, Charles Taylor notes that "the director wants us to relish the revenge taken on the Nazis." In the culminating scene of Nazi destruction, "it's the lust for vengeance that powers the film's most delirious and daring passage" (Taylor 2010: 105). As in other Tarantino movies, the dichotomy between good and evil is clear. Nazis, in fact, are a stereotypical symbol for evil incarnate. Their destruction brings justice to an otherwise chaotic and evil situation. The silver screen heroes of *Inglourious Basterds* (much like the football heroes on the gridiron) are warriors in contemporary cosmic wars—warriors who (hopefully?) judge the evildoers, destroy them, and restore order.

So, in Tarantino films we see extensive use of violence—but not violence that is completely disconnected from a conception of justice and righteous order. The violence at least implies a sense of justice, and often the connection is made explicit. While Tarantino's films seem to include a never ending cycle of violence, certain plot developments suggest ways of escaping that cycle (or, at least, the merits of doing so). In these ways, Tarantino's violence serves an ethical function.

Another way to think about the violence in Tarantino movies is related to the idea of sacrifice. As we saw with football, fans vicariously experience the violence of games. This experience is one of sacrificing the victim—the loser, the one being tackled or hit, etc. Such violent sacrifice of the victim compensates for the internal violence we must do to ourselves as members of a society (for example, repressing our instinctual desires). Through Tarantino films, we get to vicariously sacrifice victims—and even victims who really deserve such sacrifice. We particularly relish the destruction of the bad or evil characters, such as those who sought to kill Beatrix Kiddo. In a sense, these characters represent all those who have wronged us as well, and their destruction at least provides some psychological reckoning in the context of the film and perhaps also in our lives. This reaffirmation of order helps to maintain the communal value system—a system that helps to distinguish between right and wrong, good and evil.

We also are drawn to the personal sacrifices that characters make as they pursue their aims through the narrative of the films. Beatrix literally risks life and limb in order to exact her revenge. Similarly, the "basterds" in *Inglourious Basterds* are willing to risk everything in order to destroy the Nazis. As Durkheim notes, such risk-taking and willingness to bear pain raise these characters (and vicariously raise us) above our meager and profane selves (Durkheim 1995: 317–321). And, as Kerr observes, such risk-taking provides audiences with the opportunity to vicariously participate in it and thus to elevate our emotional lives out of the doldrums of contemporary existence (Kerr 2005: 118). In these ways and others, Tarantino films provide psychological benefits akin to those provided in religious settings.

Conclusion

As institutional religions come to have less influence on the majority of people in the West, popular culture comes to be the place where violence is ritualized and controlled. Whether we are watching violence in various sports or actors on television and film, violence continues to be central to our psychic and social lives. It is not gratuitous and barbaric, it is necessary and meaningful—whether that be in a religious or a secular context.

Summary

- Religion is inherently violent.
- The violence in religion serves important social-psychological functions.
- The violence in sports functions in similar ways to the violence in religion.

- The violence in popular media (television, film, etc.) functions in similar ways to the violence in religion.
- Violence in popular culture may serve as a substitute for stereotypically religious violence in an increasingly secular society.

Glossary terms

Bhagavad Gita – literally "Song of the Lord"; an Indian religious text that is the sixth part of the *Mahabharata*; the text is approximately 2000 years old.

Karma – literally meaning action, it is the Indian law of cause and effect as these pertain to individual behavior and its consequences either in this lifetime or future ones.

Manicheanism – a view attributed to the Manichees (third century) in which the world is divided into the world of light and the world of darkness, good and evil, and history is the working out of the struggle between the two.

Ritual – prescribed actions or behaviors that express communal and/or religious meanings.

Scapegoat – a surrogate victim that bears responsibility for the evil or ills faced by a community.

Totem – a natural object (typically an animal or plant) that represents the community and/or its gods.

Transcendent – Referring to that which is qualitatively different and separate from this world; for example, God is transcendent (other-worldly) even if he/she/it also works in the world.

Points for discussion

- Are human beings inherently violent?
- Is religion inherently violent?
- Is violence in popular culture a reflection of human violence or does it encourage human violence or both?
- Is violence in sports like ice hockey or football an important reason for why they are so popular?
- Is violence the key to why many films are so popular?

Further reading

Girard, René (1977) *Violence and the Sacred*, trans. Patrick Gregory, Baltimore, MD: Johns Hopkins University Press.

A classic theoretical work that has influenced numerous scholars in regard to theories of religion, ritual, and violence.

Juergensmeyer, Mark (2003) *Terror in the Mind of God: The Global Rise of Religious Violence*, 3rd edn, Berkeley, CA: University of California Press.

Perhaps the most important and frequently cited book on contemporary religious violence. A standard in the field.

Lincoln, Bruce (2006) *Holy Terrors: Thinking About Religion After September 11*, 2nd edn, Chicago: University of Chicago Press.

A powerful critique of the discourse surrounding 9/11 and how it reflects upon the study of religion.

Schwartz, Regina (1997) *The Curse of Cain: The Violent Legacy of Monotheism*, Chicago: University of Chicago Press.

A powerful genealogy of violence in the Abrahamic traditions.

Selengut, Charles (2008) *Sacred Fury: Understanding Religious Violence*, Lanham, MD: Rowman & Littlefield.

An excellent introduction to various ways of interpreting religious violence, with ample historical examples.

Bibliography

Anderson, Aaron (2004) "Mindful Violence: The Visibility of Power and the Inner Life in *Kill Bill*," *Jump Cut: A Review of Contemporary Media*, no. 47. Online. Available HTTP: www.ejumpcut.org/archive/jc47.2005/KillBill/ (accessed 21 June 2010).

Arendt, Hannah (1994) *Eichmann in Jerusalem: A Report on the Banality of Evil*, New York: Penguin Books.

Aslan, Reza (2009) *How to Win a Cosmic War: God, Globalization, and the End of the War on Terror*, New York: Random House.

Beresin, Eugene V. (2009) "The Impact of Media Violence on Children and Adolescents: Opportunities for Clinical Interventions," American Academy of Child and Adolescent Psychiatry. Online. Available HTTP: www.aacap.org/cs/root/developmentor/the_impact_of_media_violence_on_children_and_adolescents_opportunities_for_clinical_interventions (accessed 13 August 2010).

Durkheim, Emile (1995) *The Elementary Forms of Religious Life*, trans. Karen E. Fields, New York: The Free Press.

Girard, René (1977) *Violence and the Sacred*, trans. Patrick Gregory, Baltimore, MD: Johns Hopkins University Press.

Greene, Richard, and Mohammad, K. Silem (eds) (2007) *Quentin Tarantino and Philosophy: How to Philosophize with a Pair of Pliers and a Blowtorch*, Chicago: Open Court.

Gronstad, Asbjorn (2008) *Transfigurations: Violence, Death, and Masculinity in American Cinema*, Amsterdam: Amsterdam University Press.

Hari, Johann (2009) "The Tragedy of Tarantino: He Has Proved His Critics Right," *The Independent*, London, 26 August. Online. Available HTTP: www.independent.co.uk/opinion/commentators/johann-hari/johann-hari-the-tragedy-of-tarantino-he-has-proved-his-critics-right-1777147.html (accessed 27 July 2010).

Hibbs, Thomas S. (1999) *Shows about Nothing: Nihilism in Popular Culture from The Exorcist to Seinfeld*, Dallas, TX: Spence Publishing Group.

Higgs, Robert J. (1995) *God in the Stadium: Sports & Religion in America*, Lexington, KY: The University Press of Kentucky.

Higgs, Robert J. and Braswell, Michael C. (2004) *An Unholy Alliance: The Sacred and Modern Sports*, Macon, GA: Mercer University Press.

Juergensmeyer, Mark (2003) *Terror in the Mind of God: The Global Rise of Religious Violence*, 3rd edn, Berkeley, CA: University of California Press.

Kerr, John H. (2005) *Rethinking Aggression and Violence in Sport*, New York: Routledge.
Lincoln, Bruce (2006) *Holy Terrors: Thinking About Religion After September 11*, 2nd edn, Chicago: University of Chicago Press.
Mandelbaum, Michael (2004) *The Meaning of Sports: Why Americans Watch Baseball, Football, and Basketball and What They See When They Do*, Cambridge, MA: Perseus Books.
Novak, Michael (1994) *The Joy of Sports: Endzones, Bases, Baskets, Balls, and the Consecration of the American Spirit*, rev. edn, Lanham, MD: Madison Books.
Oriard, Michael (1993) *Reading Football: How the Popular Press Created an American Spectacle*, Chapel Hill, NC: The University of North Carolina Press.
Peary, Gerald (ed.) (1998) *Quentin Tarantino: Interviews*, Jackson, MS: The University Press of Mississippi.
Romanowski, William D. (2007) *Eyes Wide Open: Looking for God in Popular Culture*, rev. and exp. edn, Grand Rapids, MI: Brazos Press.
Schwartz, Regina (1997) *The Curse of Cain: The Violent Legacy of Monotheism*, Chicago: University of Chicago Press.
Selengut, Charles (2008) *Sacred Fury: Understanding Religious Violence*, Lanham, MD: Rowman & Littlefield.
Siegel, Lee (2009) "Tarantino's Hollow Violence," *The Daily Beast*, 24 August. Online. Available HTTP: www.thedailybeast.com/blogs-and-stories/2009-08-24/tarantinos-hollow-violence/# (accessed 21 June 2010).
Taylor, Charles (2010) "Violence as the Best Revenge: Fantasies of Dead Nazis," *Dissent*, Winter (accessed 21 June 2010).
Wann, Daniel L., Melnick, Merrill J., Russell, Gordon W., and Pease, Dale G. (2001) *Sports Fans: The Psychology and Social Impact of Spectators*, New York: Routledge.

Filmography

From Dusk Till Dawn, Richard Rodriguez/Quentin Tarantino, dir. (1996)
Inglourious Basterds, Quentin Tarantino, dir. (2009)
Kill Bill, Quentin Tarantino, dir. (2003)
Kill Bill 2 Quentin Tarantino, dir. (2004)
Pulp Fiction, Quentin Tarantino, dir. (1994)
Reservoir Dogs, Quentin Tarantino, dir. (1992)

6 On the job and among the elect

Religion and the salvation of Sipowicz in *NYPD Blue*

Dan W. Clanton, Jr.

Introduction

NYPD Blue, which ended its twelve-season run in 2005 as one of the most honored and influential series in TV history (the series has received eighty-two Emmy nominations, and won twenty times), premiered on 21 September 1993 to a flurry of media attention. The show's Executive Producer, Steven Bochco, had a proven track record with evening dramas such as *Hill Street Blues* and *L.A. Law*, and this new show boasted an impressive ensemble cast, along with a brand new disclaimer for night time viewers: "This police drama contains adult language and scenes with partial nudity. Viewer discretion is advised." In fact, most of the hype surrounding the show's early seasons centered on the rawness of the language and imagery, but slowly people began to take notice of the writing and acting. Specifically, fans began to watch the show to see the development of Detective Andy Sipowicz, played by Dennis Franz, a veteran of *Hill Street Blues*. The series started strangely for Sipowicz, as we're shown an irresponsible racist drunk, who'd rather spend time with prostitutes than do his job. As far as I can tell, *Blue* is one of the only, if not *the* only prime time series that shows its main character being brutally shot six times only twenty-three minutes into its very first episode. However, it's during his recovery that Sipowicz sobers up and begins to realize he wants his life to improve.

Most critics agree that even though *Blue* has one of the most effective casts in recent memory, the show really centers on Sipowicz. *Denver Post* TV critic Joanne Ostrow writes,

> We knew immediately that Sipowicz, a balding, bullying, racist pig, was offensive; we had no idea how complex or long-suffering he would be. As he inched toward reining in his twin demons of prejudice and alcoholism, we became more invested in his struggle. As the demons multiplied, the anti-hero, alternately simmering and exploding, dared us to care.
>
> (Ostrow 2005: 6)

In the same article, she quotes David Lavery, who writes, "TV may well be the only medium, and that includes literature, capable of showing, in something like real time, the making of a soul" (Ostrow 2005: 6). In a way, one of the main undercurrents of Sipowicz's character is this making of a soul, and more specifically, the move toward salvation.[1] However, the show doesn't often define salvation in a traditionally religious sense. For that matter, the presentation of religion in the series is unusual for a prime-time drama. In the case of Andy, it seems as if he is "saved" or achieves "redemption" in a more general sense via his family and his fellow officers and detectives, those characters described as "on the job." This chapter will focus on two theoretical issues—defining religion and **secularization**—before examining six examples of the portrayal of religion in *NYPD Blue*, and will conclude with a consideration of how this series understands and represents religion.

Theory and method

A definition of religion? Functional and substantive suggestions

Scholars of religion have long tried to define what religion is, exactly. After all, if one wishes to engage in a field of study, it would be useful to know what one is studying, right? However, a widely accepted definition of religion has been elusive, precisely because religion is such a splendiferous phenomenon. Oddly enough, it's much easier to define what we do when we study religion in an academic setting. In her work, Rita M. Gross defines Religious Studies as a "descriptive discipline that gathers and disseminates accurate information about the variety of religious beliefs and practices people have entertained and engaged in throughout time" (Gross 1996: 8). As fine a definition as this is, it doesn't move us closer to defining what religion actually is.

Historically, most scholars who have tried to define religion have done so by offering propositional definitions, i.e. by saying "religion is" something or other.[2] More recently, this emphasis on propositional definitions has waned in favor of what scholars call a "polythetic" approach. That is, instead of trying to say religion is, or does, one thing, some feel it is more accurate to focus on a group of characteristics. Some of these might include rituals, ethics, scripture, a specialized class of persons to assist with ritual, and so on. Even so, the vast majority of the classic definitions of religion have been propositional, and if one looks at enough of these definitions, it becomes clear that the vast majority of them either defines religion *functionally* or *substantively*. A ***functional* definition [of religion]** focuses on what religion or religious activities do, that is, their function. On the other hand, a ***substantive* definition** focuses on what makes religion different from other human endeavors, that is, it tries to discover some sort of essence or substance unique to religion. Here are some examples of these types of definitions.

Functional definitions of religion

1 Rita M. Gross: "Any belief that functions as the most significant arbiter for decisions and actions and any behaviors whose value is unlimited to the actor are religious beliefs and behaviors, whatever their content" (Gross 1996: 9).

2 Clifford Geertz: "A religion is: (1) a system of symbols which acts to (2) establish powerful, pervasive and long-lasting moods and motivations in men by (3) formulating conceptions of a general order of existence and (4) clothing these conceptions with such an aura of factuality that (5) the moods and motivations seem uniquely realistic" (Geertz 1973: 90).
3 Conrad Ostwalt: "Religion, therefore, should be considered a cultural form that is directed toward the sacred and that exists in dialectical relationship with other cultural forms that sometimes explore religious content" (Ostwalt 2003: 23).

Substantive definitions of religion

1 Friedrich Schleiermacher: "The essence of the religious emotions consists in the feeling of an absolute dependence" (Schleiermacher 1893: 106).
2 E.B. Tylor: "It seems simplest ... simply to claim, as a minimum definition of religion, the belief in Spiritual Beings" (Tylor 1871: 1:383).
3 Sir James George Frazer: "By religion, then, I understand a propitiation or conciliation of powers superior to man which are believed to direct and control the course of Nature and human life" (Frazer 1993: 46).
4 Sigmund Freud: "Religion would thus be the universal obsessional neurosis of humanity" (Freud 1961: 55).

As you can see, the substantive definitions tend to be both universal and ethnocentric in that they claim religion to be the same for everyone and they understand religion in their own terms. Functional definitions shy away from trying to specify what it is that makes religion unique in favor of focusing on what it is that religion does, that is, how religion affects people.

The importance of discussing these different ways of understanding religion in the context of discussing a television show like *NYPD Blue* is that when religion is portrayed in television shows, it is most often shown in a *functional* way. That is, due to the episodic nature of television genres like sitcoms and dramas, as well as the notoriously short-lived existence of many shows, most television series shy away from the in-depth storylines needed to portray religion as something other than a superficial character trait, along with other common motivating factors like ethnicity, familial background, and sexual identity. Put differently, television shows are more apt to treat religion as an excuse for characters to act, dress, or speak in certain ways rather than delve into complex storylines that put religion and religious identity at the fore. As we'll see, though, *NYPD Blue* is an exception to that trend.

Conrad Ostwalt and the "sacrilization of the secular"

In 2003, religion scholar Conrad Ostwalt published his book *Secular Steeples: Popular Culture and the Religious Imagination*, in which he examines the (sometimes reciprocal) relationship between religion and secularization. By secularization, he means the process by which a society embraces discourses, or ways of meaning-making, that are not based on a religious foundation, for example, science (and especially Darwinian evolution), humanism, psychology, sociology, atheism, etc. Usually, scholars have thought of religion and secularization as opponents, but Ostwalt claims not only is there not "an antagonistic relationship between secular culture and religion," but that "the secular and the religious worlds can and do coexist. In fact, they have always coexisted" (Ostwalt 2003: 3–4).

One of the most interesting themes in his book is the presence and trajectories of secularization in modern American culture. Ostwalt argues that secularization takes place in two interrelated directions in modern society. On the one hand, "there is a tendency for religious institutions to employ secular and popular cultural forms like television and the movies to make religious teachings relevant for a modern audience" (Ostwalt 2003: 7). On the other hand, Ostwalt notes that with the loss of authority experienced by traditional religious institutions, "religious concerns find expression in other cultural forms so that cultural products perceived to be secular can carry authentic and meaningful religious content and deal with sacred concerns" (Ostwalt 2003: 7). The former tendency Ostwalt terms the "**secularization of the sacred**," the latter, the "**sacrilization of the secular**" (this discussion of Ostwalt is taken from my review of his book).[3]

When discussing series or even episodes on television that portray religion, Ostwalt's theory of the "sacrilization of the secular" will allow us to talk about these popular cultural renderings as valid and sincere expressions of the religious impulses of humanity, rather than trivial or subsidiary curiosities that pale beside what goes on in more traditional religious settings, like churches. That is, Ostwalt gives us permission to: (1) analyze and discuss religion on television as primary evidence for the presence and understanding of religion in our present context; and (2) consider these as legitimate expressions of religiosity.

Case study

In order to examine the development of Sipowicz's character, as well as the way(s) in which the series treats religion in general, we will focus on six specific examples that span the entire series.

Example 1: "The Bookie and the Kooky Cookie" (Season 2; originally aired 5-9-95)

In one of the last episodes in Season 2, Andy has finally established a serious relationship with a woman, ADA (Assistant District Attorney) Sylvia Costas (played by Sharon Lawrence). They're preparing to marry, but since Sylvia is a practicing member of the Greek Orthodox Church, they meet with her priest, Father Kankarides (Jorge Montesi). In what follows, we learn that even though Andy is on his way to redemption from his past, he has lost something along the way. The Father insists on speaking with Andy alone, after Andy neglected to completely fill out a questionnaire the Father gave them. Sylvia's faith is obviously important to her, but Andy is hesitant to talk about his religious beliefs. As the Father probes more deeply, we learn that Andy has lost his faith because of what he's seen over the years as a police officer. Even so, the Father agrees to marry them after Andy assures him that he truly loves Sylvia.

In the final scene of the show, Andy and Sylvia talk about their meeting with the priest, and Andy reveals to her one of the reasons he's lost his faith, and where he now places his faith. He tells her a harrowing story about investigating a missing fourteen-month-old child. The child's father is an amateur dog trainer, and the mother is a heavy drinker. Andy becomes more and more sorrowful as he tells Sylvia that he eventually discovered the child's father had thrown the child to the ground after the child peed on him while having his diaper changed. While the mother was passed out, the father let the child bleed to death on the floor, and then fed its remains to one of his dogs. As Sylvia looks at Andy with a mixture of repulsion and compassion, Andy tells her that in the earlier interview Father Kankarides asked him if he'd lost his faith. Without revealing to her what he told the Father, Andy tells her that he has faith in her.

These scenes demonstrate that at this early point in the series, Andy's redemption is not defined in traditionally religious terms, as he doesn't discuss that part of himself with the Father. However, there's no doubt that the show portrays him as a changed man, and that change stems from the help of his fiancé and his squad. Put differently, the series shows Andy rejecting a traditional understanding of religiosity in favor of faith in his relationship with Sylvia, a relationship that he feels possesses redemptive power, even if he doesn't feel he deserves it.

Example 2: "He's Not Guilty, He's My Brother" (Season 3; originally aired 5-21-96)

In the middle of Season 3, tragedy strikes Sipowicz as his son, recently reunited with his father and preparing to start a career as a cop in New Jersey, is murdered while trying to prevent a robbery. Andy falls off the wagon, Sylvia kicks him out the house, and he's mugged for his gun and shield. In a particularly poignant scene in the previous episode ("Closing Time," originally aired 5-14-96), Father Kankarides comes to visit Andy at the Station House to check in on him, and Andy asks him where God was when his son was killed. When the Father responds that God was there, Andy responds angrily that God can kiss his ass. In this episode, Andy returns to his job, now sober and back with Sylvia, but he's still haunted by the death of his son. This episode opens with Andy talking with the Father in Church. The Father explains to Andy—and to the audience—the nature of the upcoming "**churching**" of his new son with Sylvia, a boy named Theo (a name which is, perhaps coincidently, related to the Greek word for God, *theos*). This ritual both introduces Theo to God, and serves as a re-introduction of Sylvia to God. In their talk, Andy expresses remorse for the way he behaved toward both the Father and Sylvia, after which Father Kankarides urges Andy to entrust Theo to God during Theo's "churching." It's obvious that Andy isn't comfortable talking with the Father about either the ritual or his son, and he leaves soon after.

The crime on which this episode focuses centers around two brothers who are both implicated in a robbery-homicide. One is a repeat offender and the other has no experience with crime. The former eventually decides to "take the rap" so his brother can have a chance at a normal life. Perhaps inspired by this display of altruism, Andy approaches the "churching" ceremony in a more optimistic light. It's during this ceremony at the end of the episode, which is also the end of the show's current season, that Andy begins to embrace the idea of a more traditional religious outlet for his faith. The Father assures Andy that both of his sons are present prior to the ritual, and gradually, Andy accepts that claim. We see him fumbling through the ritual crossing of himself in imitation of Sylvia, as well as praying to God. Perhaps the most moving moment in the ritual occurs when Andy asks God to watch over both Theo and his dead son, as well as to give him the strength to be a better person. The episode ends with a wide shot of the beautiful and ornate altar of the Church, and Andy whispering Amen.

At the outset of the episode, it seems clear that Andy is uncomfortable talking with the Father about either the ritual or his murdered son, but as the episode progresses, Andy becomes more open to both the efficacious nature of the ritual, and to addressing his loss through prayer. It's interesting to note here that the focus of the show isn't on the formal words and ritual practice of the churching, as the focus of both the camera and the microphones are on the reactions of Sipowicz to the ritual, as well as his own prayers to God instead of the Father. Thus, the series both (a) shows a progression in Sipowicz's faith from a more amorphous, generic variety to something within more recognizable parameters; and (b) betrays its interest not in religion as a culturally understood given, but rather as a personal character trait of certain characters, most obviously Sipowicz.

Example 3: "Lost Israel, Parts 1 & 2" (Season 5; originally aired 11-25-97 and 12-9-97)

In Season 5, *Blue* aired two episodes that are generally considered some of, if not *the*, best episodes the series has produced (as seen by the fact that these episodes were nominated for an Emmy in 1998 for Outstanding Writing, and won that year for best directing). In Part One of this episode, parents Steve and Sherrie Egan (Brian Markinson and Annie Corley) come to the 15th Detective Squad to report the disappearance of their son Brian. Detectives Bobby Simone (Jimmy Smits) and Sipowicz catch the case. Mr. Egan suggests that a homeless mute named Israel (Thom Gossom, Jr.), whom Brian befriended in Tompkins Square Park, might have something to do with the disappearance. After Detectives Simone and Sipowicz pick up Israel, they realize that he communicates mainly by pointing to seemingly obscure passages in his Bible. At the beginning of the second episode, Israel commits suicide, and Andy finds the body. He discovers that Israel had left his Bible open to **Psalm 119**:81–88, and is convinced that

Israel meant to leave him a secret message. Most of Andy's time in Part Two is spent trying to decipher this hidden message, which he claims he's not able to do, because it's not in his heart. One of the major breakthroughs in the Egan case comes when Steven admits to Detective Simone that he (Steven) was sexually abused as a child. This is obviously significant, since after finding Brian's body, the detectives were informed that Brian was sexually abused over a long period of time. After Steven admits he was a victim of sexual abuse, the detectives' suspicions about his involvement with his son's murder increase.

A major theme in Part Two is forgiveness. Bobby claims that humans can't effect their own forgiveness, and that remorse and understanding are necessary for forgiveness. The last few scenes in Part Two are the most intense, and perhaps the most important for our purposes. When Bobby and Mr. Egan are in the observation room, there is a sense in which their conversation and situation is reminiscent of a confessional. Steven, the penitent, is looking for forgiveness, and Bobby can offer it to him. Mr. Egan questions the existence of God and asks why God wouldn't want someone who's suffering to be taken away, that is, Steven implies that since Brian had suffered so much that perhaps God desired that suffering to end through Brian's death. Once Egan admits to himself that he sexually assaulted and then killed his own son, he asks Bobby to shoot him, and when Bobby refuses, he asks for help in confessing. Bobby, like most people, doesn't think there is forgiveness for what Steven did. In an ensuing conversation with Andy, Bobby says that he was trying to gain Egan's confidence by telling him that forgiveness is possible through God. However, it's clear from Bobby's impassioned speech that he lied, as he shouts to Andy that forgiveness isn't possible for such a heinous act. Bobby tells Andy that Egan will burn in Hell and that since he asked Bobby to shoot him Egan knows he can't be forgiven. Menacingly, Andy responds that Egan should have asked *him* to shoot him.

The most emotional moment in the entire episode comes when Bobby has to inform Mrs. Egan that her husband has confessed to the murder. She breaks down, wailing and crying, as Detective Diane Russell (Kim Delaney) tries to remind her that Brian's not really gone as long as she can keep his memory alive. Mrs. Egan seems inconsolable, and then—rather surprisingly—Andy recites Psalm 119:81–88 to comfort her. This psalm, which Israel had left for Andy to find prior to his suicide, is the longest in the book of Psalms, and is an extended meditation on the goodness of God and God's laws. The section that Andy reads in particular represents a supplication to God for protection because of the speaker's adherence to the law. It is a moving piece of poetry:

> My soul fainteth for thy salvation: but I hope in thy word. / Mine eyes fail for thy word, saying, When wilt thou comfort me? / For I am become like a bottle in the smoke; yet I do not forget thy statutes. / How many are the days of thy servant? When wilt thou execute judgment on them that persecute me? / The proud have digged pits for me, which are not after thy law. / All thy commandments are faithful: they persecute me wrongfully; help thou me. / They had almost consumed me upon earth; but I forsook not thy

> precepts. / Quicken me after thy lovingkindness; so shall I keep the testimony of thy mouth.
>
> (King James Version)

The sense of catharsis following Andy's reading is palpable. Andy has finally realized Israel's message and the power of the inherited, recorded experiences of one's ancestors in faith. Mrs. Egan seems to be consoled after the murder of her son by her husband, through both an identification with the suffering of the speaker in the Psalm, as well as the emphasis on keeping her son alive through her memory.

In this case, the spiritual development of Andy—while obvious, and highlighted at the climax of the episode—seems to be of minor concern overall to the episode, with its themes of forgiveness and punishment. Thus, the portrayal of religion in this episode seems to be more general than the previous examples in that all the characters are affected by the case, and all seem to have religious responses to the tragedy they investigate. As such, the series again shows religion as a personal matter, focused more on individual expressions of guilt, faith, remorse, sin, etc., rather than on more communal, formal, and traditional religious rituals or settings.

Example 4: "Hearts and Souls" (Season 6; originally aired 11-24-98)

This example is from possibly the most famous episode in the series, in which Detective Bobby Simone dies. Prior to this episode, the series had shown several of Andy's dreams/visions, in which he sees his murdered son Andy J., and two in which he actually sees Jesus. However, this episode—which won both an Emmy and a Director's Guild Award—concludes with a long (just over seven minutes) vision scene, in which the squad says goodbye to Bobby, and he converses with his old friend Patsy, who taught him how to fly and care for birds when he was just a boy. This farewell scene is one of the more moving scenes in recent television memory, as each member of the Squad enters in turn to pay their respects. As they do, we hear Patsy review the good deeds Bobby performed in his life, as well as reassure Bobby that Detective Diane Russell—now Bobby's wife—is right beside him.

Here, the emphasis isn't on traditional religion, although Bobby receives last rights and mentions his belief in God and Jesus. Rather what we're shown is an entirely secular understanding of Bobby's salvation. That is, because of the show's interest in putting forth essentially religious ideas in a secular garb, it's no wonder we have Bobby's death portrayed as a kind of release into a new horizon. As his mentor Patsy notes, when a bird flies past the horizon, it's simply going home. Following this, Patsy tells Bobby that in this new horizon, he'll be able to see his son that Diane miscarried, as well as his parents. Finally, Patsy—who seems to function as some sort of spiritual mentor or guide—tells Bobby that he has to leave, as Bobby has grown enough to be on his own. It's at this point that Bobby removes his oxygen tubes, and signals the attending doctor that he's ready to die.

Diane remains with him until the end, and for a single time in the history of the series, the screen turns a brilliant white at the end of the episode, instead of the customary black. As such, this episode renders one of the most perplexing and central religious questions—what happens when we die?—in an unorthodox and almost completely non-religious fashion. There's little to no talk of a heaven or judgment, but rather a more general sense that Bobby will be reunited with his departed loved ones as a part of him begins a journey over the horizon, like one of his beloved birds.

Example 5: "The Last Round Up" (Season 7; originally aired 5-23-00)

After the death of Simone in Season 6, and the murder of Sylvia in that same season, one might hope that Andy wouldn't have to face any more trials. But in Season 7, his son Theo becomes ill and enters the hospital for blood tests. At the same time, another detective in the squad is having serious troubles with her ex-husband, and Andy's new partner Danny Sorenson (Rick Schroeder), comes to him for help. Specifically, he wants to know how to dispose of a body. As such, Andy is distressed for his friends in the Squad, but then he also finds out Theo may have Leukemia. While at the hospital, Andy enters the chapel, and confronts God. Knowing what we do of Sipowicz's character, it comes as no surprise that Andy's monologue aimed at God is direct and profane. He initially refuses to petition God for anything, and instead tells God—whom he colloquially and colorfully refers to as a male anatomical member—that Theo shouldn't be sick. Andy also implies that it's his fault his son is sick, and if that's the case, he cries, *he* should be the one who's stricken with illness, not his son. In the end, though, Andy attempts to bargain with God, asking God what he must do in order to save his son—including preventing Sorenson from carrying out his murderous plans—and petitioning God to safeguard his son, much as he did in the earlier episode, "He's Not Guilty, He's My Brother" (Example 2).

The importance of this prayerful encounter lies in the way in which Andy talks to God. He's already been through so many crises, and has developed to the point where he's able to address God directly. Almost like **Job**, Andy rails at God for punishing his boy because of his own shortcomings, but in the end he begs God to help Theo. This example shows us the continuation of Andy's spiritual progression, and it seems as if he's building on both the experience of speaking to God in a formal religious setting—as in Theo's "churching" ceremony—as well as releasing his frustration and pain through direct address and petition, much like Psalm 119. In all this, we see the series portray religion once again as a way for characters to deal with pain and loss (a *functional* emphasis) through the use of traditional modes of religious expression with recognizable content (a *substantive* emphasis). Put differently, Andy seeks out a way to deal with the pain and uncertainty that accompanies his son Theo's medical problems (a *function* of religious beliefs and rituals), yet the setting and method he chooses (praying in a chapel) are recognizable as traditionally religious, thus signaling that the show embraces that religion contains a specific *substance*. After all, Andy doesn't go to the cafeteria in the hospital and eat chocolate cake to deal with his pain; instead, the show portrays him choosing a religiously traditional locale and form of expression to express his anxiety and worry. This choice implies that the series is not interested in what religion *does*, but what religion *is*.

Example 6: "The Vision Thing" (Season 12; originally aired 11-9-04)

In this episode, from the series' last season, things look grim for Sipowicz. The squad has a new boss, Lt. Thomas Bale (Currie Graham), who has come in from Internal Affairs, and he has a much stricter way of running the squad than Andy's used to. So, Andy not only thinks the new boss wants to get him off the job, he's beginning to think it might not be a bad idea. A rift has developed between Andy and his most recent partner, Detective John Clark (Mark-Paul Goselaar) because, ironically, Clark has begun to drink and womanize, just like Andy used to do. They catch a case in which a young man is stabbed to death on a bus in front of his wife and two kids, and the case makes Andy think about what would happen to his new family if something were to happen to him. During the investigation, Andy visits another victim of the killer in the hospital, and then has an extended (over eight minutes long) supernatural visit from an old friend, viz. Bobby Simone.

It's unclear as to what exactly the nature of the visit is, as Andy proves Bobby is clearly not a ghost by touching him. Bobby tells Andy that his own imagination summoned him there so he could advise Andy on his problems. As I noted above, Andy's concerned about how short life—and specifically his life—seems, but Bobby reassures him that life is, in fact, long in a variety of ways and effects. Andy protests that he's responsible for his new family, his boss hates him, and he can't bear any more losses like the ones he's already endured. However, Bobby both provides Andy with a new vocation—that of a teacher—and reveals to Andy that more is going on with him than he knows. Bobby relates to Andy not only that there is a God, but that God has been with Andy in times of crisis. Knowing what we know of Andy, it comes as no surprise that he questions this claim, but Bobby reassures him by both his words and his presence that God is indeed present with Andy. After all, Bobby *is* physically present and communicating with Andy. Andy persists in his concern over his future and his past losses, and Bobby again tries to reassure him by saying that he'll always be around as something like Andy's guardian angel. At that point, Andy's new partner comes in, and Bobby vanishes. After reflecting for a moment, Andy reaches out to his new partner, a signal that he intends to follow Bobby's advice and become a mentor.

This scene is a fitting ending to our examination, because it sums up the portrayal of religion in the series nicely. Bobby tells Andy that not only is there a God, but that human existence has a purpose and Andy's purpose is to be a teacher. As such, religion has both a function—to serve as a resource for healing after loss or grief—as well as a substance, i.e. there is an identifiable and recognizable content to the religious yearnings, proclamations, and settings in the series. That is, the series portrays religion as serving a purpose for the characters, but that purpose is enacted often through settings, words, and actions that would be familiar to viewers. This scene also represents a turning point for Andy. After this episode, he and Clark get along better, the boss becomes more impressed with him, and the series ends with Andy being promoted to Squad Commander of the 15th Precinct.

Conclusion

Based on these limited examples, how does *NYPD Blue* portray religion? In his work "God in the Box: Religion in Contemporary Cop Shows," Elijah Siegler argues that *Blue* "principally explores the personal, private aspect of religion. The detectives, recovering from grief, addiction, and otherwise damaged lives, seek redemption, forgiveness, second chances. Sometimes they find salvation" (Siegler 2001: 203). In the context of this chapter, we also need to ask how that portrayal affects audiences. In contrast to shows like *Law & Order*, which portray religion as solely functional (for more on this, see Clanton 2003b), *Blue*, like other series such as *The Simpsons* and *Joan of Arcadia*, portrays religion in *both a functional and substantive light.* That is, this series posits the existence of some sort of substance, or essence, to religion, even if it isn't a traditional portrayal of religion, as one might find in series like *Seventh Heaven.* Put differently, the last example we discussed above contains a fairly traditional religious message (God exists and has a plan for you, so don't despair), but that message is delivered in a police locker room via a visionary encounter with a dead man. More broadly, religion is more than an abstract trait, it serves as not only the basis for plot but also for character motivation, and it isn't devoid of content or reduced to psychological deviance, as in many series.

On the other hand, scholars like Wade Clark Roof might argue with this assessment, as he notes that usually on prime time TV, "Seldom is religion dealt with as an integrated set of religious beliefs, values, and symbols—that is, as inherited tradition—but is framed more as a moment or encounter arising out of personal experience or crisis" (Roof 1997: 66). This description certainly seems to apply to *Blue*, in that almost all of the examples of religion we've seen stem from moments of crisis. However, the sheer number of these incidents seems to belie Roof's judgment, i.e. religious belief and behavior is almost always specifically identified in terms of sect/denomination, and isn't dismissed as trivial or abnormal. Rather, religion in the series emerges from the characters' encounters with tragedy and their desire to connect with something larger, and perhaps purer, than themselves. In sum, *Blue* religion focuses on the desire of these injured characters to not only improve themselves, but to try and achieve some sort of redemption for themselves and their community, and those attempts often take place within and echo more traditional religious places and practices.

There's also something to be said for the way in which the series represents what Ostwalt calls a "sacrilization of the secular" (Ostwalt 2003: 7). One could argue that the series, despite its focus on perhaps a more traditional mode of religiosity, carries a religious meaning or delivers a traditional religious message through its portrayal of Andy's "salvation" through the ideas of family and community. That is, the series itself can be understood as disseminating messages about redemption, forgiveness, loss, pain, and wholeness—messages that traditionally were the purview of religious institutions. With reference to the series' emphasis on family and community, the latter category of discussion includes a dichotomy between those "on the job," and those who diverge from that discourse, i.e. bad cops. Those who are really "on the job" as well as Andy's family assist him in battling his personal demons, and thus save him from self-destruction. This discourse of "on the job" is highlighted by the inclusion of farewell scenes in which departing characters toast each other as well as whoever came up with the idea of being a cop. Thus, there can be multiple ways of viewing the presence of religion in the series, but they all recognize the unique, unlikely, and rich contribution this series has made to the presentation of religion in prime-time TV dramas.

Several versions of this chapter were presented in my "Religion and Popular Culture" classes at the University of Colorado, Colorado Springs and the University of Denver from 2004–2006. I would like to thank my students as well as my co-instructors for their helpful comments and suggestions.

Summary

- Substantive definitions of religion try to define what religion *is*, i.e. what is at the core of religion. Functional definitions of religion focus on what religion or religious activities *do*, i.e. their function.
- Conrad Ostwalt identifies two main trends in modern secularization: the "secularization of the sacred," and the "sacrilization of the secular."
- *NYPD Blue* treats religion both substantively and functionally, in contrast to the common trend in other series to focus solely on function.
- *NYPD Blue* is an example of the "sacrilization of the secular."

Glossary terms

"Churching" – traditionally, a ceremony in which mothers are welcomed back to the Church following childbirth.

Functional definition of religion – a definition of religion that focuses on what the phenomenon of religion does to/for a practitioner. The emphasis is on the function of religion or a particular religious ritual/practice, rather than what ideas, stories, or traditions lie behind it.

Job – a biblical book which centers on the character of Job, a man whose existence is upended when God and the Satan make a wager regarding the bases of his faithfulness.

Psalm 119 – the longest psalm and the longest chapter in the Bible, this anthological poem focuses on the highly regarded properties of Torah and Torah observance.

Sacrilization of the secular – one of two main trends of modern secularization posited by Conrad Ostwalt. This trend is defined as the tendency for secular genres of expression or discourses to impart what have been traditionally considered religious messages or claims.

Secularization – the process by which religion is gradually removed from society, and non-religious, or "secular" concerns, expressions, and bases for thought replace it. (See also the treatment of this word in the introduction and in Ch. 10, including the glossary terms at the end of each unit.)

Secularization of the sacred – one of two main trends of modern secularization posited by Conrad Ostwalt. This trend is defined as the tendency for religious groups to employ secular methods or genres to disseminate their message(s).

Substantive definition of religion – a definition of religion that focuses on the *essence* of religion or a particular ritual/practice, rather than what it does to/for a practitioner/believer.

Points for discussion

1 Questions on essay
   - How have scholars usually defined "religion"?
   - How does Conrad Ostwalt understand secularization in the modern era?
   - How does *NYPD Blue* portray religion?
   - How does the series exemplify Ostwalt's idea of "sacrilization of the secular"?

2 General questions on television and religion
   - Is there a main religious issue discussed or alluded to in the episode? If so, is it treated seriously, flippantly, or humorously? Is there one type of religiosity or religious practice that is endorsed? Does the show denigrate certain types of religious practice or belief? If so, why?
   - Do any of the characters exhibit identifiably religious behavior? How do the show and other characters react to/treat this behavior? Can we identify with any specificity the religious traditions/denominations of the characters? If so, how? Is the behavior of a religious character accurate and appropriate for the tradition being portrayed?
   - What role does disbelief and/or confusion about religion play, if any, in television?
   - Building on the work of Gregor Goethals, how does the episode/series in question mediate "faith and values in American society," and "indoctrinate us into a public system of symbols" (Goethals 1987: 212–213)?
   - Based on your viewing of these episodes, is Wade Clark Roof (1997) correct when he claims that television both: (1) flattens religion, i.e. makes all religions look so similar that it's difficult to tell them apart; and (2) reinterprets religion, i.e. views religion not as a discourse in and of itself, but as more of a psychological crutch (i.e. reductively)?
   - After watching episodes/clips discussed here, ask yourself if Roof is also correct when he writes, "Television assumes some of the functions traditionally ascribed to religious myth and ritual. But it does so in ways that are subtle and by means of vocabularies that are at best quasi-religious … Seldom is religion dealt with as an integrated set of

religious beliefs, values, and symbols—that is, as inherited tradition—but is framed more as a moment or encounter arising out of personal experience or crisis" (Roof 1997: 66).

- How can television perform both the functional and substantive aspects of religion? That is, what functions of religion might the viewing of television fulfill? How might television mediate the sacred for the viewer? Can watching television be a religious experience? If so, how? If not, why?

Notes

1 I, obviously, am not the only one to notice the emphasis the series placed on Sipowicz's redemption. In his 2004 article, "Sipowicz's Progress: A Slow Walk of Redemption," Maurice Broaddus examines this theme, as well as some of the same examples I discuss here. My work here goes beyond Broaddus', though, in (a) the theoretical concerns I raise; (b) his examination does not include any examples beyond Season Seven; and (c) he focuses exclusively on the character of Sipowicz.
2 For more specifics, see the work of D.N. Gellner (1999) "Anthropological Approaches," and M. Southwold (1978) "Buddhism and the Definition of Religion."
3 See Clanton (2003a).

Further reading

Blythe, T. (2002) "The God of Prime-Time Television," in C.K. Robertson (ed.) *Religion as Entertainment*, New York: Peter Lang.
Blythe examines four episodes/storylines from prime-time TV dramas to determine how God is portrayed in each, and concludes with a call to religious institutions to recognize and embrace the power of TV to disseminate theological images.
Clanton, Jr., D.W. (2006) "From Mr. Hankey to *The Hebrew Hammer*: Hanukkah in Pop Culture," in L.J. Greenspoon and R.A. Simkins (eds) *Studies in Jewish Civilization 17: 350 Years of American Judaism in Popular Culture*, Omaha: Creighton University Press.
I examine the presentation/understanding of Hanukkah in two TV series (*South Park* and *Friends*) as well as the film *The Hebrew Hammer*, and conclude that these representations signify a more complex relationship between Judaism and secular culture than is implied in the traditional Hanukkah narrative.
Davis, Jr., W.T., *et al.* (2001) *Watching What We Watch: Prime-Time Television through the Lens of Faith*, Louisville, KY: Geneva Press.
A methodologically helpful, faith-based examination of multiple genres and examples of TV shows informed by the claim that TV is now "America's popular religion," and as such it deserves "serious and sustained *theological* examination" (304).
Forbes, B.D. and Mahan, J.H. (eds) (2005) *Religion and Popular Culture in America*, Berkeley: University of California Press.
A collection of essays that focus on diverse genres, including TV, all of which contain helpful theoretical musings on how religion and popular culture reciprocally relate to one another.
Schultze, Q.J. (1990) "Secular Television as Popular Religion," in R. Abelman and S.M. Hoover (eds) *Religious Television: Controversies and Conclusions*, Norwood, NJ: Ablex Publishing Corporation.

Schultze examines both the secularization of religious TV programming, as well as how "secular" TV shows carry religious messages.

Suman, M. (ed.) (1997) *Religion and Prime Time Television*, Westport, CT: Praeger.

This volume contains papers/talks given at the 1995 Religion and Prime Time Television Conference, held at UCLA, and includes entries by representatives from diverse communities enmeshed in this issue, such as religious leaders/figures, academics, media critics, and speakers from within the TV industry.

Bibliography

Broaddus, M. (2004) "Sipowicz's Progress: A Slow Walk of Redemption," in G. Yeffeth (ed.) *What Would Sipowicz Do? Race, Rights and Redemption in NYPD Blue*, Dallas: Benbella Books.

Clanton, Jr., D.W. (2003a) "Review of *Secular Steeples: Popular Culture and the Religious Imagination*, by Conrad Ostwalt," *Journal of Religion and Popular Culture* 4, Online. Available HTTP: http://www. usask.ca/relst/jrpc/br4-secularsteeples.html (accessed 26 February 2011).

——(2003b) "'These are Their Stories': Views of Religion in *Law & Order*," *Journal of Religion and Popular Culture* 4, Online. Available HTTP: http://www.usask.ca/relst/jrpc/art4-lawandorder.html (accessed 26 February 2011).

Frazer, J.G. (1993) *The Golden Bough: A New Abridgement*, ed. Robert Frazer, Oxford & New York: Oxford University Press.

Freud, S. (1961) *The Future of an Illusion*, trans. and ed. James Strachey, New York & London: W.W. Norton.

Geertz, C. (1973) "Religion as a Cultural System," in *Interpretation of Cultures: Selected Essays*, New York: Basic Books.

Gellner, D.N. (1999) "Anthropological Approaches," in P. Connolly (ed.) *Approaches to the Study of Religion*, London & New York: Cassell.

Goethals, G. (1987) "Images and Values: Television as Religious Communication," in Doug Adams and Diane Apostolos-Cappadona (eds) *Art as Religious Studies*, New York: Crossroad.

Gross, R.M. (1996) *Feminism & Religion: An Introduction*, Boston: Beacon Press.

Ostrow, J. (2005) "Sipowicz a Cop for the Ages," *The Denver Post* (27 February) F:6.

Ostwalt, C. (2003) *Secular Steeples: Popular Culture and the Religious Imagination*, Harrisburg, PA: Trinity Press International.

Roof, W.C. (1997) "Blurred Boundaries: Religion and Prime Time Television," in M. Suman (ed.) *Religion and Prime Time Television*, Westport, CT: Praeger, 61–68.

Schleiermacher, F. (1893) *On Religion: Speeches to Its Cultured Despisers*, trans. John Oman, London: Kegan Paul, Trench, Trübner, & Co., Ltd.

Siegler, E. (2001) "God in the Box: Religion in Contemporary Cop Shows," in E.M. Mazur and K. McCarthy (eds) *God in the Details: American Religion in Popular Culture*, London & New York: Routledge.

Southwold, M. (1978) "Buddhism and the Definition of Religion," *Man* 13: 362–379.

Tylor, E.B. (1871) *Primitive Culture: Researches into the Development of Mythology, Philosophy, Religion, Language, Art, and Custom*, 2 vols., London: John Murray.

7 "Unlearn what you have learned" (yoda)

The critical study of the myth of *Star Wars*

John C. McDowell

Introduction

It is 25 May 1977, and little is known about the movie that opens this evening, ***Star Wars*** (hereafter this will be referred to by the abbreviation *SW*). In fact, the fear of the 20th Century Fox studio, and the movie's creator and director George Lucas himself, is that it will be a financial disaster. Lucas himself has even forgotten it is the opening night, and he is spending the evening with his wife Marcia in a restaurant near the Chinese Theatre in Los Angeles. (The limited fan base of science fiction movies in the mid-70s makes *SW* a risky project. Lucas feels it will at most appeal to the "$8 million worth of science fiction freaks in the U.S.A.," and he braces himself for the fall-out. See Kaminski 2008: 140f.) Nevertheless, "gigantic lines [have] formed … in each town, city, or suburb" as a result of word-of-mouth (Rinzler 2008: 326). Because of the lengths of the queue, only those who are near the front, and have accordingly queued longest, are lucky enough to be admitted.

The lights go out, the screen retracts fully and after attraction-promoting advertisements and a viewer health warning (the film-board classification certificate), audience anticipation builds. What appears first on screen is the impressive Studio logo—thickly blocked gold writing lit by spotlights on the ground, sitting high on a pedestal. It evokes the feeling that something magnificently grand but also important, valuable and significant is about to take place. This sense is intensified by the accompanying drum roll and the blare of the trumpets, a call to attention that evokes "a 'looking up' to where the wondrous things are" (Plate 2008: 218). It visually displays the fact that cinema has become the cultural medium *par excellence* "that changes the way we think about, interpret, and live in the world" (Miles and Plate 2004: 23).

In a consideration of the cultural significance of cinema, *SW* in particular, with its phenomenal long-lasting popularity and abundant referencing in countless other pop culture texts, has no equal. A reason often cited for this success is that, as Steven Spielberg claims, "George … created a mythology of characters—he touched something that needed touching in everybody" (Rinzler 2008: 328). In fact, because of the connection between the *SW* sensation, the prominence of Joseph Campbell's PBS interviews, and the popularity of the 1997 Smithsonian Institution's

National Air and Space Museum exhibition, "In the public's imagination, the terms '**myth**' and '*SW*' are very closely linked" (Silvio and Vinci 2007: 2).

Theory and method

"A long time ago ...": Star Wars, *genre-pastiche, and the fairy tale*

An early draft summary (May 1973) of what was then tentatively titled *The Star Wars* was set in the thirty-third century. Lucas had in mind a Buck Rogers/Flash Gordon type action-adventure, but failing in the quest to procure the rights to remake *Flash Gordon*, he began to develop an "original" hero-in-space adventure story. The story gradually moved from a future-of-this-world setting, and early in 1976 the script for *The Adventure of Luke Starkiller as Taken from the Journal of the Whills: Star Wars* opened with a longer version of the now famous scene-setting line: "A long, long time ago in a galaxy far, far away." Possibly as a result of familiarity with Bruno Bettelheim's *The Uses of Enchantment*, Lucas uses this as a conceptual link to fairy tales ("Once upon a time") and legends: in other words to the stories of our past.

Like Tolkien's *Hobbit* and *The Lord of the Rings*, Lucas had conceived of *SW* as being part of a grand narrative being recounted many years later. To that end, he developed the idea of the *Journal of the Whills*, similar in function to Tolkien's ancestral **mythology** of Middle-Earth, *The Silmarillion*. This, Lucas claims, "was meant to emphasize that whatever story followed came from a book," an inspirational piece of heroic folklore in a "holy book" (Rinzler 2008: 14). The second draft of Lucas's script even opens with a prophecy of a savior (Rinzler 2008: 361).

In the **screen-crawl** there is a reference to a "princess," but this is an echo not merely of the fairy story link but of another influence. Initially, when searching for a story to tie a few visual ideas together (principally, the cantina scene and the space battle), the story became shaped around Akira Kurosawa's sixteenth-century adventure, *The Hidden Fortress* (1958). The influence of this remains in several places in the final version: in taking the perspective of two squabbling peasants, Tahei and Matashichi (in *SW*, C3PO and R2D2); and in General Rokurota Makabe's (in *SW*, General Obi-Wan Kenobi) rescue of the young Princess Yuki (in *SW*, Princess Leia Organa) to return her to her own people (in *SW*, Leia's family on Alderaan, and then the Rebel Alliance on Yavin IV). Lucas also named his religious order the "Jedi" after the Japanese term "jidai geki," meaning period film; and the Jedi were dressed in Buddhist-like monastic robes with kimono-like garments underneath. At one stage, Lucas had even toyed with the idea of making *SW* a wholly Japanese affair.

The director from Modesto was keen, too, on the swashbuckler movies of old, such as those starring Errol Flynn, and from this comes the notion of the Jedi as *knights* and of their weapons as *sabres* (albeit a technologically sophisticated version, *lightsabers*). The eminently popular Westerns of Lucas's youth had enough of an impact upon him for *SW* to raid that particular genre, with its frontier hero-mythology, for some of its inspiration. The saloon scene in John Ford's *The Searchers* (1956) partially inspired the Mos Eisley cantina sequence; Tatooine is a frontier environment, with settlers under constant threat from nomadic indigenous peoples ("Tuskan Raiders" or "Sand People"); Han Solo is an old fashioned gunslinger, kitted out in waistcoat, boots and low hanging gun-belt; Luke's uncle Owen and aunt Beru are farmers living at the edge of civilization; and the gun-wielding gangs (the Hutts, with their hired hands, bounty hunters) are the "law."

There are also references to, among other things, Isaac Asimov's *Foundation* stories' "The Empire"; the histories of imperial Rome, Britain, and Nazi Germany; Fritz Lang's 1926 masterpiece, *Metropolis* (Lucas's C3PO); and Carlos Castaneda's *Tales of Power*.

But while *SW* involves something of a **pastiche** of genres, its eclecticism is not simple homage. Instead, its referential diversity suggests that here we have something that *sums* up all others in a single instance. This has much to do with its appeal to "myth," and the kind of myth it is largely predicated on.

George Lucas and myth

According to Lucas, "[B]eing a student in the Sixties, I wanted to make socially relevant films ... But then I got this great idea for a rock & roll movie, with cars and all the stuff I knew about as a kid" (Lucas, in Kline 1999: 89). As he was completing *American Graffiti* (1973), he began slowly designing his space-adventure. *THX 1138* (1971) had been a financial disaster two years before, and he was having problems selling the idea of *Apocalypse Now* (dir. Coppola 1979), which he had spent some of the past four years developing—Vietnam movies were too controversial for both film studios and audiences at that stage.

Star Wars was conceived against a backdrop of cultural turmoil in America—the Vietnam War limped to its ignominious end, and many in the nation suffered traumatic introspection; President Richard Nixon was implicated in the Watergate scandal (1974); and economic misery loomed on the horizon. Francis Ford Coppola had challenged his friend Lucas to make "a happier kind of film" (Rinzler 2008: 4). In response, *SW* was supposedly created to encourage wonder, an enjoyment of stories, and a fantasy imagination among the youth after Vietnam. More specifically Lucas hoped to morally *re-educate* young people, as we will see later.

To many critics Lucas's *SW*, and his claims concerning it, look like a return to the older American hero-myths. It appears to encourage a simple escapism that both emotionally comforts the traumatized American psyche and politically mitigates the possibility of learning from the mistakes that resulted in Vietnam in the first place. For instance, the Empire's Nazi-look resonates for American audiences with less morally complex wars, and thus re-romanticizes American involvement in conflict. So, influential film critic Pauline Kael even describes *SW* (and Spielberg's *Jaws* 1975) as infantilizing the cinema, reconstituting the spectator as child, and then overwhelming her with sound and spectacle, obliterating irony, aesthetic self-consciousness and critical reflection (see Biskind 1998: 344). Andrew Gordon, among others, consequently claims that *SW* responds to the need for Americans to renew faith in themselves as the "good guys" on the world scene (1978: 324).

That reading, however, should be contested. First, Lucas's politico-cultural **dystopian** *THX 1138*, adapted from his Samuel Warner Memorial Scholarship-winning student film *THX 1138.4EB/Electronic Labyrinth* (1967), is a critical observation on the United States of the late 1960s and early 70s, accusing it of promoting a dehumanizing capitalism that makes conformist "masses" no less than does the Communism it was fighting against. Secondly, when Lucas's significant involvement in originally conceiving of the politically subversive *Apocalypse Now* ended, he admits migrating several of its broad themes into *SW*. "What we had in common is we grew up in the '60s, protesting the Vietnam War" (Lucas, in Biskind 1998: 317). In particular, *America* was acting in ways similar to the "evil Empire"; the Emperor Palpatine is like Nixon; and the Rebel Alliance's guerrilla fighters reflect the Vietcong (even if they had an all-American cast). This Vietcong-versus-"imperial"-America subtext is played out again in *Return of the Jedi* (Biskind 1998: 342).

Thirdly, it is important to observe that *American Graffiti* produced the kind of fan mail that convinced Lucas that an upbeat mood movie could be more transformative of young people's increasingly fractured lives. "Traditionally we get … [moral values] from the church, the family, and in the modern world we get them from the media—from movies" (Lucas, in Kline 1999: 53). In response, among other things, Lucas lightened the serious tone by introducing more humor into *SW*'s third script-draft (1 August 1975). It consequently makes sense to understand his claims about challenging the post-Vietnam mood as an attempt to encourage a *new hope*: not a wallowing in self-pity or pacifying introspection, but a learning to be *moral* agents.

As early as 1977 (the month *before SW*'s theatrical release) Lucas declares, "I wanted to do a modern fairy tale, a myth" (Lucas, in Kline 1999: 53). What does Lucas understand by "myth" and by *SW* as updating "ancient mythological motifs" (Lucas, in Rinzler 2008: 5f.)? The discussion above provides several clues.

The first is the connection with moral truths and myths. Most commonly, the "journalistic" use of the term "myth" operates in contrast to the terms "truth" or "fact." This is largely a hangover from late nineteenth-century studies. So, for E.B. Tylor (1832–1917) myths are primitive pre-scientific explorations of the world that have to be read as literal. Accordingly they are scientifically redundant explanations of states of affairs (see Tylor 1871: vol. 2, 85). In contrast, Lucas attempts to provide what he considers to be truthful insight into the nature of things and persons, and thereby provide a context for moral reflection and education through a particular visual narrative form. In this, he builds more on twentieth-century scholarly developments.

The second is Lucas's reference to the updating of "*ancient* mythological motifs." The idea is not to generate a "new myth," since such a thing is, by the very *cultural* nature of myths, not possible anyway. Myths are stories that *cultures* tell about themselves, and expressions of what cultures deem to be valuable and meaningful (morally and spiritually). They are not narratives that flow simply from a single person's imagination or vision of the world (see McDowell 2007: Ch.1).

The third is Lucas's reference to "ancient mythological *motifs*," suggesting that myths are largely alike. In this approach, Lucas had learned from the likes of Joseph Campbell (1903–1987). Lucas explains that he had studied anthropology in college for a couple of years, and there he encountered Campbell's *Hero of a Thousand Faces* (1949). When writing *SW*, "I was going along on my own story, I was trying to write whatever I felt. And then I would go back once I'd written a script ... and check it against the classic model of the hero's journey ... to see if I had gone off the deep end, and simply by following my own inspiration ... it was very close to the model" (Lucas, in Kaminski 2008: 215). Here Lucas explicitly admits using the hero-myth as a touchstone for *SW*, checking his writing against the "classical model" (or, rather, Campbell's version), and discovering that he was already working in these terms. Consequently, when Lucas shows Campbell the "**classic trilogy**" at Skywalker Ranch in 1983, the myth-scholar apparently grandiosely remarked, "You know, I thought real art stopped with Picasso, Joyce and Mann. Now I know it hasn't" (Campbell, in Larsen and Larsen 1991: 543).

Campbell's own approach largely built on the foundations laid in 1876 by Austrian scholar Johann Georg von Hahn on the "Aryan" hero tales, and Lord Raglan's 1936 linking of the myth of the hero (the god) with ritual (following J.G. Frazer) with his patterning of mythic narrative. Campbell compares the myths of various cultures and controversially argues, following Carl Jung's theory of **archetypes**, that they are all the same "monomyth." Ignoring cultural specificities, he claims there is broadly the same hero in each one, only with this essence being displayed under different, and culturally specific, guises (Campbell 1949: 4). Yet while Campbell "cites hundreds of myths and extricates from them hundreds of archetypes ... he analyzes few whole myths," and in insufficient critical depth (Segal 1987: 137f.). In fact, Segal believes Campbell to be less interested in analyzing myths than in using myths to analyze human nature. What emerges is not the interest in the many creation, fertility, or deliverance myths, but rather in the myth of the hero's journey, particularly the psychological one from childhood to adulthood—a journey of self-discovery. Through Campbell, Lucas is able to draw from a well-stocked store of ancient possibilities for characterization and plot structuring. Campbell's "monomyth" here shapes the journey or adventures of Luke Skywalker (for a useful comparison, see Henderson 1997).

Case study

Identifying the nature of the particular mythic form in any mythic text is far from being the end of the process of myth-study, however. There are several ways in which myths can be studied, especially since they reflect the social and political values, or beliefs, of the cultures that develop and sustain them. Yet this type of exploratory work is largely ignored by much study of myth. It is generally the case, then, that "much myth criticism ignores the complicity of myth in establishing and maintaining social dominance and power structures," or how myths can "explain why those in power are in power and why those who are oppressed or dominated are (and should be) oppressed and dominated" (Wetmore 2005: 95).

There are morally significant questions about the largely hidden and otherwise unquestioned cultural assumptions of the myths that shape as well as give an audience to *SW*. These need to be exposed in order to be morally tested and possibly contested. So, for instance, does *SW* express, assume and reinforce 1970s' American patriarchalism, racism, homophobia, individualism, or American supremacism? "To dismiss the *Star Wars* films out of hand as lowbrow adventure-romance films that cannot support any meaningful analysis ... is erroneous and perhaps irresponsible. Given the saga's immense popularity, its potential cultural and psychological impact upon millions of viewers ... should not be underestimated" (Wilson 2007: 136). Therefore, critically examining the mythic underpinnings of *SW* provides an important opportunity to examine critically significant mythic shapers of American culture and consciousness.

Among these debated issues, the one that will be the case study for the remainder of this chapter is announced in the title of the *SW* movies: it is a story of violence, of war! With the US's moon landings eight years earlier—"a triumph of the spirit and will as well as a major technological feat" (Henderson 1997: 136)—for a moment Americans forgot the "Cold War" troubles and celebrated optimistically. Yet Lucas's "war" theme not only references *Flash Gordon* space-serials, Kurosawa's *The Hidden Fortress*, and the Vietnam War, but also suggests that even the new frontier (space) is not free from human conflict. After all, the "space race" was itself the fruit of the Cold "War." By setting the audience in the "middle" of war *SW*, according to many as we will see below, invites the audience to see violent conflict as being origin-less, as being the way things really are.

"You don't know the power of the Dark Side" (Darth Vader)

Biblical scholar Walter Wink has grandly identified the "myth of redemptive violence" as "the real religion of America" (Wink 1992: 13). This "enshrines the belief that violence saves, that war brings peace, that might makes right. Violence simply appears to be the nature of things. It's what works. It seems inevitable, the last and often, the first resort in conflicts" (Wink 1998: 42). A number of scholars have discovered just such a myth underlying *SW*. The critique is not about the *amount* of violence in *SW*—after all, anti-war movies like *Apocalypse Now* are full of violence. Rather, the question concerns the *purpose* of the violence, whether it portrays a violence that disturbs us into moral reflection and vigilance against pressures to violate other people in our own contexts.

Star Wars's final scene, the medal-ceremony set in the throne room of the Rebel base at an ancient Massassi temple on the fourth moon of Yavin, is instructive and emotionally climactic. Its temper is an entirely jubilant one, one of resolution achieved. (Of course, Vader's escape has notably left enough unresolved to support a sequel.) While this may reflect historic moments like those in Trafalgar Square and Times Square after the Victories in Europe and Victories over Japan in WWII (1945), it ignores the cost and traumatic loss. For instance, while Luke's good childhood friend, Biggs Darklighter, has recently been killed in the battle, not only is there no mention of this but Luke's mood on returning is an unreservedly euphoric one. Rubey sees this as romanticizing war as "tidy and uncannily bloodless" (Rubey 1978: 9), presenting it as thrilling and entertaining. Moreover, the mood celebrates a simple victory of "good" and the defeat of "evil," leading critics to complain about a morally simplistic **Manichaean** sensibility (e.g. Biskind 1998: 342f.; Henderson 1997: 117; Wetmore 2005: 96, among many others).

This is reinforced by the suggestion that *SW*'s evil is rather obvious, and is personified by flatly dark characters such as Darth Vader, and later Darth Sidious (*Return of the Jedi*, dir. Richard Marquand 1983) and Darth Maul (*The Phantom Menace*, dir. Lucas 1999). In *SW*'s second draft (1975) there was no backstory granting Vader a more complex psychology. Even when he does finally appear in the movie he, with his visual allusion to Nazism and black knight malevolence, exhibits nothing but power and the iconic presence of menace. Vader's costume itself is symbolic—a combination of Nazism (the helmet, and even the SS black), medieval monastic robes, a samurai girdle (and, again, the helmet as well, reminiscent in shape of the Japanese *kabuto*), and the black knight (the black armor), and Jack Kirby's Darkseid and Doctor Doom (see Kaminski 2008: 100; Rinzler 2008: 131; Henderson 1997: 146, 164, 189). Only the smallest glimmer of something more complex appears in Obi-Wan's earlier revelation that Vader had been "a young Jedi Knight."

Understanding a movie involves appreciating the whole ***mise-en-scène***, and the images of this particular scene are full of significance. First, Han's western gunslinger style costume refers to the violent American frontier myth that, among other things, skirts over and romanticizes the moral problems with the late nineteenth-century appeal to "**Manifest Destiny**" in settling the West (see Cherry 1998: Part Three). Critics argue that *SW* displays a vigilantist suspiciousness of authority, and thus the idea of the gunslinger's being a law-unto-himself. "The ultimate victory of good over evil finally boils down to firing laser-blasters, detonating bombs, or slicing through one's enemies with a light saber" (Stone 2000: 139).

The battle of Yavin had involved the *mass* destruction of all those on the Death Star. Is this any different in scope from the Imperial destruction of Leia's home planet of Alderaan? The difference between the two is simply one of mood and attitude, so that the latter is to be seen as an aggressive and wicked act of those who are "evil," whereas the former is a necessary act of moral virtue and heroism. It, therefore, becomes as much a "revenge narrative" as a quest and rescue story. According to Lawrence, when Luke, "with an utterly clear conscience," destroys the Death Star, *SW* helps "restore a nuclear pleasure earlier dampened by the grim awareness that hundreds of thousands of Japanese were incinerated at Hiroshima and Nagasaki" (Lawrence 2006: 85).

Second, does this religious setting in the ancient Massassi temple provide religious justification for the preceding violent action against "evil"? Critics often point to the "religious" concept of "the Force" as dividing reality into *both* good *and* evil. Luke may have used "the Force" to help him select the appropriate moment to fire his proton torpedo into the Death Star's reactor shaft, but the first occasion in the movie that "the Force" is mentioned is quite different. Vader in the Death Star Conference Room threatens the life of the religious scoffer, Admiral Motti, with the *power* of "the Force."

Third, the visual imagery substantially echoes two moments from Leni Riefenstahl's Nazi propaganda movie *The Triumph of the Will* (1934). The first is when three figures silently march between two mass ranks of troops at Nurnberg, while the other, significantly, is the concluding, triumphant scene. According to Lucas, the visual overlaps were entirely unintentional, and he had planned instead to use a set of images from Riefenstahl for "the Emperor on the Empire planet" (cited in Rinzler 2008: 325). Critics remain unconvinced!

"A Jedi uses the force for knowledge and defense" (Yoda): defensive violence

The main difficulty with this reading is that it abstracts *SW* from its historical context (the questioning of American empire), and, crucially, from the succeeding movies in the saga. The succeeding movies subvert several of the frequently offered critiques (Manichaeism, and the "myth of redemptive violence").

By *The Empire Strikes Back* (dir. Irvin Kershner 1980) Luke, the heroic destroyer of the Death Star, has become a Rebel commander, and his "Force-consciousness" has significantly improved (he "Force-grabs" his lightsaber in the Wampa's cave on Hoth). Early in the movie a ghostly Obi-Wan Kenobi instructs Luke to go to Dagobah and be trained by Jedi Master Yoda. But what the young man finds on Dagobah is far from what he had expected. The planet itself is a murky and swampy world, wholly uncivilized in a way that makes his former home-world—gangster-run Tatooine—appear cultured and sophisticated. It is not the place from which to expect a great Jedi Master.

On feeling he is being watched he swings around with blaster drawn only to see something apparently unthreatening—an unarmed diminutive green being with protruding ears. This character acts like a scavenger, uses strange grammatical syntax, is physically unimpressive, and appears more fool or jester than Jedi Master.

Later, however, he is unexpectedly revealed to be precisely the one the youth has been seeking. The problem for Luke, with his obviously militaristic notions of "power" simply is that the reality did not fit the expectation of what "a great warrior" should look like. Yoda's initial appearance could not be more contrasting with that of Vader. The masked Sith Lord arrives striding over recently slain bodies, exuding a cool and power-full arrogance, distinguished by his menacing warrior dress and with his cape flowing behind him that impressively adds to the threat of his presence. His voice and manner reveal that he is one to be obeyed because, imposing in form and character, he is eminently fearsome. Soon after, he is seen holding a Rebel commander by the neck a few feet off the ground before the sound of breaking bones can be heard. *The difference between Yoda and Vader has to do with different conceptions of power and understandings of the self*—for Vader, power is the power of force and the right of might; for Yoda, power has to do with the virtues of wisdom, self-control, and just living; for Vader, the self is to be exalted, and that at others' expense; while Yoda is a servant of "the Force," and correspondingly a servant of all living things. The Luke who *begins* in *SW* with a macho sense of the hero-myth has to be brought up short by Yoda. The fact that he can ask "is the dark-side stronger?" indicates just how difficult it is for him to move away from thinking in terms of sheer power, echoing Vader's response to Admiral Motti earlier in *SW* over "the power of the Force." Luke's sense of the Jedi way, of "the Force," is to be radically purged of inappropriate conceptions and valuations. He is forced to *unlearn* what he has learnt, to face his prejudices and misunderstandings about life. This is why Yoda later challenges him with the rhetorical question: "Judge me by my size do you?"

So Yoda responds to Luke's talk of a "great warrior" by claiming that "wars not make one great," and later instructs, "A Jedi uses the Force for knowledge and defense, never for attack." Anger, fear, hate, aggression, all those traits that are conducive to generating violence, characterize the dark side. This is why the Jedi who resort to such unrestrained belligerence suffer for their actions. Luke's aggressiveness, for instance, in later cutting his training short in order to rush off to face Vader and save his friends culminates in his losing his right hand in his defeat. In this way the saga begins to seriously expose the problems of appealing to "necessary violence." Lucas had originally planned to name his central protagonist Luke Sky*killer* and the change to Skywalker a month into shooting *SW* in 1976 itself is a significant nod towards the Jedi philosophy. Similarly, in the earlier versions of the script Lucas had a major role for a *General* (1 August 1975—"General of the White Legions"), but that character then became the Jedi Knight Obi-Wan who, although there remains a reference to him as having been a general in the Clone Wars, is now given a primary role as mentor to Luke and whose Jedi order is associated more with having been guardians of peace and justice in the old Republic. Lucas himself seems to be demonstrating an unlearning of what he had learned!

"I will not turn and you'll be forced to kill me" (Luke Skywalker): pacifism?

In many ways the mood of the third *SW* movie, *Return of the Jedi*, is very like that of the first *SW* film. Lucas appointed Richard Marquand to direct, and this was partly to guarantee that the movie's creator could have more control over the director, more than he had with Irvin Kershner, director of *The Empire Strikes Back*. Much like the first film, *Return of the Jedi* involves a high-octane race to destroy a newly operational Death Star, has a climactic battle scene, and a celebratory end. The climactic conflict is cast, though, in three different settings. First, a Rebel team on the forest moon of Endor, supported by the indigenous Ewok peoples, battles to destroy the shield generator that is protecting the incomplete Second Death Star. Second, the Rebel fleet fights to destroy that super-weapon. Finally, on the Second Death Star Luke clashes with Darth Vader in front of the Emperor.

Lucas comments that Luke "has the capacity to become Darth Vader simply by using hate and fear and using weapons as opposed to using compassion and caring and kindness" (Lucas 2004). The visual imagery is striking—Luke's Jedi clothing is now black, and his prosthetic right hand is an early reflection of his father's mechanized state. He is being urged by the Emperor to succumb to the values of the "dark side" (hate, anger, revenge and self-assertiveness), take revenge on Vader, and replace his nemesis at the Emperor's side.

This is a movie that for some time seems to have been heading for the title *Revenge of the Jedi*. Yet with the release date looming, the movie was renamed *Return*. One of the reasons given, recounted by producer Howard Kazanjian and actor Mark Hamill, is that "revenge" is not the business of Jedi (see Kaminski 2008: 282ff., 460). So Luke finally refuses to succumb to the Emperor's temptation to kill his most bitter of foes in a fit of angry aggression when he has the chance, and discards his lightsaber, thereby leaving himself defenseless against the Emperor's own destructive rage. He is prepared to sacrifice himself rather than do evil.

In his spiritual journey into a "larger world" (Obi-Wan) Luke's whole value system has to be deconstructed (or "unlearned," in Yoda's terms) and replaced with a whole new way of seeing the life and interrelations of all things. Towards the end, then, his journey seems to have brought him closer to a "pacifism" that is an active "non-violence," a purposeful action that is beyond a "bare peace." His heroic journey is into a type of "sainthood" rather than into "warrior-heroism." Of course, the Empire is defeated only through the violent act (albeit defense-of-another) of Vader/Anakin, the commando attack on the imperial shield bunker, and the torpedo from Lando Calrissian in the Millennium Falcon. Luke's action is just a hint of peace, a moment, but not any less significant for that!

Conclusion

"The films visually and through narrative are lengthy ruminations on violence and power" (Wetmore 2005: 20). But what kind of ruminations? The critics' discovery of the "myth of redemptive violence" is too simple. Certain contextualizing features must be borne in mind: for instance, Lucas's critical response to the Vietnam War, and his claims that Nixon's America embodies oppressive empire as much as the rebellion for freedom. He himself may have come from a politically conservative home, but he broke with his father's wishes, headed off to what George Lucas Sr. considered to be "sin city"—Los Angeles and the University of Southern California—became engaged in avant-garde filmmaking, and disagreed with the Vietnam War. Moreover, the post-1977 movies in the saga crucially indicate that the various features that make *SW*'s violence look like a politics of revenge against the "evil them" need to be understood differently. Taking these detailed steps enables a deeper reading of *SW* than ones often heard, and we have not even discussed the considerably more complex prequel trilogy in which the story-arc of the "classic trilogy" ("the adventures of Luke Skywalker") moves in a thematically different direction ("the tragedy of Anakin Skywalker").

And yet despite the trajectory of this deeper reading and the cautionary message about violence, there still remains a concern: *SW*'s violence is insufficiently horrifying and emotionally involving, or at least not until *Revenge of the Sith* (dir. Lucas 2005). Its form in this space action-adventure still looks too exhilarating, and children may not be dissuaded from engaging their "enemies" with a lightsaber or a blaster pistol in conscious mimicking of their swashbuckling heroes. As they mature the question remains: will they begin to learn the lessons of Jedi compassion, self-giving and other-interestedness, or will they feel the pressure of *SW*'s ambiguity in the direction of reducing moral issues to simple affairs, and using violence to settle conflicts with "alien" others?

Summary

- George Lucas conceives of *SW* as a kind of *Flash Gordon* adventure serial and space opera.
- The real-world background was the Vietnam War, and *SW* is supposedly Lucas's attempt to morally *re-educate* young people.
- The ideas for it emerged slowly (1973–77) through the influence of, among others, Akira Kurosawa, John Ford, and especially Joseph Campbell.
- *Star Wars* is influenced by other cultural myths, and many critics see it reflecting the American "myth of redemptive violence."
- However, *SW* needs to be read in its political and social context, and in the context of the other five movies that make up the *SW* saga.
- The saga displays various understandings of the social role of violence, from defensive violence to even a form of pacifism.

Glossary terms

Archetype – an original image or paradigmatic character. According to Carl Jung the archetypes are to be found in all humanity. (See also the treatment of this term in Chapter 8 and in the glossary at the end of the chapter.)

"Classic trilogy" – *Star Wars* movies Episodes IV–VI, released 1977–83 (*Star Wars* [later known as *A New Hope*], *The Empire Strikes Back*, and *Return of the Jedi*). Differentiated from the "prequel trilogy," Episodes I–III released 1999–2005 (*The Phantom Menace*, *Attack of the Clones*, *Revenge of the Sith*).

Dystopia – from the Greek literally meaning "bad place." A view of a degraded society, for instance where the government is repressive.

Ideology – a set of beliefs that reflect the beliefs and interests of a nation, political or cultural system, or groups within society and shapes the way persons in that society understand themselves and how they should act. (See also the treatment of this term in the Introduction and in the glossary at the end of the Introduction.)

Manichaeism – the religious teachings of third-century Persian prophet, Mani. Associated with cosmic dualism—a primordial conflict between light and darkness, good and evil.

Manifest Destiny – nineteenth-century belief that America is God's chosen land that has been allotted the whole of North America, and thus could rightfully spread west across the continent.

Mise-en-scène – adapted from theatrical studies, literally meaning "to put onto stage." It refers to everything that can be seen inside the frame of the film: the characters and their positioning, the props, the lighting, the costumes, as well as how the framed image is established through camera angles, and so on.

Myth – the Greek term *mythos*, meaning "speech" or "word." In early Greek literature it ranged from "a true story," "an account of facts," and so "fact" itself, to an invented story, a legend, fairy story, fable or poetic creation.

Mythology – the body of inherited myths of any culture.

Pastiche – a work of art that mixes styles, genres, and/or material from other works of art.

Screen-crawl – provides information at the opening of the *Star Wars* movies as a time-saving plot device to fill in background matters. A visual nod back to the 1930s' *Flash Gordon* adventure serials.

Star Wars – the term itself is actually complex since it covers six *SW* movies (over two sets of trilogies), and a massive series of "Expanded Universe" materials that include, among other things, several spin-off movies, two different versions of *Clone Wars* short animations series, a plenitude of computer games, novels and graphic novels. This raises intricate issues of the *SW* "canon."

Points for discussion

- What are "myths?" How do they function?
- How might the category of "myth" help us understand *SW*?
- What, if any, resources does *SW* have for (1) supporting and/or (2) resisting the "myth of redemptive violence"?
- What mythologies and sacred traditions shape *SW*?

Further reading

Henderson, M. (1997) *Star Wars: The Magic of Myth*, New York: Bantam.

The curator of the Smithsonian Institution's National Air and Space Museum exhibition (1997) discusses *Star Wars*' "mythological roots."

Kapell, M.W., and Lawrence, J.S. (eds) (2006) *Finding the Force of the Star Wars Franchise: Fans, Merchandise, and Critics*, New York, *et al.*: Peter Lang.

Moves away from myth-based criticism to ideology criticism, and critically evaluates *SW* as a cultural set of texts that demand deep critiques of its approach to issues of race, gender and sexuality, politics, economics, and religion.

Lucas, G. (26 April, 1999) "Of Myth and Men: A Conversation between Bill Moyers and George Lucas on the Meaning of the Force and the True Theology of Star Wars," *Time* 153.16, 91–4. Online. Available HTTP: www.time.com/time/magazine/article/0,9171,990820,00.html (accessed 4 April 2006).

Lucas discusses issues of myth, spirituality and religion in relation to his saga.

McDowell, J.C. (2007) *The Gospel According to Star Wars: Feeling the Force of God and the Good*, Louisville, KY: Westminster John Knox Press.

A critical theological treatment that reads *Star Wars* contextually and attempts to understand the mythologies that shape it, from Joseph Campbell and tragic drama to contemporary American myths.

Wetmore Jr., K.J. (2005) *The Empire Triumphant: Race, Religion and Rebellion in the Star Wars Films*, Jefferson, NC, and London: McFarland & Company, Inc.

A critical post-colonial reading of *Star Wars* that is concerned about Lucas's presentation of Asians, people of color, and political imperialism and rebellion.

Bibliography

Biskind, P. (1998) *Easy Riders, Raging Bulls: Sex-Drugs-and-Rock 'n' Roll Generation Saved Hollywood*, New York: Touchstone.

Campbell, J. (1949) *The Hero With a Thousand Faces*, New York: Princeton University Press.

Cherry, C. (ed.) (1998) *God's New Israel: Religious Interpretations of American Destiny*, rev. edn, University of North Carolina Press.

Gordon, A. (1978) "*Star Wars*: A Myth for Our Time," *Literature/Film Quarterly* 6.4: 314–326.

Henderson, M. (1997) *Star Wars: The Magic of Myth*, New York: Bantam Books.

Kaminski, M. (2008) *The Secret History of Star Wars: The Art of Storytelling and the Making of a Modern Epic*, Kingston, Ontario: Legacy Books Press.

Kline, S. (ed.) (1999) *George Lucas: Interviews*, Jackson: University Press of Mississippi.

Larsen, S. and Larsen, R. (1991) *A Fire in the Mind: The Life of Joseph Campbell*, New York: Doubleday.

Lawrence, J.S. (2006) "Joseph Campbell, George Lucas, and the Monomyth," in Matthew Wilhelm Kapell and John Shelton Lawrence (eds) *Finding the Force of the Star Wars Franchise: Fans, Merchandise, and Critics*, New York, *et al.*: Peter Lang, 21–33.

Lucas, G. (2004) "Commentary," DVD of *The Empire Strikes Back.*

Miles, M.R. and Plate, S.B. (2004) "Hospitable Vision: Some Notes on the Ethics of Seeing Film," *Crosscurrents* 54.1 (Spring): 22–31.

Plate, S.B. (2008) "Filmmaking and World Making: Re-Creating Time and Space in Myth and Film," in Gregory J. Watkins (ed.) *Teaching Religion and Film*, Oxford: Oxford University Press, 219–231.

Rinzler, J.W. (2008) *The Making of Star Wars: The Definitive Story Behind the Original Film*, London: Ebury Press.

Rubey, D. (1978) "Not So Far Away," *Jump Cut* 18: 8–14.

Segal, R.A. (1987) *Joseph Campbell: An Introduction*, New York: Garland.

Silvio, C., and Vinci, T.M. (2007) "Introduction. Moving Away From Myth: *Star Wars* as Cultural Artifact," in Carl Silvio and Tony M. Vinci (eds) *Culture, Identities and Technology in the* Star Wars *Films: Essays on the Two Trilogies*, Jefferson, NC: McFarland and Company Inc., 1–8.

Stone, B.P. (2000) *Faith and the Film: Theological Themes at the Cinema*, St. Louis, MO: Chalice Press.

Tylor, E.B. (1871) *Primitive Culture: Researches into the Development of Mythology*, Philosophy, Religion, Art, and Custom, 2 vols, London: Murray.

Wetmore Jr., K.J. (2005) *The Empire Triumphant: Race, Religion and Rebellion in the Star Wars Films*, Jefferson, NC, and London: McFarland & Company, Inc.

Wink, W. (1992) *Engaging the Powers: Discernment and Resistance in a World of Domination*, Minneapolis, MN: Fortress.

——(1998) *The Powers That Be: Theology for a New Millennium*, New York: Doubleday.
Wilson, V.A. (2007) "Seduced by the Dark Side of the Force: Gender, Sexuality, and Moral Agency in George Lucas's *Star Wars* Universe," in Carl Silvio and Tony M. Vinci (eds) *Culture, Identities and Technology in the* Star Wars *Films: Essays on the Two Trilogies*, Jefferson, NC: McFarland and Company Inc., 134–152.

Filmography

American Graffiti, George Lucas, dir. (1973)
Apocalypse Now, Francis Ford Coppola, dir. (1979)
Attack of the Clones, George Lucas, dir. (2002)
Electronic Labyrinth: THX 1138.4EB, George Lucas, dir. (1967)
Flash Gordon, Mike Hodges, dir. (1980)
Jaws, Steven Spielberg, dir. (1975)
Metropolis, Fritz Lang, dir. (1926/1927)
Return of the Jedi, Richard Marquand, dir. (1983)
Revenge of the Sith, George Lucas, dir. (2005)
Star Wars, George Lucas, dir. (1977)
The Empire Strikes Back, Irvin Kershner, dir. (1980)
The Hidden Fortress, Akira Kurosawa, dir. (1958)
The Phantom Menace, George Lucas, dir. (1999)
The Searchers, John Ford, dir. (1956)
THX 1138, George Lucas, dir. (1971)
Triumph of the Will, Leni Riefenstahl, dir. (1934)

8 Religion and video games

Shooting aliens in cathedrals

Rachel Wagner

Introduction

When we play video games, we also engage with powerful, world-orienting stories. The typical video game reflects a fantasy world with well-developed characters, engaging tales of triumph and woe, challenges to overcome, enemies to be defeated. Such myths show up too in religions around the world, showing us how supernatural beings—gods and goddesses—defeat forces of evil or overcome great challenges, often in order to protect humanity. Even those world religions that focus on a single god have stories about how that God acted on earth for humanity. In Judaism, for example, there is the story of the Exodus; in Islam, there is the story of Muhammad's divinely guided escape from Mecca when his life was in danger. Christianity offers stories of a savior who, although he was killed two thousand years ago, will eventually return to defeat his enemies in the end times. Apocalyptic literature provides us with story after story of the violent defeat of masses of evil entities, who, while intent upon destroying humanity, instead find themselves crushed at the hands of God's warriors.

Through their shaping of our experience through guided actions, video games reveal a kinship with religious ritual. Rituals are often, for all the other things they may also be, myths in action—that is, deeply meaningful and often interactive retellings of foundational stories. Religious rituals can be a means of taking a religious myth and providing a set structure for ritual participants to engage with that myth themselves, via gestures and/or re-enactments, perhaps even costumes and props. For example, the Exodus story is retold in the ritual of the Passover meal (**Seder**) and all its associated activities; the death of Jesus is retold in the ritual of the Eucharist (the Christian ritual meal), as well as in the procession through the Stations of the Cross practiced by Catholics (the series of images from the story of the death of Jesus). Some Muslim pilgrims end their **hajj** (ritual journey to Mecca) with a trip to Medina, following in the footsteps of Muhammad. The story of Hanuman (a famed Hindu deity) is retold in the Balinese Monkey Dance. These rituals walk participants through a sacred story via a fixed procession of events associated with traditional gestures, thereby teaching participants how to see themselves in relationship to the story, and allowing them to immerse themselves in it, as if they were actually "there" (i.e. witnessing or participating in the originating events). Video games, too, have "ritual" components in their fixed structures, set storylines with room for certain choices but not others, and they invite us to engage with those stories via prescribed gestures and movements. Of course some video games are more story-driven than others, just as some rituals are more driven by myth than others. But the kinship seems apparent: both are fixed scripts that often involve stories, and that invite our interactive engagement with them.

Sometimes, the connection between religion and video games is explicit, as in the case of those games that use religious ideas or places as backdrop to the video game's own in-world story. These kinds of religious games can create new contexts and new gestures and acts to be performed in relationship to depicted sacred spaces. But what is the relationship between sacred space in real life, such as a church or temple, and a virtual version of this same space, when it is digitally replicated and put into a video game? Who decides if and to what extent such spaces are sacred in their new environment? Virtual portrayals of sacred space can be puzzling for players if they aren't sure whether to see the religious images in-game as relating *only* to the game or also having some implications for real life. Take, for example, the controversy caused in 2002 by *Hitman 2: Silent Assassin* (Eidos Interactive). The game requires the player to murder "terrorists" wearing turbans and hiding in the Golden Temple in Amritsar. For real-life Sikhs, the scene evoked memories of a massacre of Sikhs in 1984 when Indian troops stormed the Temple on suspicion of military activities ("Shops," *BBC News* 21 November 2002). One obvious problem here is the memory of real violence that the game evokes. But games like this that present virtual replays of real violence also make some people worry that the game may evoke real life violence again, in that the game may encourage players to enact in real life what they are doing in the game. Concerned about both issues, some Sikhs requested a recall of *Hitman 2* and removal of the digital Temple from the game.

In 2007 a similar controversy erupted as a result of the digital depiction of a real-life Anglican cathedral in another first-person shooter video game created for Sony's PlayStation 3. *Resistance: Fall of Man* is set in an imagined alternative backdrop of Britain in the 1950s. World War II never happened in this game's world, and Britain is threatened by hostile invasion by alien creatures called Chimera, bred in Russia but now running amok. Britain is the last European stronghold against the creatures, and American army ranger Nathan Hale is sent on a messianic rescue mission to help defend Britain against otherwise certain destruction. *Resistance: Fall of Man* raised the hackles of the Church of England[1] not long after its release due to an intensely violent shootout in the game staged in a perfect digital replica of Manchester Cathedral.[2] The Church responded with anger, public castigation, and threats of a lawsuit, arguing that the Cathedral's image was used without permission and claiming that the violence in the digital cathedral was in bad taste. The game raises powerful questions about the nature of sacred space in virtual form, about the power of virtual storytelling and ritual, and about player immersion when playing video games. The considerable and carefully considered exchange that took place between the Church of England and Sony reveals for us the intense and as-of-yet unresolved questions that portrayals of sacred space in virtual reality evoke, especially when these sacred spaces appear in violent video games.

Theory and method

What is a video game anyway? If we are to make sense of how video games relate to religion, we should first of all figure out what other things video games are most like. Is a video game like a board game or a theatre performance or a game of tag? Is it art or entertainment, or can it be both? Is it a very loosely scripted performance of the sort that might occur in impromptu street theatre? Is a video game like a novel, with a narrative form that unfolds a story that we "read"? Or is a video game most like one of those *Choose Your Own Adventure* books from the 1980s, where you make choices and turn to different pages in the book based on your decisions?

In some ways, video games are very much like films. After all, video games, like films, rely on a visual screen to relay most information. Films, like video games, can be viewed as the product of a sort of game-play by the director, who takes certain visual raw materials and shapes them into his own version of the story he wants to tell. Video games even use some of the same techniques as film, such as computer-generated "virtual zooms" and "tracking shots" of the kind that would occur if a real, moving camera were following a particular image (Lahti 2003: 162). Nevertheless, there are some crucial differences. Although in both mediums the viewer-player can *relate* with the experiences of characters on-screen, in many video games passive identification with characters is replaced with what Miroslaw Filiciak calls "introjection," in which "the subject is projected inward into an 'other.' ... The subject (player) and the 'other' (the on-screen *avatar*) do not stand at the opposite sides of the mirror anymore—they become one" (2003: 91). As such, the "player" is inserted, so to speak, into the screen's activity, and *participates* in the manipulation of the virtual space, at times seeming to become so fused with the virtual persona in the digital space that she participates in some way in the actions performed in that virtual space. In a video game, the player often participates in the very staging of the experience as well, since as Torben Grodal notes, "the user/player is able to change the visual appearance of a computer screen (and/or sounds from speakers) by some motor action via an interface" (2003: 142). When playing video games, we all become directors to some degree—a role that some have suggested is eerily god-like.

However, the video game format resembles cinematic representation only imperfectly, as Bob Rehak observes when he describes the first-person shooter's "direct (visual) address, updated in real time, [which] presents one ongoing and unbroken half of the shot-reverse-shot construction, enabling a snug fit between the player and his or her game-produced subjectivity" (2003: 119). In cinema, the point of view of the camera, and thus of the viewer, can roam from character to character and beyond. In the typical first-person-shooter game, despite the interchangeability of personas one might select at the beginning of a game, the player can *only* view the virtual world from the perspective of the *avatar* holding the weapon. Through deep immersion of this sort, games can accomplish what cinema cannot—they provide a "sense of literal presence, and a newly participatory role for the viewer," such that the player also resembles an actor in a play, but with a very fluid script (Rehak 2003: 121). Along with this increase in agency, one must ask if it then makes most sense to think of the player primarily as a spectator, as a producer, as an actor, as a participant, as an artist, or simply as an observer, and what these roles may mean in terms of experience and effect—especially if the game is a violent one.

One of the most fascinating things about video game analysis is the way that video games confound what we think we know about storytelling and experience. There is no single way of making sense of them, and they consistently and sometimes deliberately blur the boundary between our day-to-day world and the "world" of the game. Because video games are so complex, we are best served in using a toolbox of analytical methods rather than counting on just one. A video game is not just theatre, art form, medium, novel, board game, or film, yet it is a little of each, distinguished most clearly by its open-ended form and the enhanced role of the player in determining the experience; in short, the video game is the ultimate postmodern experience: it is relative, difficult to define, echoes the real, and yet resists being identified with the real.

Interestingly, religious rituals are equally difficult to define in any single way; they too evoke elements of theatre, art, storytelling, games, and visual media. Some of the best tools for ritual analysis and for video game analysis draw on multiple fields of study; and as scholars are increasingly realizing, these may be the exact same tools for analyzing both! Accordingly, I draw here from several fields, in an interdisciplinary way, as a means of making sense of the controversy surrounding *Resistance: Fall of Man*. The most helpful concepts include: (1) Johan Huizinga's work on the "**magic circle**" of play; (2) Mircea Eliade's theoretical (and theological) development of the distinction between "sacred" and "profane"; and (3) the notion of "**procedural rhetoric**" as defined by game theorist Ian Bogost.

The "magic circle"

Johan Huizinga's writing reveals his deep interest in how religious activities can resemble play. In his famous work, *Homo Ludens* (1955), Huizinga coins the term "magic circle" to identify an activity present in both ritual and play—namely, the demarcation of a region marked off from other realms of life in which temporary and special activities occur. Huizinga explains play in ways that highlight its kinship with ritual. He says: "All play moves and has its being within a play-ground marked off beforehand either materially or ideally, deliberately or as a matter of course." This can include, says Huizinga, an arena, a table, or even "the temple, the stage, the screen," and a host of other defined spaces. In fact, he claims, all of these play spaces are "temporary worlds within the ordinary world, dedicated to the performance of an act apart" (1955: 10). Of course, Huizinga lived decades before video games would become popular, but his observations are prescient. Video games, perhaps even more so than board games or athletic games, are increasingly dedicated to "temporary worlds" that are "apart" from our ordinary lives, separated from us by the digital screen but still evoking our engagement with them and the "playgrounds" they create for us. This means that video games can be viewed as play *and* as ritual—at the same time.

Religious ritual spaces, of course, are similarly "marked off" for acts "apart." Thus, in Huizinga's list of places where we will likely find the "magic circle," the temple is included. Huizinga describes play as "a free standing activity quite consciously outside 'ordinary' life as being 'not serious' but at the same time absorbing the player intensely and utterly. It is an activity connected with no material interest, and no profit can be gained by it." For Huizinga, play "proceeds within its own boundaries of time and space according to fixed rules and in an orderly manner. It promotes the formation of social groupings, which tend to surround themselves with secrecy and to stress their difference from the common world by disguise or other means" (1955: 107). Both rituals and play are characterized by rules that must be followed within these "magic circles," such that a temporary world is created by our experience of this separate space and time.

Drawing on Huizinga, contemporary game theorists agree that video games often demarcate separate spaces and times for play, what they call "frames." Game theorists Katie Salen and Eric Zimmerman explain that: "[T]he frame of a game is what communicates that those contained within it are 'playing' and that the space of play is separate in some way from that of the real world." The frame of a game "creates the feeling of safety" and can even be physically designated by taking place in a theatre, playground, or other defined space (2003: 94). It is easy to see how play serves some of the same functions as ritual, which also is set outside "ordinary life," which also proceeds according to generally fixed rules, and which also encourages social groupings in distinction from the larger social world. Much of religious ritual even takes place in a physical space that is set apart from everyday life. Stanley Tambiah's definition of ritual highlights these similarities:

> Ritual is a culturally constructed system of symbolic communication. It is constituted of patterned and ordered sequences of words and acts often expressed in multiple media, whose content and arrangement are characterised in varying degree by formality (conventionality), stereotype (rigidity), condensation (fusion) and redundancy (repetition).
>
> (1981: 119)

This definition of ritual could as easily describe play, especially video-game play, in which formality (fixed patterns), stereotyping (predictable experiences or images), and redundancy (repetition) are typically part of the design. As we will see in our analysis of *Resistance: Fall of Man*, sometimes people decide for themselves how to view a scripted experience, and whether to see it as play or ritual. Accordingly, a lot depends upon whether or not one defines the making of a "magic circle" as an act of ritual construction or merely as an act of temporary game-play. But in both cases, the "magic circle" identifies an experience that evokes a different world, or at least a different mode of being, temporarily entered into by participants.

Sacred space

One of the most useful theorists for making sense of the *Resistance: Fall of Man* controversy is the Romanian thinker Mircea Eliade, and his work on "sacred space." Ritual theorist Jonathan Z. Smith has remarked on what he calls the "audacity and industry" of the project that most occupied Mircea Eliade, who "forge[d] a coherent whole out of apparently disparate items" in the construction of his well-known theory of "chaos to cosmos" and his views about "the sacred" and "the profane" (2005: xii). Eliade identifies the "sacred" as "the sphere of the supernatural, of things extraordinary, memorable, and momentous. While the profane is vanishing and fragile, full of shadows, the sacred is eternal, full of substance and reality" (Pals 2006: 199). For Eliade, the construction of sacred space is *itself* a hierophany, or "an irruption of the sacred that results in detaching a territory from the surrounding cosmic milieu and making it qualitatively different" (1987: 26). That is, we can see sacred space as an appearance of something perfect within the imperfect world. Hierophanies are viewed as manifestations of the heavenly or the otherworldly (which is often viewed as structured, predictable, and orderly) into the worldly (which is often viewed as in need of structure, predictability, and order). Such a function may be played by a beautiful religious building via its architecture, by a god or angel speaking to a human recipient, by the awe inspired by a vast mountain range, or even by a powerful dream.

Eliade describes how hierophany is an instantiation (realization) of the "Real" within the profane world. When people make a church or temple, he suggests, they are also creating a point of order, a place that is "real" and thus evokes our ideas of perfection, or perhaps even heaven, as contrasted with our hectic, often troubled, and chaotic lives:

> [H]ierophany has annulled the homogeneity of [profane] space and revealed a fixed point ... [T]he sacred is pre-eminently the *real*, at once power, efficacity, the source of life and fecundity. Religious man's desire to live *in the sacred* is in fact equivalent to his desire to take up his abode in objective reality, not to let himself be paralyzed by the never-ceasing relativity of purely subjective experiences, to live in a real and effective world, and not in an illusion.
>
> (1987: 28)

According to Eliade, a profane thing (such as a building) becomes "sacred" when the sacred enters into it and "saturates" it with "being." The object "appears as a receptacle of an exterior force that differentiates it from its milieu and gives it meaning and value" (2005: 4). Temples are hierophanies, or earthly receptacles of the Sacred, but they are also modeled after a "celestial prototype," which not only "precede[s] terrestrial architecture," but is "also situated in an ideal (celestial) region of eternity" (2005: 7–8). All sacred things on the earth (below) have "an extraterrestrial **archetype**, be it conceived as a plan, as a form, or purely and simply as a 'double' existing on a higher cosmic level" (2005: 9). The construction of sacred space, for Eliade, is a physical imitation of the movement from "chaos to cosmos" enacted by divine forces in primordial time. That is to say, it is a gesture of sacred order-making in a chaotic, disordered world. Today, such movement takes place when people build beautiful architectural structures like Manchester Cathedral, and the veneration of such structures is an ongoing means of maintaining one's sense of order in the world.

Eliade's view has garnered more than its share of criticism, assuming as it does the *actual* heavenly existence of the Sacred (the Real) as the model upon which human religious activity is based. Since not all people believe in an actual heaven or an actual "Sacred" origin for things, some have complained that Eliade's theories are only useful to believers. However, J.Z. Smith gestures towards a theoretical rehabilitation of Eliade when he suggests that we might readily "grant" the "cogency of Eliade's description" but "reverse the polarities of the maxim 'as above, so below,' yielding the formula 'as below, so above' thereby suggesting some theory of projection in the service of legitimating human institutions and practices" (2005: xv). In other words, regardless of whether or not there really is a god or a heavenly realm, we can still look at what people are *doing* to reinforce their own desire for cosmic order, and consider why and how they are doing it.

This reversal allows us to view the construction of sacred space as a *human-initiated* religious orienting procedure. Whether there is a "Sacred" out "there" or not, the human *building* of sacred space *is* a religious act, in that it reflects the religious *intent* to orient, the conviction that construction can imitate the Real and in so doing can also generate meaning. Human beings build sacred places and engage in sacred ritual as a way of "projecting" or enacting their own *desire* for meaning, their own *hope* that there is indeed a "Sacred" beyond worldly, profane existence. If Eliade is right, then people make beautiful cathedrals and gold-covered temples as a means of approximating what they think heaven might be like. They build places that are "heavenly" as a means of providing themselves with a sense of safety in the chaos on earth.

And as we will see in our analysis of *Resistance: Fall of Man*, for the admirers of such spaces, who see them as a sort of reflection of heaven on earth, it may not matter if they are digitally constructed or made out of real stone or brick: both can be seen as sacred in Eliade's sense. Both kinds of spaces—virtual and physical—have the ability to evoke and/or reflect the idea of "Perfection," and thus, for those who adhere to such beliefs, any violence done to such "sacred" buildings—whether they are merely digital or are made of brick—is an act of "profanity," a disrespectful disruption of centuries (even millennia) of constructive gestures toward perfection. One of the key questions raised by an application of Eliade to video games, then, is to what degree digital replicas of real sacred spaces *retain* their sacredness when placed within new imaginative story environments like the one created for Sony's video game. Our next theorist, the game designer Ian Bogost, offers help with understanding better the role of the new video game context into which the "sacred" Manchester Cathedral is put in *Resistance: Fall of Man.*

Procedural rhetoric

Whereas some analysts of video games are most interested in the images they portray, others focus on how video games can teach us things about the world via the *processes* they evoke as they lead us through interactive storytelling experiences. Game theorist Ian Bogost invites us to consider what he calls the "software authorship" of video games. In order to compose something "procedurally," an author creates (authors) a code that "enforces rules to generate some kind of representation" (2007: 4). Procedural systems like video games, Bogost points out, "Generate behaviors based on rule-based models" and in so doing, "run processes that invoke interpretations of processes in the material world" (2007: 4–5). As a means of explaining this process, Bogost coins a new term, *procedural rhetoric*, which he applies to video games. Procedural rhetoric is "the practice of persuading through processes in general and computational processes in particular." It is "a technique for making arguments with computational systems and for unpacking computational arguments others have created" (2007: 3). In other words, video games lead us through predictable scripted experiences, give us limited choices and urge us to act in certain ways. Video games present us with a "procedural rhetoric," an argument that is presented to us via processes and interactive experiences (like computer-generated choices in programs and games). Rituals, interestingly, do the same thing—they give us a story, invite our interaction with it, and use this interaction to shape how we see the world. In both rituals and games, then, we can say that the parameters of our interaction have been pre-established and limited by the creators of the game or ritual.

Bogost argues that procedural rhetoric is a much more "vivid" experience than the passive viewing of images, indeed that procedural rhetoric is the *most* vivid of experiences one can have apart from actual experience. Video games can "muster moving images and sound" that are "in accordance with complex rules that simulate real or imagined physical and cultural processes." Bogost convincingly argues that procedural rhetorical claims are "every bit as logical as verbal arguments—in fact, internal consistency is often assured in computational arguments, since microprocessors and not human agents are in charge of their consistent execution" (2007: 36). In other words, the reasoning of procedural processes is as powerful as any other kind of verbal or experiential persuasion. We are led to do things in a certain way, with certain images in mind, and certain goals predetermined. This kind of experience, Bogost claims, shapes how we view what we are doing and what we think about it afterwards.

Put another way, for Bogost, we learn by *doing*, and any images used in this process are contextualized by fixed structures of interactivity. The fixed process or "procedural rhetoric" of a video game is part of what marks what we could call its "ritual" quality, especially in the sense that some rituals are deeply integrated with fixed storylines meant to *teach* us the "rhetoric" of the religious tradition they evoke. Procedural rhetoric, then, is the means by which creators of fixed experiences like video games and rituals imbue those experiences with processes meant to shape how we see the world. Bogost's work is especially useful in interpreting the *Resistance: Fall of Man* controversy because it encourages us to ask exactly what arguments a ritual or game is making about how we should see the world. Using these three powerful conceptual tools of analysis—the magic circle, sacred space, and procedural rhetoric, we can now turn our attention to the controversy surrounding the virtual shootout in Manchester cathedral in Sony's popular video game.

Case study: *Resistance: Fall of Man*[3]

Resistance: Fall of Man was released in Japan and the United States in 2006, and in Europe on 23 March 2007. By early June, the game was noticed by Church of England officials who were already dealing with several recent shootings in the city of Manchester. Church officials were told about the game, and took a look themselves via a scene captured and uploaded to YouTube.com. Dean Govender of Manchester Cathedral quickly responded to the footage, speaking for himself and his fellows: "We are shocked to see a place of worship, prayer, learning and heritage being presented to the youth of today as a location where guns can be fired … Every year we invite hundreds of teenagers to come and see the cathedral so that they might appreciate an alternative to the violence that they experience in their daily lives. It is a shame to have a game like this undermining such important work" (Sugden 11 June 2007). The Church then issued a public letter to Sony in which it demanded the removal of the games from store shelves and requested a donation be made to the Cathedral for the prevention of future gun violence. Church representatives also claimed that Sony had not secured its permissions for portrayal of the Cathedral, and threatened legal action ("Talks," *BBC News* 10 June 2007).

Sony's European representative, David Reeves, replied to the Church's representatives in some detail with the following letter:

> Dear Dean Govender,
>
> Thank you for your email of 11 June 2007. Please understand that Resistance: Fall of Man is a work of science fiction. It is fantasy entertainment set against a backdrop of an alternative reality of 1950's [sic] Britain. History has been rewritten and the Second World War has not happened but a race of alien creatures has attacked the earth and the human race is engaged in a struggle to defend itself from this alien invader. Early in the time line of the story, Manchester Cathedral is utilised as a field hospital to tend to the human casualties of the war. When the story line reaches chapter 8, the Cathedral is empty and abandoned, no longer used as a place of worship and the sequences that take place inside are to defend the building from the aliens.
>
> We do not accept that there is any connection between contemporary issues of 21st century Manchester and a work of science fiction in which a

fictitious 1950's [sic] Britain is under attack by aliens. We believe a comprehensive viewing of the work will make its content and context clear.

Accordingly we would be pleased to demonstrate it to you at a mutually convenient time.

It was not our intention to cause offence by using a representation of Manchester Cathedral in chapter 8 of the work. If we have done so we sincerely apologise.

In conclusion we note that you are consulting lawyers. We confirm that it is our policy to seek all necessary permissions for our products and services, and we believe with this particular work we have done so.

Yours sincerely,
Dr David A Reeves
President
Sony Computer Entertainment Europe

("Church of England" 2011)

As it turned out, the representatives of Manchester Cathedral were not able to sustain any claims of legal offense, and were left with only moral complaints. Nonetheless, the issue did not die away easily. In July 2007, Manchester Cathedral issued a set of "sacred digital guidelines" to prevent "virtual desecration" of religious structures. The Dean of Manchester Cathedral, Rogers Govender, defined four rules of conduct that he argued all video game designers should follow:

1 Respect our sacred spaces as places of prayer, worship, peace, learning and heritage.
2 Do not assume that sacred space interiors are copyright free.
3 Get permission from the faith leaders who are responsible for the building interiors you want to clone.
4 Support the work of those engaged in resisting the culture of gun crime and those involved in promoting the work of conflict resolution.

(Gledhill 6 July 2007)

On the first day of the Full Synod of the Church of England in 2007, the issue was raised again by Mr. Simon Butterworth of Manchester, who asked the Presidents of the Archbishops' Council about the ordeal with Sony. The question was slated after several questions about women bishops and before one about clergy sexual orientation, placing it in the company of highly controversial church topics. Ann Sloman replied to Mr. Butterworth, describing the uncomfortable and largely unsettled outcome of all the negotiation:

> Sony has unreservedly apologized for using the cathedral in the game and has acknowledged that they did not seek permission to use the Cathedral's interior: they have undertaken not to use the Cathedral in [the] future. However, they assert that there is no legal requirement for them to seek such permission. Sony has refused either to withdraw the game or to make a donation to

> community groups nominated by the cathedral. Sony has also refused to sign up to the guidelines proposed by the Cathedral calling for undertakings over permission to use sacred spaces and support for those resisting the culture of gun crime in their communities.
>
> (Church of England Website, General Synod Proceedings: July 2007)

David Reeves spoke again to the press on July 6, attempting to respond to the moral complaints issued by Manchester officials, but remaining firm in his defense that the game's fictional nature provided some degree of insulation from real violence: "We do not accept that there is any connection between contemporary issues of twenty-first-century Manchester and a work of science fiction in which a fictitious 1950s Britain is under attack by aliens. We believe a comprehensive viewing of the work will make its content and context clear" (Gledhill 15 June 2007). Nonetheless, soon after, Reeves also accepted that "the connection between the congregation and the cathedral is a deeply personal and spiritual one" and acknowledged that Sony had "offended some of the congregation by using the cathedral in our science fiction game." He asserted that "[i]t was never our intention to offend anyone in the making of this game, and we would like to apologise unreservedly to them for causing that offence, and to all parts of the community who we might also have offended" (Osuh 6 July 2007). Reeves's comments seem sincere, but the careful insertion of the phrase "science fiction game" betrays a certain reserved friction; he seems to be trying to make the point, however implicit, that *Resistance* is, in fact, "just" a game and that it draws on a fictional universe that has nothing to do with the real-life cathedral. Dr Reeves also said that Sony would ensure that Manchester Cathedral was not used in any of its games again.

The legal issues regarding digital representation of the Cathedral are thorny and exceedingly complicated, and turned out not to be worth the fight for the Church of England. The bottom line appears to be that buildings can only be copyrighted in the UK for the first 70 years, and the Cathedral, being much older than that, is apparently simply available for public use (Parfitt 15 June 2007). Photographs are another matter. However, since there was no evidence Sony had taken any photographs or used pre-existing copyrighted photographs, there wasn't anything the Church could do. The matter appears to have ended there, mostly unresolved.

Analysis

We can make some sense of the controversy sparked by *Resistance: Fall of Man* by considering the different ways that people engaged in the discussion encountered the "magic circle" of play. In the theoretical section, we looked at how the "magic circle" can be recognized in various activities that "set apart" performances that are experienced as different from ordinary life, and we saw the similarities that the magic circle exhibits with more formalized ritual experiences in religious contexts, the latter of which also create their own "magic circle" of sorts. The similarities games have with religious ritual are not lost on Huizinga, who follows with the observation that in a sacred performance, the participants are:

> Convinced that the action actualizes and effects a definite beatification, brings about an order of things higher than that in which they customarily live. All the same this "actualization by representation" still retains the formal characteristics of play in every respect. It is played or performed within a playground that is literally "staked out" ... A sacred space, a temporarily real world of its own, has been expressly hedged off for it. But with the end of the play its effect is not lost; rather it continues to shed its radiance on the ordinary world outside ...
>
> (1955: 108)

So here is one possible difference between ritual and game-play, and one that has significant bearing on how we interpret the events relating to the digital shoot-out: for Huizinga, in play the changes in behavior and rules are *temporary* and often viewed without lasting consequence, whereas in religious ritual, the changes are often meant to be *longer-lasting* in effect; they teach us how to be in the world, how to see ourselves in relationship to the ultimate in a life-altering kind of way. Which kind of event was the digital shoot-out? Was it a fleeting moment of inconsequential play, or a ritualized glorification of violence in a sacred (if still virtual) space?

Unfortunately, this crucial difference between ritual and play appears to depend largely upon the *intent* with which one enters into the experience, since as Stanley Tambiah notes, "we cannot in any absolute way separate ritual from non-ritual" (1981: 116). Players and/or ritual participants themselves will decide how "seriously" to take the experiences in which they engage. David Chidester claims that in today's mediated society, the sacred is increasingly something "negotiated" by individuals—the sacred is in fact produced "through the religious labor of interpretation and ritualization" (2005: 19). If Tambiah and Chidester are right, we simply *choose* what to see as a ritual, and what to see as play. Thus, it seems that we may be able to *choose* whether or not the activity will have a lasting effect on us. We can, accordingly, choose whether or not the violence portrayed in the Cathedral will have any bearing on our everyday lives. It will *not* have an effect if we see the video game as *just* a game. It *will* have an effect if we see the violent game-play as having a ritual component that spills its effects over into our daily lives.

To make things even more complicated, certain kinds of religious rituals even encourage symbolically violent or taboo behavior, such that the lasting effect (once the ritual is over) is to reorient us to the status quo. This means that one could argue that a violent video game, if it is viewed as a ritual, might even have a positive social role to play by giving people a temporary outlet for relieving stress. Ritual promotes what Victor Turner identifies as **communitas**, a "sacred" time and space that "transgresses or dissolves the norms that govern structured and institutionalized relationships and is accompanied by experiences of unprecedented potency" (1969: 128). Abiding in such a liminal (in-between) space can give people the freedom to do otherwise taboo things, giving them an outlet and voice so that when they return to ordinary time they are more content with existing social structures. Turner even gives us a reason to understand the comradeship that sometimes builds around those who engage in such taboo rituals, and we can apply his ideas to video games as well, since in both situations the "modality of relationship" appears to "flourish best in spontaneously liminal situations—phases betwixt and between states where social-structural role-playing is dominant, and especially between status equals" (1969: 138). Put simply, video games encourage us to temporarily leave aside our normal social hierarchy and see everyone playing a game as equal; therefore any violence that happens in a video game is just a sort of purging experience in which negative emotions are released in a safe environment. Such a disruption of social norms is by nature temporary, protected within what we might call the "magic circle" of the ritual experience. For Turner, then, the spillover effect of some rituals or games is simply that they give us a way of purging negative or unacceptable emotions, allowing us to return to our daily lives with greater acceptance of the limitations in them.

If we apply Turner's work on ritual to *Resistance: Fall of Man*, the argument might go something like this: games aren't ordinary life situations. Anything that happens in the game-space is simply part of a temporary (liminal) leveling of society, a sort of breakdown of normal taboos, such that we can "do" things we would not normally do. This includes the violent shootout in the cathedral. In fact, such an activity (in this view) is a healthy expression of frustration with hierarchical social structures like the church, in that it allows participants to let off steam without doing any real harm. For Turner, liminality in rituals of communitas temporarily grinds all participants down to the same level, so that the most powerful are subjected to the temporary and usually playful derision of the least powerful, representing the communitas, or interrelatedness, of all members of a group. Although no clergy are actively targeted in the game, the violence in the cathedral itself, in this safe environment, can then simply be viewed as a sort of temporary disruption of authority.

How we frame the magic circle matters a lot too, and can help us to understand why there could be such diverging views about the use of Manchester Cathedral in *Resistance: Fall of Man*. Whereas the Church of England's representatives strongly maintain that the digital *representation* of violence in the Cathedral is an offense against the *real* Cathedral, Sony holds that the game itself—as a *whole*—is its very own "magic circle," devoid of any judgments that might be made from without the game's confines. David Wilson, speaking for Sony, said in response to the Church's complaints that the shootout in the Cathedral "is game-created footage, it is not video or photography. It is entertainment, like *Doctor Who* or any other science fiction. It is not based on reality at all" (Curtis 14 June 2007). For Wilson, the game is a perfectly separate realm, a magic circle that is unaffected by and does not affect real life in any way.

So does the ritual space of the real Cathedral, a sort of special "magic circle," consist only of the physical brick and mortar building? Or do its *digital* replicas *also* exude a sort of sacredness, making any digital versions of the cathedral also a "magic circle"? Or, should we (with Sony's representative David Wilson) define the "magic circle" at work here as the *game itself*, such that any actions taken in the game have no bearing whatsoever on the real-life cathedral? It turns out that

Huizinga's ability to notice the framing and "setting apart" of ritual and play does little to help us define when we are viewing one and when we are viewing the other, or what to do when people define these arenas differently. Ultimately, it comes down to an individual's choice to define one situation as ritual and another as play.

Game theorist Chris Crawford views games in a way that more accords with Sony than with the Cathedral's representatives. For Crawford, games are closed formal systems with a fully intact magic circle, and so they *require no external referent*: "The model world created by the game is internally complete; no reference need be made to agents outside the game" (1982). The Cathedral's representatives view the violence of the shootout scene as of profound and damaging significance because of their views of the digital Church as representing the "Sacred" beyond the game; Sony, supported implicitly by Crawford, views this violence simply as one interactive scene in a very long and fictional game that has no external referents. Focusing on the "magic circle" helps us to understand Sony's defense. However, we can come closer to making sense of the Church's stance in this dispute by returning to Eliade's work on sacred and profane spaces.

If, as Eliade argues, brick and mortar sacred structures echo heavenly structures, then we could say that the physical, real-life Manchester Cathedral becomes "real" only insofar as it imitates the ultimate "Real," that is, heavenly structures like God's throne, or the heavenly Temple. A new problem emerges, however, when we consider virtual representations of sacred spaces: What are we to make of *copies of copies of* the "Real," like Sony's digital rendering of Manchester Cathedral? In other words, if the "Real" is beyond our profane world, and we can only imitate it in the building of sacred spaces that *gesture toward* the "Real," what are we to do with digital doubles of sacred spaces, like Manchester Cathedral in *Resistance: Fall of Man*, which must then be viewed as a *gesture toward a gesture toward* the "Real"? There's an odd kind of sacred "nesting" that happens here, such that the virtual Cathedral is a copy of the physical Cathedral, which is a copy of the heavenly Cathedral. How can we make sense of this? One possible answer, building upon Eliade, is that the physical copy (Manchester Cathedral) of the "Real" (the heavenly Temple) *and* the virtual copy of the physical copy of the "Real" (the virtual/video game version of Manchester Cathedral) are *both* copies, and therefore both can be seen as echoes of the "Real." This means that both can be viewed as equally sacred—since both can just as easily gesture toward the heavenly Cathedral.

The perplexing problem of how earthly sacred space relates to digital replicas of earthly sacred space lies behind the Church of England's visceral response to *Resistance: Fall of Man*'s use of Manchester Cathedral in the shootout scene. As *The Times* reports, Manchester Cathedral has in recent years worked very hard to disrupt the pattern of gun violence in the youth community of Manchester, holding special services each year in the cathedral for the families of those who have lost loved ones to gun crime (Gledhill 6 July 2007). Manchester's Dean Govender said: "We have been dismayed at those in the computer industry who have defended the use of Manchester Cathedral in this violent game. We fear that the next buildings to be cloned for virtual desecration could be a mosque, synagogue, temple, or other churches" (Gledhill 6 July 2007). Such claims depend very much upon the kinds of arguments Eliade makes, since "virtual desecration" would not be possible unless the digitized Cathedral were sacred in some way.

This point of view can be seen in the "Sacred Digital Guidelines" drawn up by the Cathedral Chapter at Manchester, which call for "respect" of physical spaces as "places of prayer, worship, peace, learning and heritage" but extend this demand for respect to include digital replicas of sacred spaces too (Gledhill 6 July 2007). Here is reflexivity at its best: the Church believes that sacred buildings are echoes of the "Sacred," so they believe that digital buildings are *also* echoes of the "Sacred"; thus, to fight in a sacred building, digital or not, is sacrilege. Sony, on the other hand, claims implicitly that the shootout falls within the "magic circle" of a fantasy game, and has no bearing on the physical cathedral at all; thus, to fight in such a digital building is acceptable. It all depends on how you look at it. Who could have predicted that video games would cause us to question the very notion of what it means to call something sacred, and relativize the answer to different situations?

If we return to Bogost's notion of "procedural rhetoric," then we find some additional clues for how to make sense of the *Resistance: Fall of Man* controversy. It seems that part of the issue here is the role of sacred space in storytelling, especially in new interactive video-game based storytelling. We can, for example, compare the digital construction of Notre Dame Cathedral in the online world *Second Life* with the digital construction of Manchester Cathedral in *Resistance: Fall of Man* as reflecting different procedural rhetoric. The *Second Life* cathedral has caused nary a stir among religious conservatives. Perhaps this is because any violence in *Second Life*'s Notre Dame Cathedral is not procedural (that is, not predetermined by a fixed script or gaming process enacted by programmers), but must be attributed to the digital shenanigans of renegade *Second Life* scripters. In *Second Life*, there is no overarching storyline determining player interactions with the Cathedral. Any violence performed against sacred space in *Second Life* is incidental, typically individual, and ephemeral.

In *Resistance: Fall of Man*, however, the violence is procedural, systemic, and obligatory in order to successfully complete the game. Put another way, the violence in *Resistance: Fall of Man* is required to make it through the interactive story, and thus every single player will wield the weapon and destroy digital church property. They have to; they have no choice if they want to win the game. The implicit sense that to perform the violence in the video game is somehow also to symbolically perform it in some real or meaningful way is the clincher here. For those who see sacred spaces as symbolically meaningful, it may not matter if the gun is symbolic too—it all has meaning, and it all says something about how the universe works and how we find ourselves in it. In other words, for the representatives of Manchester Cathedral, virtual violence is meaningful, even if nobody real is directly harmed.

The disagreements between the Church of England and Sony over *Resistance: Fall of Man* have a lot to do with the place where procedurality and the "magic circle" of play intersect. The church focuses on the *procedurality* of violence in a digitized sacred space and does not acknowledge the "magic circle" of the fantasy. Sony (and avid game-players in support of Sony) fiercely contend that the game is merely fantasy, safely ensconced in the magic circle, and therefore, they claim, it makes no difference where the battle was staged, church or not: it's all make-believe and irrelevant to daily life. For Sony's supporters, the procedurality of violence can be easily explained within the storyline of the game, and that's enough. One discussant, Daniel Carew, explains the violence: "The only way to remove these aliens from the cathedral is to use army-grade weaponry, which is exactly what the main character does." For him, one need only look at "what kind of action happened in the game, in the cathedral," to see that "Sony has done nothing wrong" (Osuh 2007). For Carew and other Sony supporters, within the magic circle of the game, the violent procedural goal of ridding a sacred area of vicious aliens is justified.

Part of the disagreement may be attributed to the fact that the Church of England's representatives were not gamers and simply watched a video of game-play that included only the level in question. Therefore, their consumption of the violent shootout was distinct from the "magic circle" of the full gaming experience, and without an appreciation for the complete procedurality of the game. It would be interesting to know if these same representatives would maintain their critiques if they became experienced enough to make it through a complete play of the game. However, the dispute may also be tapping into something even more fundamental—the way that games and religion both provide us with rules, with rituals, and with what seem to be other worlds, experienced via the imagination. Both draw upon the human desire to escape our daily lives by imagining other places, to immerse ourselves in the identity of characters that have abilities that we do not, and to create for ourselves some sense of order and meaning. Both, it seems, may be doing a kind of religious work. And as we have seen, whether or not people see a particular experience as a game or a ritual depends a lot upon the attitude with which they approach it. And similarly, whether or not they see the images portrayed in a virtual experience to be insulated from the real world or deeply connected to it depends a lot upon personal approach and perspective.

The *Resistance: Fall of Man* controversy raises a number of powerful questions about the relationship between religion and virtual reality. Representatives of Manchester Cathedral and representatives of Sony reflected very different opinions about the ability of the video game to reflect an impermeable "magic circle" of play. Representatives argue that even a digital representation of the Cathedral has "sacred" qualities that spill over into everyday life, no matter where the image is digitally portrayed. Accordingly, they argue that the "procedural rhetoric" of *Resistance: Fall of Man* has profound implications for how real people might think of the brick and mortar Cathedral situated in the streets of Manchester. Sony, on the other hand, argues that the "procedural rhetoric" of the game placed the digital Cathedral in a brand new fictional context that has no bearing whatsoever on real-life Manchester. The questions raised by this case raise even more profound issues that remain unresolved, revealing for us the complex intersections of the religious and the virtual today and refreshing age-old disputes about what is "real": Is the sacredness of a virtual space dependent upon it having a real-life original? Must sacred space be inhabitable by a physical body before we can see it as "space" and thus also as "sacred space"? What is the difference between ritual and play? How does the magic circle compare to ritual space and to sacred space? It seems that a lot depends upon how one feels about particular sacred spaces, on how one views the difficult and complex relationship between ritual and play, how one defines the relationship of real-life events to virtual ones, and indeed, even how one defines what is "real." Perhaps what is most telling about this controversy is the idea that "sacredness" today is a matter of much more negotiation and individual opinion than it used to be. What do you believe?

Summary

- Video games and religious ritual both evoke an experience of "other worlds," evoking in us a desire for temporary escape from daily life.
- In those games that depict real-life sacred spaces, new issues of interpretation arise, and those involved will likely not agree on how to settle these issues.
- Mircea Eliade's work on "sacred space" offers us a means of understanding why the Church of England was so upset about *Resistance: Fall of Man*, and thus in a more general sense, helps to enhance debates about virtual sacred space in new gaming environments.
- The concept of the "magic circle" as articulated by John Huizinga invites us to think about the close relationship between ritual and play. Those using this tool as a means of analysis would do well to think about how the frame of the magic circle is defined, and to think carefully about what (if anything) makes a particular magic circle seem insulated from the real world, and how the magic circle relates to rituals and/or to sacred space.
- Ian Bogost's work on "procedural rhetoric" invites players and critics to consider what arguments are made about the world via a particular digital gaming experience, and how these arguments may be made by the processes in which the game involves us and the choices it asks us to make. Some may argue that these choices have real-life implications in the way that they shape player perspectives about others, about the sacred, and about themselves.
- There is no easy answer to the problem of digital representation of sacred space in video game contexts; too much depends upon the opinions of the players and viewers on how video games work, on what constitutes sacred space, and on how we learn. This controversy suggests that we are just beginning to think about how virtual sacred space draws from but also complicates age-old beliefs about what is sacred and indeed, about what is "real."

Glossary terms

Archetype – an idea or image of something that is believed to be an ideal form of the thing; an original from which other copies are made.

Hajj – the hajj is the symbolically important and real life journey of Muslims to the Great Mosque in Mecca, Saudi Arabia, in which resides the black stone, believed to have been delivered from God to earth, and around which Muslims walk in worship of God as the singular Creator of the universe.

Magic circle – a term first used by Johan Huizinga to describe the idea that ritual and play both demarcate separate spaces or times in which activities happen that are insulated from the real world.

Procedural rhetoric – a term coined by game theorist Ian Bogost to describe the means by which computerized processes can argue for particular views of the world or ways of acting by leading us through predetermined and scripted interactive experiences.

Seder – a symbolically rich meal eaten by Jewish families during the celebration of Passover, which evokes memories of the safe passage of the Israelites out of bondage in Egypt and as they moved toward the Promised Land of Israel.

Points for discussion

- Can you think of any other video games or online environments that depict sacred spaces? What issues come up when you try to decide if a particular digital depiction of a sacred space is appropriate or not? Who gets to decide? Think also of other ways that media can reflect "the sacred" in profane ways, such as *South Park*'s depictions of Cartman dressed as the pope, or similarly problematic depictions in media of important religious figures like Muhammad or Buddha. Is there a significant difference between video game depiction of sacred people or things and those you find in less "interactive" media like literature, film, television, or stand-up comedy?
- Think of some examples of religious rituals. Which of them includes prescribed gestures, stories, or activities? Do you see any similarities between the "magic circle" of rituals and the "magic circle" of video game play? Why or why not?
- An interesting problem emerging today is in the matter of permissions for staging of sacred space in filmic and virtual contexts. In order to make the *Harry Potter* movies, for example, the producers had to change venues for the building upon which they intended to model Hogwarts School from the Canterbury Cathedral to the Gloucester Cathedral, because the dean of the former refused permission to film there. In video game reproductions of cathedrals, however, no such permissions are (currently) required. Should both kinds of images be subject to protections? Is there a difference between placing a sacred building in a film versus placing one in a video game?
- Sony claims that the violence that takes place in the Cathedral has nothing to do with contemporary events, since "*Resistance: Fall of Man* is a fantasy science fiction game and is not based on reality" ("Cathedral Row," *BBC News* 12 April 2011). What do you think of this claim? Does the fact that Manchester has been struggling with urban gun violence matter when considering that Sony staged this shootout in a digital version of a well-known sacred landmark?

Notes

1 For further information on the Church of England, see the Church of England Website: www.cofe.anglican.org/news/prmancath.html.
2 For further information on Manchester Cathedral, see the Manchester Cathedral Visitor Centre Website: www.mcvc.info/?s=copy.
3 Comments in this chapter regarding the extent of lawful public use of a Cathedral are the views of the author and do not necessarily represent the Church of England.

Further reading

Bogost, Ian (2007) *Persuasive Games: The Expressive Power of Videogames*, Cambridge, MA and London: The MIT Press.

This groundbreaking book offers the theoretical foundation for much of what is possible in the intersection between gaming theory and ritual theory. Bogost coins the term "procedural rhetoric," and even offers a few religious examples in the midst of his larger goal of urging critical thinking about interactive digital experiences.

Grimes, Ronald (2006) *Rite Out of Place*, Oxford University Press, 2006.

World-respected ritual theorist Ronald Grimes here applies some of his foundational ideas to emerging media, thinking especially about how television and other visual popular media can work like rituals for us, suggesting that we may be getting our religious fix in new places today, while utilizing millennia-old structures of construction and recognition of ritual.

McGonigal, Jane (2011) *Reality Is Broken*, New York: Penguin Press.

McGonigal's book is an unashamed apologetic for the socially positive possibilities of gaming. McGonigal argues that deliberately evoking gaming structures in the midst of everyday life can motivate us to create life-changing, community-building experiences. She refers only occasionally to religion, but the main interest here is how she suggests, without saying so directly, that gaming can work like religion today, and may already be doing so.

Wardrip-Fruin, Noah, and Harrigan, Pat (eds) (2004) *First Person: New Media as Story, Performance, and Game*, Cambridge, MA and London: The MIT Press.

This collection of essays by top game studies theorists and scholars in related fields will introduce you to key issues that have indirect but obvious implications for religious studies, including: narrative theory; discussions about interactivity; and debates about virtual identity.

Wolf, Mark J.P. and Perron, Bernard (eds) (2003) *The Video Game Theory Reader*, New York and London: Routledge Press.

Want to understand how storytelling is different when comparing films, video games, and written media? Want to think about how different degrees of immersion affect how we interpret gaming experience? This excellent collection of essays represents some of the best emerging theory on video games.

Bibliography

Bogost, Ian (2007) *Persuasive Games: The Expressive Power of Videogames*. Cambridge, MA and London: The MIT Press.

"Cathedral Row over Video Game" (9 June 2007) *BBC News*. Online. Available HTTP: http://news.bbc.co.uk/2/hi/uk_news/england/manchester/6736809.stm (accessed 12 April 2011).

Chidester, David (2005) *Authentic Fakes: Religion and American Popular Culture*, Berkeley, CA: University of California Press.

Church of England Website, General Synod Proceedings. Online. Available HTTP: www.cofe.anglican.org/about/gensynod/proceedings/july2007/ (accessed 6 January 2011).

The Church of England Website, News. Online. Available HTTP: www.cofe.anglican.org/news/prmancath.html (accessed 6 January 2011).

Crawford, Chris (1982) *The Art of Computer Game Design*, Currently maintained online by Washington State University Vancouver. Available HTTP: www.vancouver.wsu.edu/fac/peabody/game-book/Coverpage.html#TOC (accessed 23 June 2008).

Curtis, Gretta (14, June 2007) "The Church of England Urges Japan to Join Campaign Against Sony," *Christian Today*. Online. Available HTTP: www.christiantoday.com/article/the.church.of.england.urges.japan.to.join.campaign.against.sony/11127.htm (accessed 6 January 2011).

Eliade, Mircea (1987) *The Sacred and the Profane*, Houghton, Mifflin, Harcourt.

——(2005) *The Myth of the Eternal Return: Cosmos and History*, trans. Willard R. Trask, Bollingen Series, Princeton: Princeton University Press.

Filiciak, Miroslaw (2003) "Hyperidentities: Postmodern Identity Patterns in Massively Multiplayer Online Role-Playing Games," in Mark J.P. Wolf and Bernard Perron (eds) *The Video Game Theory Reader*, New York and London: Routledge Press, 87–102.

Gledhill, Ruth (15 June 2007) "Sony Apologises Over Cathedral Computer Game," *Times Online*. Online. Available HTTP: www.timesonline.co.uk/tol/comment/faith/article1940286.ece (accessed 23 March 2008).

——(6 July 2007) "Manchester Cathedral Says Sony Apology Not Enough and Issues New Digital Rules," *Times Online*. Online. Available HTTP: www.timesonline.co.uk/tol/comment/faith/article2036423.ece (accessed 20 March 2008).

Grodal, Torben (2003) "Stories for Eye, Ear and Muscles: Video Games, Media, and Embodied Experiences," in Mark J.P. Wolf and Bernard Perron (eds) *The Video Game Theory Reader*, New York and London: Routledge, 129–155.

Huizinga, Johan (1955) *Homo Ludens: A Study of the Play Element in Culture*, Boston: Beacon Press.

Lahti, Martii (2003) "As We Become Machines: Corporealized Pleasures in Video Games," in Mark J.P. Wolf and Bernard Perron (eds) *The Video Game Theory Reader*, New York and London: Routledge Press, 157–170.

Manchester Cathedral Visitor Centre Website. Online. Available HTTP: www.mcvc.info/?s=copy (accessed 20 February 2011).

Osuh, Chris (6 July 2007) "Sony Says 'Sorry,'" *Manchester Evening News*. Online. Available HTTP: http://menmedia.co.uk/manchestereveningnews/news/s/1010/1010666_sony_says_sorry_.html (accessed 11 August 2010).

Pals, Daniel (2006) *Eight Theories of Religion*, New York: Oxford University Press.

Parfitt, Ben (15 June 2007) "A Legal View on the Sony Church Row," *MCV*, 15. Online. Available HTTP: www.mcvuk.com/news/27531/A-legal-view-on-the-Sony-Church-row (accessed 18 October 2010).

Rehak, Bob (2003) "Playing at Being: Psychoanalysis and the Avatar," in Mark Wolf and Bernard Perron (eds) *The Video Game Theory Reader*, New York and London: Routledge, 103–128.

Salen, Katie and Eric Zimmerman (2003) *Rules of Play: Game Design Fundamentals*, Cambridge, MA and London: The MIT Press.

"Shops Take Hitman 2 Game off the Shelves" (21 November 2002) *BBC News*. Online. Available HTTP: http://news.bbc.co.uk/cbbcnews/hi/sci_tech/newsid_2500000/2500199.stm (accessed 4 March 2011).

Smith, Jonathan Z. (2005) "Introduction," in Mircea Eliade, *The Myth of the Eternal Return: Cosmos and History*, trans. Willard R. Trask, Bollingen Series, Princeton: Princeton University Press.

Sugden, Joanna (11 June 2007) "Church Threatens to Sue Sony Over 'Sick' Video Game," *Times Online*. Online. Available HTTP: www.timesonline.co.uk/tol/comment/faith/article1916001.ece (accessed 14 October 2010).

"Talks Over Cathedral Gun Game Row" (10 June 2007) *BBC News*. Online. Available HTTP: http://news.bbc.co.uk/2/hi/uk_news/england/manchester/6738669.stm (accessed 7 July 2009).

Tambiah, Stanley (1981) "A Performative Approach to Ritual," in *Proceedings of the British Academy* 65, Oxford: Oxford University Press, 113–169.

Turner, Victor (1969) *The Ritual Process: Structure and Anti-Structure*, Chicago: Aldine Publishing Company.

9 The Coca-Cola brand and religion

Jeffrey Scholes

Introduction

Brand logos are now so ubiquitous in Western society that it is difficult to imagine our visual landscape and our lives without them. From the Golden Arches to the Ford logo on the front of a car to an apple on the outside of a laptop to Ralph Lauren's Polo insignia on each piece of clothing they make—corporate brands are everywhere you look. Brands do not show up only on the outside of a product though. They appear in television commercials. They are found on billboards that dot our highways. They are plastered all over race cars. They can even be a "character" in movies that have conspicuous product placements shown on the screen. Some people view the brand saturation of our public spaces as an annoying, even immoral, intrusion, some barely notice brands at all anymore, and some gladly use brands to help them express themselves or to direct them on what to buy.

Corporate brands are unique cultural expressions. Unlike some forms of music, movies, television shows or professional sports to name a few, brands rarely enter the realm of pop culture haphazardly, organically or reluctantly. Brands are signs, logos, symbols, etc., that serve as the *identity* of a product or service. Hence brands are carefully constructed by companies and their marketing/advertising apparatus to generate the kind of meaning that will garner consumer loyalty. This is not to say that music bands and sports teams don't use brands to sell their wares—they often do. But with music and sports, a brand is usually not the *principal* medium through which these cultural forms are sold—it is the music or performance of a team itself that makes them popular. With major brands like Coca-Cola, the taste of the drink and the look of the bottle matters but they matter less than the *meaning* of the brand, which encourages consumers to think of the relationship between themselves and the product in a deeper way.

Deep, yes, but "religious deep"? James Twitchell says yes:

> Brand stories act like religion not just by holding people together but also by holding individual experiences together … We cluster around them [brands] as we used to cluster around sacred relics; we are loyal to them the way we are loyal to symbols such as the flag; we live through, around, and against them. Brands have become members of the new and improved family of man.
>
> (Twitchell 2004: 24–25)

Have brands integrated into our lives to the point that they "act like religion"? Or stated in another way, does the power that certain brands have to hold people and individual experiences together constitute *religious* power? If so, what is the nature of the relationship between a secular brand like Coca-Cola and religion?

This chapter will first address the issue of corporate brands as a popular cultural product and whether we need to ask different questions of brands than we do other, less debatable expressions of popular culture such as movies or books. Then it will examine David Chidester's definition of religion and his method for integrating popular culture and religion that he puts forth in his book *Authentic Fakes* (2005). Based on both his definition and method, Chidester boldly states that Coca-Cola "does the work of religion," and is even religion itself. The chapter will end with an analysis of the relationship between corporate brands and religion with suggestions on how we can understand the relationship using Chidester's approach.

Theory and method

First we need clarification on the meaning of the word, "brand." It is true that almost all businesses, no matter the size, present some kind of sign to the public (even if it is only the name of the business in plain font) that not only identifies the business but also distinguishes it in some way. Think of McDonald's arches or the arrangement of "V" and "W" in the logo for Volkswagen. In addition, each product or service provided by the company is also accompanied by its own sign to distinguish it from similar goods and services provided by competing companies. A brand, of course, needs to be recognizable, but according to Douglas B. Holt, a brand has success in the marketplace when, "various 'authors' tell stories that involve the brand" or a collective narrative or story begins to build around the brand (Holt 2004: 3). The storytellers can be customers, critics, sellers or the company itself, and it is in and through these stories that a brand embeds itself into the personal narrative of a consumer—often without anyone noticing the intrusion. Holt writes, "Brand stories have plots and characters, and they rely heavily on metaphor to communicate and to spur our imaginations. As these stories collide in everyday social life, conventions eventually form" (Holt 2004: 3).

Holt adds that successful brands typically perform something for the consumer that would otherwise go unaccomplished or not be recognized at all as something that needs to be accomplished. Beyond conveying the mere use value of the product or service, successful brands communicate a deeper value to consumers. In fact, modern branding has less and less to do with the product and more and more to do with generating a profound meaning around a product (Klein 2002: 4).

These brands not only have to "embody the ideas [that consumers] admire," but also "help [consumers] express who they want to be" (Holt 2004: 4). A deeper need is met here by brands that contribute to one's identity or this sense of who one is, brands that Holt calls "identity brands" (Holt 2004: xi). There are a few identity brands that graduate into what Holt calls "**iconic brands**" when they appeal to larger segments of the society, or actually contribute to the identity of a community, even a nation (Holt 2004: xi). Apple, Nike, Budweiser, McDonald's, Coca-Cola and a few others are iconic because they act as a medium through which consumers can construct desirable identities for themselves, and they do it by creating a mythical aura around the brand. This aura, whether it be historical (how the brand came to be), character-driven (who is running the company, who is buying the product), or functional (what the product can do for you), helps make a brand iconic through the use of legendary stories, whether they are actually true or not. And it is these legendary stories that we as consumers tell, as we attempt to locate the brand in our own story.

Think of the Apple computer brand. The advertising campaign for its Mac computer asks viewers to identify either with the cool "Mac guy" or the awkward "PC guy." Once I say or think that "I'm a Mac person too!" then the Mac is, to a degree, now a part of my personal narrative. I not only may buy a Mac to ensure that in fact I'm a Mac person, but I also will use what it means to be a "Mac person" to differentiate myself from "PC people." Thus the story of the Apple brand becomes my story. Other storytellers add to my story and before long, a more collective, more compelling story builds around the brand. For instance, the band Atomic Tom gained fame after their video of playing a song on a New York City subway using only their Apple iPhones as instruments went viral.[1] In this case, an Apple product acts as the medium through which the members of Atomic Tom were able to express and promote themselves. In addition, the iPhone also helps bridge the band to its fans, who may admire their use of the devices and use iPhones themselves just like the band! In both of these ways, the iPhone, and by extension the Apple brand, becomes an integral part of the story that the members of Atomic Tom and its fans weave for themselves, tell themselves, and understand themselves through.

Even if we grant that iconic brands are able to do some of the serious work of identity construction for their loyal users, this does not necessarily mean that iconic brands are automatically a part of popular culture. John Storey's tentative list of criteria that cultural items need to possess in order to be popular is helpful here. For starters, the definition of "popular" dictates that popular cultural items need to be "favored or well-liked by many people" (Storey 2009: 5–6). We would have trouble saying that a poem read by one's girlfriend is popular in any meaningful sense. Yet problems accompany this simple criterion such as the hazy determination of the threshold of people needed to make something "popular" or the difficulty connecting raw numbers (sales of an album, for instance) with the kind of likeability of a cultural product to justify its entrance into the realm of pop culture. Despite these legitimate concerns, Story asserts that any definition of popular culture "must include a quantitative dimension" (Storey 2009: 7). Otherwise the term "popular" is meaningless. It is safe to say that iconic brands by definition have already reached a large audience that likes the product, as displayed through purchasing decisions. Therefore iconic brands are already popular cultural icons once having reached the iconic level.

Most would answer the question of whether Coca-Cola is a part of popular culture in the affirmative. Not only is it the most popular brand on Facebook (based on how many people "like" it),[2] but it has also been ranked as the most powerful global brand in terms of its financial worth.[3] Yet the Coca-Cola logo is not merely some writing on the side of a red can. Nor is Coke merely the brown, carbonated liquid inside each can or bottle. The recognizable insignia is used by its marketing department and advertising agency to convey ideas of happiness, American patriotism, and belonging to a global community that come along with drinking Coke. When we "participate" with the Coca-Cola brand, we may be able to participate in these ideas too. And based on its popularity, apparently the Coca-Cola brand is and has historically succeeded in making the Coca-Cola brand into something that far transcends a can of Coke. Indeed, the Coca-Cola brand is as popular as ever *and* has entered culture in a profound way.

In addition to consumer likeability of Coke, the producers of Coca-Cola contribute to its status as a popular cultural item. Iconic brands such as Coca-Cola are produced for a mass audience—another of Storey's possible requirements for entrance into popular culture (Storey 2009: 8–9). Perhaps more than any other cultural expression, iconic brands are modified throughout their tenure to trigger the most general, yet still deeply felt needs in the largest number of consumers possible. Because advertising departments cannot feasibly tailor a product or ad to each individual consumer, brands are meant to appeal to general needs and desires of a mass (or undifferentiated) audience. The difference between iconic corporate brands and most other cultural symbols that resonate in a healthy number of people is that iconic corporate brands (their physical markings and message) are constructed by corporations *solely* in order to reach a mass audience. Other kinds of cultural products that have similarly reached a mass audience such as movies or music or sports teams may have been produced with the hope of appealing to such an audience, but this is not necessarily the sole motive guiding all successful artistic ventures. Not so with iconic brands.

As the name "popular culture" suggests, that which "originates from 'the people'" seemingly should be a natural candidate for entrance into popular culture (Storey 2009: 12). In fact, as Storey points out, some consider the culture that is being produced by the people, instead of "something imposed on 'the people' from above" to be the only kind of popular culture (Storey 2009: 12). Think of folk music as opposed to a boy band assembled and packaged by a music studio. If Storey is correct in connecting popular culture with that which comes from the people, then brands may not fit this bill since they clearly have a "top-down" delivery system to the consumer.

But, Storey asks, what does it mean to say that something "originates from 'the people'" in today's culture? Perhaps in days past and in some small pockets of Western society today, cultural items were actually produced by the common person or community. However, in today's society, it is nearly impossible to find cultural materials with which to express yourself or your group that have not been touched or more likely, produced by a corporation (think Facebook). Storey writes, "The fact remains that people do not spontaneously produce culture from raw materials they make themselves. Whatever popular culture is, what is certain is that its raw materials are those which are commercially provided" (Storey 2009: 12). In almost all certainty, the music of today's folk musician is played on a commercially produced instrument. In other words, it is near impossible to avoid some element of "top-down" commercialization in the production of cultural items these days.

In the case of brands, those who take the stance that popular culture *must* "come from the people" would more than likely balk at the suggestion that brands are a part of popular culture because they come directly from corporations. On the other hand, some would argue that brands do come from the people because we make or break a brand through our purchasing power. Another way to look at popular culture is "as a site of struggle between the forces of resistance of subordinate groups in society, and the forces of incorporation of dominant groups in society" (Storey 2009: 13). Brands and those who own/control them are clearly one of these sites of struggle, with the battle lines being drawn between the producers of the product/brand and the consumers.

There is no doubt that a "top-down" strategy meant to cultivate the popularity of a brand is employed by corporations. Through the look and feel of the product/brand, the seductive psychological tactics used to promote the brand, and the level of brand saturation in public spaces, corporations possess quite a bit of control over how popular their brand becomes and remains. While it is true that corporations extensively use focus groups composed of regular people to guide some of their decisions, there is no question as to who has the *final* say on the brand's marketing image.

Alternatively, the consumers who buy the products of iconic brands certainly help with the brand's success. Aside from the power wielded by the consumer at the point of purchase, consumers can manipulate the image of a brand in order to communicate a different message than the company wants to send with its brand. In one example, the magazine *Adbusters* printed a mock poster of a runner wearing Nike shoes, and over her image was a message about how Nikes are produced in Indonesian sweatshops.[4] The famous Nike swoosh is at the bottom of the image and the lettering looks official at first glance. Yet *Adbusters* uses the Nike logo merely to expose the company's alleged exploitative manufacturing practices. The meaning of the Nike brand, when appropriated in this way, is the prize in a contest over control of the brand between the corporation and the people. Brands, then, also fit Storey's definition of pop culture as a "site of [ideological] struggle" (Storey 2009: 12–13).

Storey cites several more possible criteria for considering something as popular culture, but these three already cited are enough to classify brands, especially iconic brands, as legitimate candidates for popular cultural status. But the question still remains as to whether brands, as popular cultural expressions, have anything to do with religion. This is where the work of David Chidester, one of the preeminent commentators on religion and popular culture, is most helpful. While Chidester is not the only scholar to inquire into the religious significance of brands, he is one of the few who has attempted to integrate in his analysis the three components of religion, popular culture, and corporate brands. We'll now look at Chidester's definition of religion as well as his method of integrating popular culture and religion before we look at how Coca-Cola fits into his work.

Chidester offers a **functional definition of religion**: it provides "ways of being a human person in a human place" (Chidester 2005: vii). This definition is functional because it defines religion by saying what it *does* as opposed to what religion *is*. Chidester claims that a part of being a human entails the reckoning with the sheer limits of being human. We struggle with restrictions placed upon our freedom, we suffer and we die. Religion helps us to cope with these human realities by being "an arena of human activity marked by the concerns of the transcendent, the sacred, the ultimate—concerns that enable people to experiment with what it means to be human" (Chidester 2005: 1). All three "concerns" of religion, the transcendent, the sacred, and the ultimate, put us into a certain relationship with our ordinary, mundane concerns.

> Religious ways of being human engage the transcendent—that which rises above and beyond the ordinary. They engage the sacred—that which is set apart from the ordinary. And they engage the ultimate—that which defines the final, unavoidable limit of all our ordinary concerns.
>
> (Chidester 2005: 1).

When we engage any of these three, we gain a perspective, a bird's-eye view if you will, on our ordinary human situation, which can be instructive to us about what it means to be a human that otherwise could not be perceived. Thus, when religion puts us into contact with that which is "set apart from the ordinary," it opens up new ways of being a human in a human place. For example, the burning bush put Moses into contact with God by elevating him above his ordinary existence in the desert (Exodus 3:1–6).

Chidester contends that religion accomplishes its main function by doing three primary tasks. Religion helps us to be human in a human place by forming a human community, focusing human desire, and entering us into human relations of exchange (Chidester 2005: 2, 5). To extend the burning bush example, the bush, as a **mediator** of religion, focuses Moses' desire immediately and profoundly. This focus, unlike the kind homed in on ordinary bushes, is the kind that puts Moses in a position to experience the divine. Here, religion focuses desire through ordinary materials (a bush and a fire) in a unique way that allows Moses to encounter the sacred.

A burning bush is one thing, but a popular cultural item is something altogether different ... or is it? Chidester contends that popular culture can act as a go-between from humanity to the transcendent/sacred/ultimate. Yet he anticipates the question: "How does the serious work of religion, which engages the transcendent, the sacred, and the ultimate meaning in the face of death, relate to the comparatively frivolous play of popular culture" (Chidester 2005: 1–2)?

Chidester admits that popular culture is an odd mediator of religion at first glance. Unlike the mediators which have been legitimized and upheld by traditional, long-standing religious institutions (the Church as the institution and priests as its mediators, for example), pop culture expressions seem to come and go based on the whims of an impatient public. The fleeting authority of many pop culture symbols seem to make them unreliable foot soldiers in the building of communities, whether they actually have staying power (think James Dean) or not (think Paris Hilton). Odd as they may be as mediators of religion, Chidester firmly maintains that popular culture can do religious work.

He looks at baseball as a church (human community), Coca-Cola as a religious **fetish** (focuses human desire) and rock 'n' roll as that which gives itself freely to fans (brokers human relations of exchange) in order to argue that these and other expressions of popular culture do indeed perform religious work. But again, how could anyone find any semblance of authentic religion in popular culture? Chidester seems to sympathize with the spirit of this question when he states that,

> Baseball is not a religion; Coca-Cola is not a religion; and rock 'n' roll is not a religion. But then all kinds of religious activity have been denied the status of religion ... What counts as religion, therefore, is the focus of the problem of authenticity in religion and American popular culture.
>
> (Chidester 2005: 9)

Here, Chidester is stating that "Coca-Cola is not a religion," not to blatantly contradict his previous statement that Coke is a religion, but to make a larger point. Of course Coca-Cola is not a religion by most accounts, but then again Christianity was also not considered legitimate in its early stages. Hence the rejection of some practice, belief, or in this case, a brand as a religion may be short-sighted. What matters for Chidester is the *process* by which we arrive at the truth. When we ask whether Coca-Cola (or early Christianity for that matter) is a religion or not, the answer to the question matters less than whether popular culture can help us arrive at the truth about religion. Thus, even clear fakes, forgeries, or inauthentic mediators can still carry us towards the truth as well as purported authentic ones.

For instance the founder of the intentionally subversive "Holy Order of the Cheeseburger," a new religion originally created on the internet as a joke, actually used this "fake" religion to find the truth about religion in general. The founder states, "I originally started this site to give people an alternative to crazy religions with an even crazier religion ... So my journey began" (Chidester 2005: 208). Even though the journey began as a satirical knock on what he considered "crazy religions," the HOC founder moved from a tongue-in-cheek internet offering to pursue a real search for one true religion. Then another turn of events occurs, as Chidester recounts:

> As a result of that search for the one authentic religion in the world, the founder of the HOC decided to shut down the fake religion he had created in the virtual world of the Internet. As a result of what he had learned through his personal search for the one true religion, he was no longer prepared to offer an invented religion as if it were true. "My search has yielded the following results," the founder of the order revealed. "Religion is bullshit!"
>
> (Chidester 2005: 208)

Despite the anarchic, iconoclastic conclusion reached by the founder, Chidester uses this example to support the claim that even fake popular cultural expressions can serve as mediators of religious truth. Granted, the founder's journey does not lead him to belief in one true religion or even in religion at all. But the result counts less for Chidester than the fact that it was a phony internet religion that initiated and mediated a serious search for a true religion. We could easily speculate that the HOC helped form a community (the followers of the religion on the net), focus desire around a silly object posing as a religious object, and put the founder into human relations of exchange with the HOC's members to whom he finally reveals the truth about religion. Finally, it is the HOC that helps carry the founder from a position of mockery to seriousness regarding religion. This path ultimately leads to total cynicism, but it is the creation of a frivolous internet religion that initiates the serious religious work and culminates in a realization of the truth about religion for him.

Chidester asks us to treat inauthentic cultural expressions which make up much of popular culture with a kind of equanimity. To reject the possibility that fleeting, often silly and even fake expressions of popular culture can function religiously is to forget that the entire project of searching for authentic religion is widely varied. Chidester is not making any kind of metaphysical association between religion and popular culture; the current role of popular culture in mediating religion is a contingent one. Yet no matter for Chidester—he is merely shedding light on examples from popular culture that perform the work of religion as he defines it.

David Chidester and the religious work of Coca-Cola

Chidester claims that the Coca-Cola brand has similarly accomplished and continues to accomplish the tasks of religious work by presenting its primary product as a kind of global fetish. A fetish is a material object that is believed to possess supernatural or magical power or even power that goes beyond what the material object is capable of generating given its material properties alone. Introduced as a term to describe the practices of some West African tribes in the 18th century, a fetish can be anything from blood to bones to man-made objects that can be worshipped, feared, or believed to perform magic. Today, the word "fetish" is often either associated with abnormal sexual proclivities or with the behavior of practitioners of indigenous religions who mistakenly think that crystals or voodoo dolls hold the power to affect the material world.

Yet as Chidester reminds us, many more kinds of objects are fetishized whether we realize it or not. For instance Marx's famous exposure of commodities produced in capitalistic economies as fetishes, what he calls **"the fetishism of commodity,"** helps Chidester make the point that the material products of certain brands can act as fetishes for consumers (Marx 1992: 163–165). It is branding that endows a commodity like a Polo shirt with more power than an insignia-less shirt from the Gap, despite the fact that both shirts are made of the same material. Or it is advertising plus branding that converts another commodity like an Apple computer into an item that tells people who they are or who they should be. In this way, material objects transcend their mere material properties and can actually "provide ways of being a human in a human place." Hence for Chidester,

> [A]dvertising-as-religion has turned "fetishism of commodities" into a way of life. In the symbolic system of modern capitalist society, which advertising animates, commodities are lively objects. Like the fetish, the commodity is an object of religious regard.
>
> (Chidester 2005: 42)

Granted, a Mac(intosh) may not cause the immediate and profound reaction that a burning bush would, but it does allow new ways of creating human identities through the focusing of desire on a material object. And for Chidester, this is all that is necessary for a religious fetish to do its work on us.

And because commodities transcend their mere use value as a material item when we differentiate them based on nothing more than the brand, Chidester has trouble distinguishing West African fetishes from branded items in any meaningful way. Hence in the consumption of the products of iconic brands or in the consumption of popular cultural items, "ordinary objects can be transformed into icons, extraordinary magnets of meaning with a religious cast. In conjunction with these objects of popular culture, the term religion seems appropriate because it signals a certain quality of attention, desire, and even reverence for sacred materiality" (Chidester 2005: 34). Not all commodities as fetishes are created equal, though.

A bottle of Coke—if you only consider its material properties, such as the glass, bottle cap, writing on the side, and the cola inside the bottle—does not have the ability alone to become a fetish. However, as Chidester points out, "from the beginning, the beverage was enveloped in a sacred aura" (Chidester 2005: 40). Its flavoring formula, shrouded in secrecy since the drink's inception in 1886 (and including cocaine from 1886 to 1902), created a unique taste combined with a promise of medicinal healing properties (Pendergrast 2000: 57). But for Coke to become more than a tasty medicine (or for it to become truly fetishized) the Coke brand needed to seep deeper into people's consciousness—or become iconic.

Echoing Holt, Chidester cites historic examples of the Coca-Cola brand becoming a part of national and personal narratives, thereby further protecting the "sacred aura" of Coke from scrutiny or cynicism (it's only cola after all!). For instance, Coca-Cola became a beacon of the American dream to soldiers serving overseas during World War II. It almost single-handedly created the plump, jolly, bearded image of a man that Americans now know as Santa Claus.[5] This countered earlier representations of Santa as a thinner, somewhat dour figure, and helped connect Coke to Santa as a jovial giver of gifts. As the "pause that refreshes," it helped break postwar work routines that tended towards monotony. And in the 1960s, Coke promised to "build a better world in perfect harmony" with the use of diverse peoples holding hands in a circle at a time of cataclysmic social strife in America (Pendergrast 2000: 300). These purported effects, the cult-like atmosphere that protected its secrets from the public, and of course, Coca-Cola's growing ubiquity through advertising and mere presence in soda fountains in the late nineteenth century United States all conspired to build, protect, and maintain the sacred aura that turns Coke into a fetish. And as fetishes "focus desire" for Chidester, Coca-Cola has done a stunning job of fetishizing itself. As Constance L. Hays writes,

> [A]round the world, Coke crossed the line between consumer product and object of desire. It imprinted itself upon cultures everywhere, appearing in movies, in literature, in paintings and sculpture, and in the lyrics of songs. Well before the Coca-Cola Company marked its one hundredth anniversary, all kinds of people could see that Coca-Cola possessed an image that exceeded the sum of its parts.
>
> (Hays 2005: xi)

Unlike the "church" of baseball or the "unconditioned gift" offered by rock 'n' roll, Coke-as-fetish mediates our relationship to the sacred through a material object (Chidester 2005: 33–34). Chidester contends that Coca-Cola is a sacred sign. It is:

> The fetish of a global religion, an icon of the West, a symbol that can mark an initiatory entry into modernity. Through massive global exchanges and specific local effects, the religion of Coca-Cola has placed its sacred fetish all over the world.
>
> (Chidester 2005: 42)

Chidester cites the 1980 movie, *The Gods Must Be Crazy*, as proof positive that the aura surrounding Coke's genesis and the aggressive advertising strategy to maintain the aura has worked to fetishize the Coca-Cola brand. It is a Coke bottle that falls out of the sky into the middle of an African Bushmen village in the movie. The bottle becomes an object of curiosity and worship for the villagers—a fetish (Chidester 2005: 42). Yes, for the villagers, any soda bottle (or even any foreign object) falling out of the sky could have presumably been fetishized. But for the movie audience, it is a Coke bottle in particular that adds to the fetish quality of the object both for the villagers and for the audience too. Why?

Chidester notes that the Coke brand represents something beyond its sheer novelty in the African bush: "Here we find Coke as a sacred sign, a sign subject to local misreading, perhaps, but nevertheless the fetish of a global religion, an icon of the West, a symbol that can mark an initiatory entry into modernity" (Chidester 2005: 42). The fetish quality of the bottle, then, is expressed in Coca-Cola's ability to carry symbolically a group of people out of the past and into the future—even if this is only transmitted symbolically to the movie audience. Either way, whether an African tribe is brought into modernity by a Coke bottle or the Coca-Cola brand acts as the carrier of the tribe to the movie audience, the Coke bottle is acting as a fetish that focuses the desire of both groups in order to convey something about what it means to be a human being.

Another way to look at the Coca-Cola brand in the movie is that it can relieve the pressure placed on developing countries to cross the threshold of the global market (and way of life). As at different junctures in American history, Coca-Cola has had and continues to have the power to forge communal bonds through the shared experience of drinking Coke. Virtual, abstract, and imagined as this kind of community is, it is a community nonetheless, Chidester contends. And based on his definition of religion, we know that the work of religion—brokering relationships between humanity and the sacred—occurs in and through communities. A fetish is what focuses the collective desires of a community, which then not only helps to bind a community but also transports the members of the community from mere material concerns to question their place in the global community. For Chidester, this is the primary function of religion, and the Coca-Cola brand, which fetishizes Coke products, does this especially well.

Fetishes, like popular cultural artifacts, however, are inherently unstable. The instability of the fetish is again attributable to the process in which it comes about; fetishes are typically either "made" by human hands or are material in nature. Either way, a fetish will not last forever because of its inextricable tie to materiality. Hence the surplus meaning that they carry is constantly under the threat of being exposed as an artificial product of human beings or a mere material object that will undergo deterioration. Though predictably, Chidester views this relationship between Coke-as-fetish and religion as one not to be rejected for its instability but further investigated.

He concludes by using Clifford Geertz's classic definition of religion as a point of departure for what he really wants to say. Geertz defines religion as:

> (1) a system of symbols which acts to (2) establish powerful, pervasive, and long-lasting moods and motivations in men by (3) formulating conceptions of a general order of existence and (4) clothing these conceptions with such an aura of factuality that (5) the moods and motivations seem uniquely realistic.
>
> (Geertz 1977: 90)

Chidester lifts the part about "moods and motivations" to make a point about the unique religious quality of fetishes.

> Unlike the historical continuity and social solidarity represented by the church, there, instability is the inherent nature of a religion modeled around the fetish. As an object of indeterminate meaning and variable value, the fetish represents an unstable center for a shifting constellation of religious symbols. Although the fetishized object might inspire religious moods and motivations, it is constantly at risk of being unmasked as something made and therefore as an artificial focus for religious desire. The study of religion in popular culture is faced with the challenge of exploring and explicating the ways in which such "artificial" religious constructions can generate genuine enthusiasms and produce real effects in the world.
>
> (Chidester 2005: 43)

Instead of harboring suspicion that a Coca-Cola bottle can create "pervasive and long-lasting" moods and even forge stable communities, thus do real religious work in Geertzian fashion, Chidester uses our own suspicion that Coca-Cola can act as a religion to inquire into what authentic religion is. Again "inauthentic" products of popular culture, such as the Coca-Cola brand, can "produce real effects" even if only temporarily. The task is not to spurn such popular cultural expressions for their shallowness, instability, or their short shelf-lives but to learn more about how authentic religion can possibly emerge from such inauthentic processes. If we agree with Chidester that religion brokers a relationship with the transcendent/sacred/ultimate, then we may have to admit that even secular and fleeting cultural expressions can perform this task. And if we admit this, then Coca-Cola is certainly performing this task well.

Commentary

Is Chidester onto something here? Is he providing a unique as well as profound way to understand religion's relationship with popular culture? Or instead is he exaggerating the power of popular culture and its branded fetishes to do actual religious work? Can unstable carriers of religion transport passengers to the stable shores of the transcendent?

First, Chidester should be commended for mining the popular cultural terrain for its encoded religious messages. Too often, the world of pop culture is dismissed by scholars and lay practitioners alike for its seeming disconnect from anything holy. It is true that one has to look harder for the religious elements of *Star Trek* than for those in the Lord's Prayer. Yet Chidester not only looks hard, he gives us a way to describe religion that permits the kinds of points of contact between religion and popular culture that he is after.

Chidester also addresses the thorny problem brought forth by the skeptic who justifiably questions whether any iconic brand, so produced and packaged to woo customers, can have anything to do with religion. He plays the skeptic when he writes,

> In the best tradition of American advertising, the Coca-Cola Company has created the desire for a product that no one needs. Even if it has led to the "Cocacolonization" of the world, this manipulation of desire through effective advertising has nothing to do with religion.
>
> (Chidester 2005: 42)

So the skeptic can rightfully claim. Yet for Chidester, skepticism comes at the cost of ignoring the pervasive reality and scope of brand saturation and penetration that can only have profound effects on all of us, both positive and negative. So instead of pretending that brand culture (and popular culture by extension) is a phase that must be overcome if true religion is to be sought, Chidester resigns himself to the reality that religion exists in this most unlikely realm of popular culture.

He could have also answered the skeptic by arguing that religion has *always* been mediated by cultural forms. Whether it be icons in particular or simply the general culture at any given time that acts as the lens through which religious objects are viewed or the crucible in which religious practices gain their time-bound character, religion and culture have always been inextricably tied (Davaney 2001: 9). That popular culture generally, and iconic brands specifically, are currently powerful, even totalizing social forces is no reason to suddenly abandon the historical truth about the culture/religion relationship. Pop culture is simply what we have at this moment to guide us into the places where religion is still occurring.

Chidester's valorization of popular culture as it pertains to religion may not pose any real theoretical problem. In addition, his exposing of an inconsistency at the heart of arguments that reject popular culture as too shallow and artificial to do religious work is helpful. Established, legitimized methods of finding and then authenticating religions have long been under attack (Smith 1988: 102–120). Through honoring even the most deceptive, slick, and fraudulent popular cultural expressions, Chidester makes clear that religion can be authenticated and judged by its fruits, not its roots.

There is a problem, however, with Chidester's claim that the Coca-Cola brand is able to do the work of religion which has to do with the way that the fetish is created as well as Chidester's own definition of religion. Chidester downplays the need for fetishes to generate long-standing, stable religious belief systems and communities. As long as "moods and motivations" are produced by a fetish that clarifies what it means to be a human in a human place, even for a brief time, Chidester would claim that religious work is going on—even if the motivation created is to drink Coke. Hence in his push to question the methods we use to judge religious authenticity, Chidester leaves out the adjectives that Geertz uses to describe real religious moods and motivations: "powerful, pervasive, and long-lasting." Geertz attaches these attributes to religion for one main reason. The transcendent/sacred/ultimate is, in a sense, powerful, pervasive and long-lasting (or infinite for some). Thus any mood or motivation that is religious in a meaningful way must also have these traits. He writes that, "motivations are 'made meaningful' with reference to the ends toward which they are conceived to conduce" (Geertz 1977: 97). The ends, as Chidester also claims, of religion are sacred things, hence truly religious motivations are meaningful when they are powerful, pervasive and long-lasting. Otherwise, we would have trouble differentiating religious motivations from short lived motivations such as to eat a cheeseburger or buy a Coke. Geertz again claims: "A man [sic] can indeed be said to be 'religious' about golf, but not merely if he pursues it with passion and plays it on Sundays; he must also see it as symbolic of some transcendent truths" (Geertz 1977: 98). Coca-Cola may invoke passion in some, but as an unstable fetish, it does not sustain a kind of long-lasting motivation that rightly connects it to transcendent truths—Coke as a brand and the transcendent are incompatible here.

It is true that some fetishes are able to sustain a relationship with the sacred for long periods of time. However in the case of a statue of the Virgin Mary or a totemistic animal used by indigenous religions, these fetishized objects are believed to act as a window to the sacred. Or they are transparent to an eternal God or an eternal ancestral spirit. The sacred undergirds and sustains pervasive, long-lasting religious beliefs, motivations and actions that are aided by a relationship to a fetish. Therefore, belief in the power of religious fetishes, whether they actually reveal the sacred or not, can be pervasive and long-standing, despite the fact that the material that makes up the fetish will break down with time.

Coca-Cola as a fetish does not enjoy such a transparent relationship with the sacred because it lacks the credibility needed for someone to believe that it is a window to the sacred. If Coca-Cola is transparent to anything, it is to its corporation, which is behind everything that the brand means. As noted earlier, with iconic brands, there are several storytellers who create the meaning of the brand. And while consumers and critics do contribute to the meaning of an iconic brand, the unquestioned champion storyteller is the corporation itself (Ewen 2001: 51–55). The production, advertising, marketing, and distribution are all activities geared directly to making Coca-Cola into a fetish that transcends Coke as a mere product in order for more Coca-Cola to be sold. And lest there be any doubt about who is in charge of the meaning of the Coca-Cola brand, Hays sets us straight.

> Through relentless advertising, clever marketing, and sometimes plain old luck, Coke came to stand for the glamorous, prosperous, flag-waving side of America, the part that always looked forward, not back … The men of Coke [Coke executives] could have found themselves pouring all their effort into an unresponsive nation, but people returned the affection.
>
> (Hays 2005: x)

All of these meanings of Coca-Cola may be responses to consumer needs at the time, but the efforts to envelop Coke with these meanings precede the needs of the consumer and are strictly manufactured by the controllers of the Coca-Cola brand. If this were not so, then there would need to be something in a soft drink that is able to accomplish these social tasks. Since there is nothing inherent in a soft drink or any other commodity that is able to do this on its own, a soft drink needs much help—help it gets in the form of the brand.

And because the source of the meaning of the Coca-Cola brand is a corporation that only wants to make money off of consumers, the Coca-Cola fetish has a kind of "double instability"—an instability that inheres in the meaning of a made object and an instability based on the fact that the fetish points not to a long-lasting sacred object, but to a corporation looking out for its bottom line. The Coca-Cola Company is long-standing in one sense; it's been around for 125 years (longer than some religions). However Coke (and Apple and Ralph Lauren and …) will always have trouble doing the kind of religious work that corresponds to the sacred because it can never escape the fact that its fetishized product was and is created by a group of human beings motivated by very human things.

Perhaps the real problem with Chidester's analysis of Coca-Cola and religion has to do with his own definition of religion. "Ways of being a human in a human place" is so broad of a functional definition of religion that it can include Coca-Cola as that which does religious work. Yet, along the lines of Geertz's golf analogy, what cannot be religious based on Chidester's definition? If religion has to do with the transcendent/sacred/ultimate, then cultural forms that betray only the immanent/profane/contingent will have real trouble doing real religious work. Fetishes can do religious work, but not all fetishes are created equal. In fact the more that a fetish is cloaked in meaning that we deem inauthentic or fleeting, the more we may start looking for authenticity elsewhere. Stuart Ewen puts it this way:

> Each time that the Coca-Cola Bottling company informs us that their product is "The Real Thing", implicit is the message that it isn't the real thing after all; and what is more, people do feel the need for the actual real thing.
>
> (Ewen 2001: 189)

And popular cultural products that are made in order to manipulate consumers into buying the products lack the ability to convey that they are as real as the company says they are.

So finally, there is much to compliment in Chidester's effort to challenge the binary between authentic and inauthentic religion and its search. His method is original and exciting as it opens up brand new avenues to understanding the relationship between popular culture and religion. But his conclusions about Coca-Cola's true religious quality belie the merits of his methodology. If real religious work can be performed via a commodity produced and packaged by a corporation, whose only intention is to make money off of consumers, then there is little room for the kind of irony that Chidester asserts about the difference between authentic and inauthentic religious expressions. The problem with Coca-Cola as a religion is not with its fetish quality in itself. The problem lies in the source of the material product and in the employment of the people pulling the strings to make it into a fetish. Such a fetish may get people to drink Coke, but getting those same people to interact with the sacred through Coca-Cola is another matter altogether.

Summary

- Brands are the "meaning-carriers" of products and services that can have a profound effect not only on what we buy, but also on who we are.
- Certain iconic brands are a part of popular culture, as defined by John Storey. They are liked by many people, are mass produced, and are a site of struggle over who controls their meaning.
- David Chidester defines religion functionally and broadly as providing "ways of being a human in a human place" which allows brands to do religious work.
- Chidester also claims that the traditional methods for determining which religions are authentic or inauthentic are problematic. By exposing these methods,

perceived inauthentic cultural expressions, such as many popular cultural ones, can be religious.

- Coca-Cola does religious work, for Chidester, by acting as a religious fetish—one that transcends the material substance of the beverage by focusing human desire in a way that informs one of the human condition.
- We can raise questions about Chidester's stance on the relationship between religion and Coca-Cola based on the kind of instability that Coca-Cola exhibits as a fetish.

Glossary terms

Brand – the identity of a product, service or business. Some brands convey a meaning of a product, service or business that is meant to attract consumers.

Fetish – a material object that is believed to possess supernatural or magical power or even power that goes beyond what the material object is capable of generating given its material properties alone.

Fetishism of commodity – idea put forth by Karl Marx that proposes that commodities are fetishes, or that commodities represent something beyond their mere use-value, based on the way they are produced and sold in a capitalistic economy.

Functional definition of religion – a definition of religion that focuses on *what* the phenomenon of religion does to/for a practitioner. The emphasis is on the function of religion or a particular religious ritual/practice, rather than what ideas, stories, or traditions lie behind it.

Iconic brand – a brand whose meaning helps consumers construct desirable identities for themselves. Iconic brands usually have a mythical aura that helps their function.

Mediator – something that mediates or is a "go-between" between two entities. Religious mediators often broker the relationship between humanity and the transcendent realm or sacred things.

Points for discussion

- Based on your knowledge, both personal and intellectual, do certain iconic brands have the power to construct and/or contribute to personal identities? If so, which current iconic brands are the most effective at doing so?
- What are some of the problems with including corporate brands as a part of popular culture? How does the process by which brands enter the cultural landscape differ from other, perhaps more easily accepted cultural productions, such as music or movies? And if there is a difference, does this make a difference in deciding whether brands are a part of popular culture?
- What do you make of Chidester's definition of religion?
- Does Chidester have a point when he claims that the founder of the "Holy Order of the Cheeseburger" finds a kind of religious truth through the establishment of a fake religion on the internet? If so, why? If not, why?

- Is the term "fetish" appropriately applied to Coca-Cola products? Is the definition of fetish provided in this chapter too broad or too narrow—does it include so many things that almost anything can be called a fetish, or are fetishes not as inclusive as the given definition suggests?
- In order to connect people to transcendent/sacred/ultimate things, do cultural mediators need to be similarly profound? What does the shelf-life of a cultural product have to do with its ability to convey religious truth, or in Chidester's words, "do religious work"?

Notes

1 www.cbsnews.com/stories/2010/11/01/earlyshow/leisure/music/main7010938.shtml.
2 www.msnbc.msn.com/id/40823461/ns/business-consumer_news/.
3 www.interbrand.com/en/best-global-brands/best-global-brands-2008/best-global-brands-2010.aspx.
4 www.adbusters.org/node/2105.
5 See www.thecoca-colacompany.com/heritage/cokelore_santa.html.

Further reading

Allen, Frederick L. (1995) *Secret Formula: How Brilliant Marketing and Relentless Salesmanship Made Coca-Cola the Best-Known Product in the World*, New York: Harper Paperbacks.

An inside look at the inner politics of the Coca-Cola Company. It focuses on the near obsessive protection and promotion of the "secret formula" of Coca-Cola.

Carrette, Jeremy, and King, Richard (2005) *Selling Spirituality: The Silent Takeover of Religion*, New York: Routledge.

The authors take a hard look at the odd relationship between religion and the capitalistic market. They put forth a critique of the industries that put up religious ideas for sale under the guise of spirituality.

Lasn, Kalle (2000) *Culture Jam: How to Reverse America's Suicidal Consumer Binge—and Why We Must*, New York: Quill.

Lasn, editor of the magazine *Adbusters*, explains the phenomenon of "culture jamming" where consumers attempt to take back control from the producers of commodities by altering brand logos, establishing "commercial-free zones" in public spaces, and exposing the dark side of the mass production of the goods we consume.

Miller, Vincent J. (2004) *Consuming Religion*, New York: Continuum.

Miller looks at the relationship between religion and popular culture (and culture in general) and pays special attention to the means by which religion is being increasingly co-opted by the dictates of consumer culture.

Ritzer, George (2004) *The McDonaldization of Society*, Thousand Oaks, CA: Pine Forge Press.

This book examines the global reach of the McDonald's restaurant chain and its disturbing cultural impact. Specifically, Ritzer uses Max Weber's theory of rationalization to both illuminate the tactics and effects of McDonald's as well as offer his own point of departure from Weber.

Storey, John (1999) *Cultural Consumption and Everyday Life*, London: Arnold.

Another work by Storey that centers on the ways in which we consume cultural artifacts. Storey looks at cultural consumption from the perspective of varied academic disciplines.

Thomas, Mark (2008) *Belching Out the Devil: Global Adventures with Coca-Cola*, New York: Nation Books.

Investigates the untold story of the Coca-Cola Company. From poor working conditions in the sugar cane fields in El Salvador to Indian workers who are exposed to toxic chemicals, Thomas exposes some of the production costs involved that belie the global image put forth by the company itself.

Bibliography

Chidester, David (2005) *Authentic Fakes: Religion and American Popular Culture*, Berkeley: University of California Press.

Davaney, Sheila Greeve (2001) "Theology and the Turn to Cultural Analysis," in Delwin Brown, Sheila Greeve Davaney, and Kathryn Tanner (eds), *Converging on Culture: Theologians in Dialogue with Cultural Analysis and Criticism*, Oxford: Oxford University Press.

Ewen, Stuart (2001) *Captains of Consciousness: Advertising and the Social Roots of the Consumer Culture*, New York: Basic Books.

Geertz, Clifford (1977) *The Interpretation of Cultures*, New York: Basic Books.

Hays, Constance L. (2005) *The Real Thing: Truth and Power at the Coca-Cola Company*, New York: Random House.

Holt, Douglas B. (2004) *How Brands Become Icons: The Principles of Cultural Branding*, Boston: Harvard Business School Press.

Klein, Naomi (2002) *No Logo*, New York: Picador.

Marx, Karl (1992) *Capital: Volume 1: A Critique of Political Economy*, New York: Penguin Classics.

Pendergrast, Mark (2000) *For God, Country and Coca-Cola: The Definitive History of the Great American Soft Drink and the Company That Makes It*, New York: Basic Books.

Smith, Jonathan Z. (1988) *Imagining Religion: From Babylon to Jonestown*, Chicago: University of Chicago Press.

Storey, John (2009) *Cultural Theory and Popular Culture: An Introduction*, 5th edn, Essex: Pearson Education Unlimited.

Twitchell, James (2004) *Branded Nation: The Marketing of Megachurch, College Inc., and Museumworld*, New York: Simon and Schuster.

10 What makes music Christian?

Hipsters, contemporary Christian music and secularization

Courtney Wilder and Jeremy Rehwaldt

Introduction to hipsters and Christian music

Some artists perform songs that are played regularly on mainstream Christian radio and climb the Billboard charts, where they might remain for more than a year! Other artists identify themselves as Christians and are well-loved by their audiences, as evidenced by album sales, but receive little radio play on either Christian or secular stations. What can the difference between these two groups tell us about the relationship of religion and popular culture? In particular, what can the relationship between groups popular in contemporary Christian music (CCM), on the one hand, and "**hipster**" Christian artists, on the other, tell us about processes of **secularization**?

For several centuries, scholars have predicted the secularization of society, that is, a diminishment of the importance of religion, and they have discussed and analyzed a range of theories about this process. Conrad Ostwalt argues that secularization is not a one-way street from religious to nonreligious, as early theories had contended, but can be best understood as a transformation of the relationship between religion and society in which "not only do we see religious institutions becoming more like the secular world, we also see secular forms of entertainment and culture carrying religious messages" (Ostwalt 2003: 31).

This chapter explores music as a cultural and religious phenomenon, specifically using the concept of secularization to focus on the relationship and the blurred line between two kinds of musicians: first, artists or groups who identify as Christian and who perform "Christian music," and second, artists or groups who fall into the "hipster" aesthetic, who identify as Christian, and whose music may or may not be overtly religious. We begin by laying out the history of secularization and Ostwalt's reformulation, then turn to a comparison of contemporary music. We will also define **evangelicalism** and **hipsters** before turning to specific songs to demonstrate differences in their approach and their relevance for understanding secularization. We argue that the phenomenon of hipster Christian music functions in a way that illuminates the interaction between religious and nonreligious realms. In this genre, there is no sharp contrast between the religious and the secular; instead, the sacred and the secular simultaneously influence one another, in a **bidirectional** relationship, just as Ostwalt describes in his analysis of secularization.

Theory and method

Questions about the relationship between the sacred, or the religious realm of human existence, and the secular, or the nonreligious realm, are longstanding within Christianity. For centuries, thinkers in the Western world have predicted the rise of secular society and the fall of religion (Stark 1999: 249). Modern sociologists of religion offer a variety of analyses of the relationship between the sacred and the secular. Early forms of secularization theory, which have been very influential, argue that Western society is gradually and irreversibly becoming less religious. In response, some scholars have argued that societies move through cycles of religious decline and revival; others have argued that secularization moves with starts and stops, progress and reversals, in which "social movements in the direction of secularization spawn religious countermovements in the direction of sacralization" (Goldstein 2009: 175). Still others argue that the premise of most secularization theory, that the power and importance of religion is declining, is itself flawed, and that religious participation in previous historical periods tends to be overestimated and thus modern people are as religious as ever (Stark 1999). This argument presents serious problems for proponents of early secularization theory, as historical data appears to conflict strongly with the claim that religion is in decline (Berger 2008).

Conrad Ostwalt, in his recent book *Secular Steeples*, offers an analysis of the relationship between the sacred and the secular that accounts for the interaction between religious and nonreligious cultural expressions and does not rely on the premise that Western culture is in the process of religious decline. Ostwalt argues that secularization is a bidirectional movement in which, "not only do we see religious institutions becoming more like the secular world, we also see secular forms of entertainment and culture carrying religious messages" (31). Thus, the broader world becomes the setting for spiritual experiences (31). Ostwalt's position contrasts most strongly with the understanding of secularization that prevailed in the 1960s, articulated prominently by Peter Berger in *The Sacred Canopy*. In this book, Berger argues for inevitable, one-directional religious decline and says that modern societies are becoming irreversibly less religious over time. In his more recent writing, Berger says that modernity generates not a loss of religion, but rather an increase in religious pluralism.

In contrast to Berger's position in *The Sacred Canopy*, Ostwalt says:

> Contemporary American culture witnesses secularization occurring in two directions: 1) the churches and religious organizations are becoming increasingly more attuned to the secular environment, particularly to popular culture, and are in some cases trying to emulate it in the effort to remain relevant; 2) popular culture forms, including literature, film, and music, are becoming increasingly more visible vehicles of religious images, symbols, and categories. These two directions of secularization demonstrate the blurred or malleable boundaries between religion and culture—the sacred and the secular—that define the relationship of religion and culture in the postmodern era.
>
> (29)

In other words, on Ostwalt's account, we should expect to see instances of religious communities drawing on secular forms to maintain people's interest in their message, while, at the same time, we ought to see the diffusion of religious ideas in the broader cultural environment. Popular Christian music provides a test case for Ostwalt's theory, and we turn there next.

Setting up the case study

The two modes of interaction between religion and popular culture that Ostwalt describes above are visible in two very different kinds of Christian music. First is contemporary Christian music (CCM), an enormous industry with annual sales of about $500 million (Gospel Music Association 2009). There are also "hipster" Christian artists whose work falls outside of this CCM mainstream. In order to lay out the relationship between these two groups, we will begin by explaining who evangelicals are, what contemporary Christian music is, and who hipsters are. Following these brief definitional sketches, we will analyze the particular features of the music in light of Ostwalt's concept.

What is an evangelical?

There is significant overlap between consumers of contemporary Christian music (CCM) and evangelical Christians. The latter term is by no means a straightforward or clear-cut descriptor; Robert Johnston offers an analysis of evangelicalism among Christians in the United States that serves both to illuminate the concept and to explain many recurring features of CCM. Johnston argues that the word "evangelical" has many different, sometimes competing, definitions, often employed by evangelicals themselves (Johnston 1991: 253). Johnston offers a solution: he argues that the term "evangelical" ought to be understood as describing a set of family resemblances, or shared qualities and characteristics. For instance, you might resemble your parents, siblings, cousins, aunts and uncles, and grandparents by virtue of shared physical traits, shared family names, traditions, and cultural practices. According to Johnston, evangelical churches and denominations are similar in that they resemble each other without being identical.

What are these shared features of evangelicals? And how do they influence popular Christian music? A combination of doctrines and practices, including methods of reading the Bible, make up the features that form this family resemblance (260). Johnston sums them up: "An emphasis on personal religious experience, an insistence upon witness and mission, a loyalty to biblical authority, an understanding of salvation by grace through faith" (259). We can add to this summary an emphasis on living a life of personal piety and holiness. All of the above features are visible within the CCM genre.

What is contemporary Christian music?

If evangelicals can be understood as a family of Christians emphasizing an overlapping set of doctrines and perspectives, what kind of music do they listen to?

Christian rock music emerged as a distinctive genre in the 1960s, and Christian popular music rapidly expanded into other musical genres as well. As Ostwalt observes, "From light rock to rap to punk to hard rock—these forms have been adopted by the contemporary Christian music scene. The popularization of Christian rock/pop music witnesses to a purposeful adaptation of a secular medium for the propagation of the Christian message. The strategy is to tap into youth culture and Christianize it" (193). In other words, CCM developed in order to provide a "safe" alternative for Christian youth, on the one hand, and to spread the gospel to the "unsaved," on the other. Contemporary Christian music was thus born of a desire by some Christians to avoid "worldliness" and to create an alternative set of cultural products that would be attractive to young people while maintaining a separation from the mainstream, just as Ostwalt describes.

To make the boundaries of its genre clearer, in 1998 the Gospel Music Association defined Christian music, for the purposes of the GMA Awards (formerly known as the Dove Awards), as follows:

> music in any style whose lyric is substantially based upon historically orthodox Christian truth contained in or derived from the Holy Bible; and/or an expression of worship of God or praise for his works; and/or testimony of relationship with God through Christ; and/or obviously prompted and informed by a Christian worldview.
>
> (Beaujon 2006: 177)

While this definition was later changed to be less restrictive, it provides important information about the perspective of the CCM industry and its associated radio stations.

What is a hipster?

The hipster aesthetic is everywhere around us. It's gone mainstream. And it has entered the Christian tradition, most notably in the form of what we might call "Christian hipsters," a slippery category that encompasses those who participate in both the Christian tradition and the hipster "lifestyle." Hipsters—a social and intellectual group heir to the aesthetic of the **beatnik** and employing the philosophical tools of **postmodernism**—are increasingly intersecting with Christianity.

The subculture of "hipsters"—a term emerging in the 1950s describing those who are "hip," which is to say, on the cutting edge of "cool"—is associated with a particular aesthetic, evident in clothing and media tastes, as well as with a particular ideological stance vis-à-vis mainstream cultural tastes and positions. The word "hip" is likely adapted from the west African term "hipi," referring to seeing or opening one's eyes. Hip's common elements—"a love of the outsider; a straddle of high and low culture; a grimy sense of nobility; language that means more than it says"—have been visible throughout the changing landscape of U.S. culture, yet the hipster subculture has again entered the public consciousness full force in the last decade (Leland 2004: 10; e.g. Fletcher 2009).

As with evangelicals, hipsters can perhaps best be defined through a series of family resemblances, in this case based in large part on lifestyle preferences. Robert Lanham, author of *The Hipster Handbook* (2003), describes the hipster lifestyle as centered on three core themes: (1) an emphasis on "stuff," that is, a particular aesthetic linked to consumer products—clothes, music, and so on; (2) the development of cultural "pastiche," which is "the hodgepodge blending of elements from pop culture to create a sensibility" or strong stylistic preference; and (3) **irony**, which refers to their cynical detachment and critique of **mass culture** (Lanham 2009). And some hipsters are Christian; in one of his blog entries examining the phenomenon of Christian hipsters, Brett McCracken provides some definitional clues:

> Christian hipsters tend not to like contemporary Christian music (CCM), or Christian films (except ironically) ... They prefer "Christ follower" to "Christian" and can't stand the phrases "soul winning" or "non-denominational." ... Christian hipsters like music, movies, and books that are well-respected by their respective artistic communities—Christian or not ... Christian hipsters love thinking and acting Catholic, even if they are thoroughly Protestant ... Christian hipsters love breaking the taboos that used to be taboo for Christians. They love piercings, dressing a little goth, getting lots of tattoos ... and many of them play in bands.
>
> (McCracken 2009)

In order to understand the phenomenon of hipster Christian music, which is less likely to be visible on the top of the radio charts, we took the route often used by hipsters themselves—word of mouth. We interviewed a number of musicians and music lovers who had a hipster aesthetic, we read blogs and music review websites, and we listened to hipster music (see Rehwaldt-Alexander and Wilder 2010).

Case study

Having set out definitions of the key concepts in our analysis, we turn to the music itself, beginning by describing the musical styles more generally before analyzing particular songs. At issue is the relationship between the sacred and the secular in both CCM and hipster Christian music. We argue below that CCM, as a genre, is an attempt to use popular cultural forms to remain relevant in the face of what seems to be widespread secularization, and that hipster Christian music, in contrast, uses popular culture to engage in religious reflection.

Analyzing contemporary Christian music

In order to get a handle on the content and style of recent CCM music, we examined the top Christian radio hits in late 2009. Selecting one week at random during each of five months in 2009 (June through October), we found a total of only twenty-eight artists represented during that period in the "top 19" song lists of K-LOVE, a national Christian radio network (www.klove.com). Of these artists, *all* have had songs in the top 25 of the Billboard Christian charts, based on "radio airplay audience impressions" (www.billboard.com). Moreover, more than 85 percent—all but four of the artists—have been nominated for the Gospel Music Association's Dove awards, a significant means of recognition for CCM artists (www.gospelmusic.org). Of the four who were not nominated, one performed at the 2010 awards ceremony and the other three were all newcomers, with one commentator putting two of the three on the list of expected nominations (Unthank 2010).

From this data we note several things. First, there is wide overlap among three key indicators of popularity for CCM—play on major radio stations, presence on the Billboard charts, and awards from the Gospel Music Association. Second, this overlap illustrates that those artists that make it big on Christian radio are also those that fit the narrow criteria set out by the GMA, as described earlier, and are likewise additionally supported by the GMA itself through award nominations.

Do these artists have anything else in common beyond receiving the blessing of the CCM industry? In order to analyze the lyrical content and musical style of the top hits, we chose a week toward the end of the GMA awards' nomination period, in October 2009, and selected the ten songs that had stayed on the top 20 list for the longest period at that point, with the length of time for these songs ranging from a high of more than a year—fifty-eight weeks ("By Your Side," Tenth Avenue North)—to nineteen weeks ("Hold My Heart," also by Tenth Avenue North) (www.billboard.com). Given the consistency of song and artist popularity among CCM radio stations and listeners, we chose a sample of popular songs for the purpose of analyzing their lyrics, musical styles, and theological content.

Songs found on Christian radio have an identifiable "adult contemporary" style, and all ten of the songs in this longest-on-the-charts group fall into that stylistic range: highly "produced," slow to mid tempo, with guitars, background strings, and swelling choruses. Lyrically, the songs also fall into a relatively narrow range of topics and approaches, with a couple of exceptions. All are explicitly about God. Three have lyrics aimed toward God, with God the second-person recipient of the message. For instance, "Revelation Song," performed by Phillips, Craig and Dean, talks of praising and adoring God, who is referred to as "You" (Riddle 2004). Only one of the ten—Jonny Diaz's "More Beautiful You"—has a "plot," with an explicit story being told, in this case about a young woman unhappy with her body and how she is treated by men (Diaz 2009). Other songs are exhortative, providing a narrow range of theological instruction. The key lesson is often this: We are broken. Jesus has died for us, providing for our brokenness to be healed. Because of this, some day we will be in heaven. As one CCM fan described the typical lyrical style,

> If they're really a Christian band, and they're trying to win people over to Christ, there's no blurry lines … The truth is bold. I don't think people who

hear a song should have to *do something* to find out what it means … Irony in Christian music would not be good.

(Radosh 2008: 4–5)

The usual means of establishing who is "really a Christian band" within the CCM industry is to draw sharp lines between what is Christian and what is too worldly, and then market the former as affirming of faith and safe for children. This technique includes counting the times a particular song mentions the name of Jesus, known as the "JPMs" or "Jesus Per Minute." Too few JPMs can endanger radio play on CCM stations (Radosh 2008: 177). The genre itself is designed to meet the perceived religious needs of listeners. Thus both the musical style and the purpose of the lyrics in CCM songs differ from those of indie music with Christian spiritual or religious meaning. Music that gets airplay on Christian stations tends to be explicitly religious, invoking the name of Jesus and affirming the most basic form of the Christian relationship to God: Jesus loves me, Jesus died for my sins, I love Jesus. Artists who are popular on the CCM charts affirm this style of sharing their faith, and the public identity of CCM artists tends to emphasize strongly their personal virtue and pursuit of holiness. For example, Matthew Paul Turner, then-editor of *CCM*, a magazine covering Christian music, relates a story of being forced by his publisher to ask Amy Grant to apologize several years after the fact to the readers of *CCM* for her 1999 divorce. When his story did not portray Grant as sufficiently apologetic, he says, it was rewritten with fabricated apologetic quotes to placate *CCM*'s publisher, and, presumably, its readers (Turner 2010).

Hipster Christian music

In contrast to songs in the mainstream of CCM, the artists who are Christian and are creating "hipster" music with Christian themes are not receiving radio play, yet they do have a place in the marketplace. Derek Webb, a solo artist and member of Caedmon's Call; David Bazan, a solo artist formerly of Pedro the Lion; and mewithoutYou, fronted by Aaron Weiss, serve as three examples of such "hipster" Christian artists. All three have albums that have charted in the Billboard 200, which is based on album sales rather than radio play (www.billboard.com). Both mewithoutYou and Derek Webb have had albums appear high on the Billboard Christian album chart (#3 and #2, respectively). David Bazan's solo release, *Curse Your Branches*, appeared as #14 in Billboard's Independent category. All three have also been frequently profiled on indie Christian music blogs and websites, as is evident from even the most cursory web search.

Interestingly, however, *none* of the three has had a song appear on Billboard charts based on radio play. In other words, the groups have a substantial following—people are purchasing their albums—but they are excluded from the contemporary Christian music industry, as evident in the lack of radio play they receive and the limited availability through Christian media distribution channels, such as Christian Book Distributors, "today's leading resource for Christian goods," which does not carry mewithoutYou's most recent CD nor David Bazan's solo album, but does carry Derek Webb, though after requiring one song to be removed from the album for its content (www.christianbook.com). The anecdote about Amy Grant described above highlights CCM strictures; many hipster Christians are unwilling to change their approach to fit the mold. The hipster Christian genre, although much less formally organized than CCM music, demonstrates an understanding of the sacred/secular relationship that reflects Ostwalt's second mode of secularization. That is, while the CCM industry sees secularization as a one-way eroding of the power of religion and religious institutions, hipster Christian artists and their listeners affirm a model of musical self-expression, and especially songwriting that speaks deeply to religious problems and questions using secular modes of expression.

Bringing religious ideas into secular culture

For Christian hipster musicians, recognizing God's presence throughout creation, including the "secular" world, is a key impetus for their creative endeavors. This comports closely with Ostwalt's theory, which sees religious ideas engaging the broader cultural context. As he explains, "Secular and popular culture might contain more authentic belief than official religious theologies, because it is in the popular culture that one can encounter belief and values apart from and freed from paternalistic religious doctrine and dogma" (7). This theme of seeing God in all of creation was repeated again and again in our interviews and in the comments of noted musicians and leaders. For instance, Rob Bell, the pastor of the wildly successful and hipster-friendly Mars Hill Church near Grand Rapids, Michigan, put it this way: "My understanding is that to be Christian is to do whatever it is that you do with great passion and devotion" (Bell 2006: 84). In a recent interview he elaborates:

> I don't believe in Christian art or music. The word *Christian* was originally a noun. A person, not an adjective. I believe in great art. If you are an artist, your job is to do great art and you don't need to tack on the word *Christian*. It's already great. God is the God of Creativity. Categories desecrate the art form. It's either great art or it isn't. Followers of Jesus should have the first word instead of coming late to the game with some poor quality spin-off.
>
> (Blaney 2007)

Bell's position was also forwarded by several of our informants; Marcus (our interview subjects have been provided with pseudonyms) couched his analysis in the historic creeds of the church:

> I find myself using the phrase "first article" things, as in the first article of the creed: "I believe in God the Father almighty, maker of heaven and earth." Which just includes the principles of what makes good art. That's a first article item. God has made it all. Can God be praised in a good chord progression or does it have to say "Jesus"? Or a narrative story that's a redemption story but nobody comes to the altar?

The aesthetic criteria of the secular world are God's, as creator of all things. Thus Christians need not listen to music specifically labeled "Christian," or attend only films specifically labeled "Christian," in order for their well-being to be fostered. Derek Webb makes a similar point:

> I have never, ever felt like a "Christian artist." I don't live like that, I don't create that way; those categories mean nothing to me. I don't think they mean anything to anybody. I don't think they're real. I don't think there's any such thing as Christian art or secular art. I think there are Christian and secular people, who make art, and all art tends to reflect the people who make it, but there's no such thing as "redeemed art."
>
> (Wofford 2009)

An emphasis on creativity is evident in the songs we examined. Most of the songs tell stories; occasionally the songs are exhortative and narrated in the second person. The lyrics are complex, both stylistically complex, without standard verses and choruses, as well as linguistically complex, with an array of interpretive possibilities. Many of the lyrics evoke uncertainty about the human ability to know fully God, and they pose the questions as more important than the answers, a marked contrast with mainstream CCM, in which certain and simplified answers are foregrounded.

Comparing specific songs

The narrative point of view and message of music found on most contemporary "Christian" radio stations stands distinct from the music made by Christians on the margins or outside of the CCM industry. To illustrate this phenomenon, we will look at several songs, first focusing on two songs in particular, one by Wes King, entitled "I Believe."[1] King has a long history in the CCM industry; his song "This is Your Time," performed by Michael W. Smith, won the 2000 Dove Song of the Year Award, and he had a song on the 1994 Praise and Worship Album of the Year as well as many Christian radio hits (see www.doveawards.com; Powell 2002: 488–489). The other song is by David Bazan, whose band, Pedro the Lion, was a fixture of the indie Christian scene. The expulsion from the Garden of Eden is the narrative core of both songs, yet they approach the story from radically different points of view.

Both begin with stories of an idyllic paradise. In "Hard to Be,"[2] David Bazan sings: "Once upon a garden we were lovers with no clothes/Fresh from the soil we were beautiful and true," while King's song identifies a literal reading of the story of Adam and Eve in Genesis as one of many narratives essential to Christian faith: "I believe/in six days and a rest/God is good/I do confess I believe in Adam and Eve/In a tree and a garden/In a snake and a thief" (Bazan 2009; King 1993). Both artists identify the narrative of Adam and Eve as meaningful and as an opportunity for human beings to better understand their relationship to God. But then the stories and concerns diverge. For King, Adam and Eve, along with Noah,

Isaiah, and Jesus, are historical human beings, whose lives demonstrate the power and goodness of God. The chorus emphasizes the role of the modern Christian: "I believe, I believe/I believe in the Word of God/I believe, I believe/'Cause He made me believe" (King 1993). God is affirmed as Creator and Redeemer, and as the source of faith. This faith, however, does not entail questioning or deep reflection; it is a straightforward affirmation of the doctrine that the Bible is historically true and that God is its source.

In contrast, Bazan follows the initial story of the fall with this: "Wait just a minute/You expect me to believe/that all this misbehaving grew from one enchanted tree/And helpless to fight it we should all be satisfied/With the magical explanation for why the living die." Rather than accepting this particular narrative at face value, he challenges the literal reading normative for CCM and begins asking difficult questions about the relationship between the story of the Fall and human experience today, in which it is, in his words, "hard to be a decent human being." One song is focused on Jesus's role in mending the rift created by an initial sinful human choice, while the other is focused on doubt, on the difficulty of the human condition, and on the ongoing search for knowledge. One is played regularly on mainstream Christian radio, the other receives little if any airplay. Why? Certainly, an advertising line repeated frequently on Christian radio stations provides a clue: "positive and encouraging," "safe for the whole family" (www.klove.com; www.klty.com).

We can see, in this comparison of Wes King and David Bazan, key differences in their theological approach and in the way that secular and sacred intersect. King exhibits some of the features of evangelicalism, including a literalist reading of the Garden of Eden story, an unquestioning affirmation of biblical authority, and a proclamation of a very specific understanding of salvation (that Jesus came to earth to save human beings from sin, the origins of which can be traced back to the actions of two historical human beings, Adam and Eve). In turn, Bazan looks very much the hipster here: he offers an ironic analysis of the Garden of Eden story, employs a critical comparison between the traditional reading of the story and his experience of the human condition, and offers questions rather than proclaiming answers.

A common approach among CCM artists is to make declarations about the nature of Christian faith, posited as simple propositions that the listeners are implicitly encouraged to accept. Songs often remind listeners of the need to believe in Jesus, Jesus's atoning sacrifice on the cross, and his bodily resurrection. The doctrinal tropes mentioned earlier emerge in lyrical content that is simple, repetitive, propositional, and in the second person. For instance, in the megahit "Indescribable,"[3] Chris Tomlin sings, "You placed the stars in the sky and you know them by name./You are amazing God/All powerful, untameable,/ Awestruck we fall to our knees as we humbly proclaim/You are amazing God" (Story 2004). The song promotes the idea that God is "indescribable," yet seeks to provide a simple, vague description that evokes a response of praise.

In contrast to this doctrinal affirmation and evocation of a narrow range of personal feeling and experience, Weiss's music with mewithoutYou is full of questions, doubts, and narrative descriptions of the questions of life and the nature of God. For instance, in "The King Beetle on a Coconut Estate,"[4] the song refers to something called the "Great Mystery," probably to be understood as the human relationship to God. The lyrics compare it to coconut palm leaves being burned as refuse on a plantation, a fire that a beetle colony is attempting to wrap its collective mind around. The song is both lyrically and musically complex, with more than 500 words and a song structure without a chorus. Weiss's approach to the nature of God can be inferred from this section of the song in which the first two beetles, one a professor and the other a military officer, fail in their quest to understand the mysterious fire. Weiss sings,

> But for all the lieutenant's conceit
> He too returned singed and admitting defeat
> "I had no choice, please believe, but retreat
> It was bright as the sun, but with ten times the heat
> And it cracked like the thunder and bloodshot my eyes
> Though smothered with sticks, it advanced undeterred
> Carelessly cast an ash cloud to the sky, my lord
> Like a flock of dark vanishing birds."
>
> (Weiss 2009)

The song is not a straightforward description, not a set of propositions, but a fable that illustrates the fact that despite our best efforts to comprehend it, the nature of the universe remains always a mystery.

While not every possibly-Christian artist whose music is too controversial for CCM radio play fits into the hipster paradigm, hipster music tends to exclude itself from such radio play. The hipster emphasis on authenticity of self-expression, coupled with a willingness to use a variety of cultural elements and an ironic rejection of superficial popular culture, lends itself to music that is "an outlet for religious yearning," a rather different goal from the CCM music described earlier (Ostwalt 2003: 98). For Christian hipsters, the criteria used by the secular world to judge beauty and goodness are God's, as creator of all things. These criteria are often visible in their music, in stories about the broader world, seen through the eyes of people who are Christian or narrating an experience that carries spiritual meaning. As we argue in the conclusion of this chapter, while CCM music typically reiterates one of a few straightforward themes, hipster music strives to embody the complexity of the world in both musical style and lyrics.

Thus both hipsters and evangelicals can be identified according to their respective family resemblances, and these features are visible in hipster Christian music and in CCM. In addition, the respective genres of music suggest very different concepts of the relationship between the sacred and the secular. To return to the metaphor of family resemblances, while CCM music emerges from a "family" that harbors suspicion about secularization, hipster music reflects a consistent and intentional use of various religious and nonreligious cultural elements in shaping religious self-expression. What light does this comparison shed on the strength of Ostwalt's description of secularization?

Conclusions

Ostwalt identifies secularization as bidirectional, meaning that religious culture can affect secular culture and vice versa. Hipster Christian artists are a good illustration of his theory: although they typically do not make music that fits the CCM model, many hipster artists ask questions of the Christian tradition and analyze it critically, using the various cultural and intellectual tools at their disposal in order to be true to their artistic vision—in other words, to create deeply religious music. Hipster Christian music, because of its tendency to interpret critically and its willingness to engage a wider array of topics, a broader swatch of the human condition, provides an opportunity to contribute substantively to contemporary Christian practice in ways that are at odds with the boundaries typically drawn around CCM, highlighting the complexity, mystery, and doubt inherent to religious life. Ostwalt's method of analysis offers a more accurate and revealing understanding of this phenomenon than unidirectional models, suggesting that his understanding of secularization is a better analytical tool. As Ostwalt argues,

> Whereas sacred music is defined by, bounded by, and limited by doctrine and dogma, secular music has no such limitations. Thus, according to Spencer, it is in secular music that we learn what we really believe, and it is through our response to secular music that we can fashion an ethic that is meaningful and relevant. Secular music, therefore, provides a more reliable measure of authentic belief, relevant ethics, and real commitment than sacred music, which can be defined by standards of belief that are no longer owned by those in the tradition.
>
> (197)

Summary

- For several hundred years, the decline of religion in Western society has been predicted. In the 1960s, sociologies of religion, following the lead of Peter Berger, developed a theory of secularization, arguing that Christianity is in decline in the United States and Europe, and that this process is irreversible. Sociologist of religion Conrad Ostwalt argues instead for a bidirectional relationship between the sacred and the secular.
- To analyze Ostwalt's theory, the chapter examines contemporary Christian music (CCM) and its relationship with American evangelical Christianity, as well as hipster Christian music and its relationship with both Christianity and broader secular culture, especially hipster culture.
- A comparative analysis of CCM and hipster Christian music suggests that CCM reflects the perspective of earlier sociologists on secularization, while hipster music reflects Ostwalt's theory.

- Ostwalt's description of secularization accounts more successfully for the phenomenon of Christian hipster music than other forms of secularization theory, and his analysis contributes to the ongoing problematizing of the larger claim that society is becoming less religious over time.

Glossary terms

Beatnik – a person associated with a movement of counterculture artists, writers, and musicians of the late 1950s, including, in particular, writers Jack Kerouac and Allen Ginsburg, emphasizing creativity and nonconformity with social norms, including mores about sex and drugs.

Bidirectional – moving in two directions; here, Ostwalt argues that sacred and secular forms of culture influence each other, and thus the interactions are bidirectional.

Evangelicalism – a Christian religious movement that includes some or all of the following: an emphasis on personal religious experience, an insistence upon witness and mission, a loyalty to biblical authority, an understanding of salvation by grace through faith, a literalistic interpretation of the Bible, an emphasis on leading a life of personal holiness.

Hipsters – participants in an intellectual and social group that employs irony and cultural pastiche, embraces postmodernism, and values indie music, literature, and film; hipsters may or may not be Christian.

Irony – contrast between the apparent meaning and the real meaning; intentional subversion of ordinary expectations. (See also the treatment of this word in Chapter 1, including the glossary term at the end of the chapter.)

Mass culture – set of ideas and products detached from local cultural traditions and created to maximize consumption by a wide audience.

Postmodernism – an intellectual movement that critically reappraises various modern assumptions about culture, identity, religion, gender, and language. (See also the treatment of this word in Chapter 13.)

Secularization – a diminishment of the importance of religion, especially in terms of social power or influence.

Points for discussion

- How do you choose music? What genres of music do you find most meaningful? Why?
- Ostwalt suggests that artists who do not identify their music as Christian or religious, per se, might still be addressing issues of spiritual and religious importance. Do you agree? Can you think of examples?
- Do you think analyzing music and other forms of popular culture can reveal something about religious beliefs? Why or why not?
- What makes something (a song, book, poem, image) religious or nonreligious?

Notes

1 Extract from 'I Believe', words & music by Wes King & Fran King. © Universal Music Careers, USA. Universal Music Publishing Limited. All Rights Reserved.

International Copyright Secured. Used by permission of Music Sales Limited and Hal Leonard Corporation.

2 Extract from 'Hard to Be' written by David Bazan. © 2009 Eat My Flesh Drink My Blood (BMI)/Administered by Bug Music. All Rights Reserved. Used by permission of Hal Leonard Corporation.

3 Extract from 'Indescribable' by Laura Story, add. lyrics by Jesse Reeves. © 2004 worshiptogether.com Songs/sixsteps Music/Gleaning Publishing/Kingswaysongs. Adm. by worshiptogether.com songs excl. UK & Europe, adm. by Kingswaysongs, a division of David C Cook tym@kingsway.co.uk. Used by permission.

4 Extract from 'The King Beetle on a Coconut Estate' Mazzotta/Weiss/Weiss/Jahanian. © 2009 Jesus Have Mercy On Me A Sinner, Spinning Audio Vortex Inc./EMI CMP/Small Stone Media BV, Holland. Adm. Song Solutions Daybreak www.songsolutions.org. Used by permission.

Further reading

Beaujon, A. (2006) *Body Piercing Saved My Life: Inside the Phenomenon of Christian Rock*, Cambridge, MA: Da Capo Press.

In this engaging book, Beaujon provides a history of Christian rock music, exploring the array of styles and perspectives; in the process, he interviews leading musicians and others in the industry.

McCracken, B. (2010) *Hipster Christianity: When Church and Cool Collide*, Grand Rapids: Baker Books.

McCracken's book explores the emergence of "Christian hipsters," the factors leading to the subculture, and its implications for the Christian tradition.

Ostwalt, C. (2003) *Secular Steeples: Popular Culture and the Religious Imagination*, Harrisburg, PA: Trinity Press International.

Ostwalt lays out a model of secularization, as described in this chapter, then uses it to examine an array of spaces, texts, and images in popular culture.

Radosh, D. (2008) *Rapture Ready! Adventures in the Parallel Universe of Christian Pop Culture*, 1st edn, New York: Scribner.

Radosh provides a glimpse into the contemporary evangelical subculture, spending time analyzing Christian music festivals, Christian theme parks, celibacy clubs, and much, much more.

Stark, R. (1999) "Secularization, R.I.P." *Sociology of Religion* 60, no. 3: 249–273.

In this important article, Rodney Stark analyzes and deconstructs early theories of secularization, arguing that they do not adequately account for the data on religious participation and belief, either now or historically.

Bibliography

Bazan, D. (2009) "Hard to Be," [Song, performed by David Bazan on *Curse Your Branches*, Barsuk] Los Angeles: Bug Music.

Beaujon, A. (2006) *Body Piercing Saved My Life: Inside the Phenomenon of Christian Rock*, Cambridge, MA: Da Capo Press.

Bell, R. (2006) *Velvet Elvis: Repainting the Christian Faith*, Grand Rapids: Zondervan.

Berger, P.L. (2008) "Secularization Falsified," *First Things*, February, 23–27.

—— (1990) *The Sacred Canopy*, New York: Anchor.

Blaney, F. (2007) "Rob Bell on Sex, God, and Sex Gods," *Wittenburg Door*, 14 November. Online. Available HTTP: www.wittenburgdoor.com/interview/rob-bell (accessed 15 February 2011).

Diaz, J., and York, K.E. (2009) "More Beautiful You," [Song, performed by Jonny Diaz, on *More Beautiful You*, Sony Records] Mobile, AL: Integrity Media.

Fletcher, D. (2009) "Hipsters," *Time*, 29 July.

Goldstein, W.S. (2009) "Secularization Patterns in the Old Paradigm," *Sociology of Religion*, 70, no. 2: 157–178.

Gospel Music Association (2009) "GMA Industry Overview 2009." Online. Available HTTP: www.gospelmusic.org/resources/industryFacts.aspx (accessed 15 February 2011).

Johnston, R.K. (1991) "American Evangelicalism: An Extended Family," in D.W. Dayton and R.K. Johnston (eds), *The Variety of American Evangelicalism*, Downers Grove, IL: InterVarsity Press, 1991.

King, Wes (1993) "I Believe" [Song, performed by Wes King on *The Robe,* Reunion Records] Santa Monica, CA: Universal Music.

Lanham, R. (2003) *The Hipster Handbook.* 1st edn, New York: Anchor.

——(2009) "Look at This Fucking Hipster Basher," *Morning News*, 29 June. Online. Available HTTP: www.themorningnews.org/archives/op-ed/look_at_this_fucking_hipster_basher.php (accessed 15 February 2011).

Leland, J. (2004) *Hip: The History*, New York: Ecco.

McCracken, B. (2009) "Are You a Christian Hipster?" *The Search*, 27 February. Online. Available HTTP: http://stillsearching.wordpress.com/2009/02/27/are-you-a-christian-hipster (accessed 15 February 2011).

Ostwalt, C. (2003) *Secular Steeples: Popular Culture and the Religious Imagination*, Harrisburg, PA: Trinity Press International.

Radosh, D. (2008) *Rapture Ready! Adventures in the Parallel Universe of Christian Pop Culture*, 1st edn, New York: Scribner.

Rehwaldt-Alexander, J., and Wilder, C. (2010) "Christians in the Hipster Subculture: What Does the Gospel Have to Do with Skinny Jeans, Irony, and Indie Bands?" *Lutheran Education* 143, no. 2: 112–120.

Riddle, J. (2004) "Revelation Song," [Song, performed by Phillips, Craig & Dean on *Fearless*, Ino/Columbia, 2009] Mobile, AL: Integrity's Praise Music.

Stark, R. (1999) "Secularization, R.I.P." *Sociology of Religion* 60, no. 3: 249–73.

Story, L.M. (2004) "Indescribable," [Song, performed by Chris Tomlin on *Arriving* Six Step Records] Brentwood, TN: EMI Christian Music.

Turner, M.P. (2010) *Hear No Evil: My Story of Innocence, Music, and the Holy Ghost*, Colorado Springs: WaterBrook Press.

Unthank, C. (2010) "2010 GMA Dove Awards—Editor's Predictions," *The Bridge: The Link Between Faith and Culture.* Online. Available HTTP: http://thebridgelive.net/index/features/comments/1224 (accessed 1 June 2010).

Weiss, A. (2009) "The King Beetle on a Coconut Estate," [Song, performed by mewithoutYou, on *It's All Crazy! It's All False! It's All A Dream! It's Alright*, Tooth & Nail].

Wofford, J. (2009) "Not Asking for a Black Eye: Derek Webb Discusses His New Album *Stockholm Syndrome*," *Patrol*, 17 August. Online. Available HTTP: www.patrolmag.com/arts/1778/derek-webb-interview (accessed 15 February 2011).

11 Lord of the Lembas

A study of what's cooking in pop culture

Jonathan Sands Wise

Symbols and suppers: introduction to the use of food as a symbol

The pungent onions obediently form piles of pearly whiteness beneath her as Julia Child's knife dexterously slices and dices, competitively practicing the intricate dance steps of food preparation as her eyes stream and arms strain. In a food movie's version of Rocky's training montage, we watch as Child, played by Meryl Streep in the film *Julie and Julia* (2009), victoriously chops onions faster than the men in her class, cooks a better omelet, or poaches a perfect egg. The victory tune is not the steroid-pumping strains of "Eye of the Tiger," (Survivor, *Eye of the Tiger*, 1982, Scotti Brothers) but the bouncy and tantalizing symphony described by Julia's husband: of wooden spoons clicking, of metal spoons dipping into a casserole and swooping up to the mouth for a taste, of salt liberally pinched and broadcast both into the casserole and over her shoulder, or of fingers grabbing a cannelloni out of boiling water. Though the music is of instruments (spoons and pots), the cooking is conspicuously done largely with bare hands: it is sensuous and tactile, but speedy and sure. Every lump of dough is a back rubbed by an expert masseuse, and every soup is an artist's masterpiece, with ingredients added in mad dumps and sprays by the expert artist chef. In the recent spate of popular food movies, food is earthy art, both a high culture that only the true aesthetes can appreciate, and a sensuous engagement with the flesh and body that can unify and redeem even the lowest and most crass eaters.

And this, these films helpfully remind us, is what we are, if not at our most basic level, then close to it: we are eaters (cf. Ferry 2003: 2, 7; Bower 2004: 3). As such, what we eat, when we eat, how we eat, and with whom we eat, goes far to define who and what we are as creatures, and our eating can be both a moment of cultural and personal achievement and fulfillment, as it is for both Julia and, ultimately, Julie, or a demonstration of our failures. Food is at the intersection of culture and nature: we must eat because we are animals, but it is our cooking and our sharing, our waiting for others to eat and our asking a blessing on our food—in short, the cultural practices that surround our eating—that sets us apart from other animals and even from each other (Kass 1994, ch. 4). Eating is a defining act of humanity; it defines us culturally, personally, and ethically, as well mannered or wild, as patient or fiery, and perhaps even as good or evil.

But again, food, precisely because it plays this central role in both our natural and our ordered lives, is equally a symbol of both power and depth, which is to say that it is not only central for defining us culturally and ethically, but it is equally central to our religious lives. Of course, how could it be otherwise? The very division is itself artificial and partial at best, for our religion is always bound up with our culture and our ethics, and at best defines them both. This is perhaps most obvious in the Christian and Jewish religions; as *Babette's Feast* (1987), one of the first great food movies powerfully argues, food is not only an occasion for sensual pleasure, but a symbol and occasion of grace, communion, redemption, joy, and the commitment of loving servitude. In all food movies, food is an intricate task of art and skill, but so long as it is just that, it is not good food; good food comes from love and commitment and passion, and is itself, therefore, a powerful and lasting symbol of the deepest commitments of a human heart, and this is our religion.

In a widely shared and well-known foundational story in Western culture, it is when one man and one woman, wandering about in a garden, eat a fruit that was forbidden to them, that sin and evil first enter into the world and human heart (Genesis 3). Later, in his covenant with his chosen people, Israel, God commands them to keep three annual feasts, including the Feast of Unleavened Bread, or Passover, with which they are to remember that he passed over, or spared them, in Egypt (Exodus 34:18–24), and God also commands Israel to observe carefully the eating of specific foods in specific ways. It is at the observance of the highly ritualized and symbolically ordered Feast of the Passover that Jesus later institutes a new covenant, one that is still commemorated today with the Eucharistic Feast (Matthew 26:20–30). In this Eucharist, or Communion, Jesus's followers eat broken bread, Christ's body, and drink wine, his blood, and in partaking of their lord, they seek not to consume him, but to be consumed by him (Augustine 1960: 171). Finally, in both the Jewish and Christian traditions, the final revealing of God, the apocalypse, is envisioned variously as a peaceful age of eating one's own bread and wine where even the dietary habits of wolves and lions are changed (Isaiah 65:17–25), or as a wedding feast to which even the beggars are invited (Matthew 22:1–14). For many religions, but especially for these, every great moment of religious time, from the fall to redemption to the unveiling of the new age, is instituted, founded, ritualized, and accomplished with eating.

It is both as a natural indication of our ethical state and as a symbol of our deepest religious beliefs that we turn now to the place of food in pop culture. For the pop culture artist, eating presents a great opportunity and a great challenge: a great opportunity because with this one essential act, the artist can accomplish so much in defining the cultural milieu of his creation, including the aspirations and morality of its characters, while simultaneously referencing a depth of other stories that both deepens and broadens the current scene. This presents a great challenge, though, because such powerful acts and symbols must be handled with great care, or they can undercut what the artist is trying to achieve. In what follows, I will suggest some specific ways that movies can use eating and food to show us what sort of characters we are dealing with—good or evil, strong or weak—and as religious symbols that imbue these scenes with important meaning. Our central text will be the movie trilogy, *The Lord of the Rings*, but we will refer freely to other works as necessary to spice up our conversation.

Theory and method or two pinches of allegory and a dash of gluttony: a medieval recipe for reading

The basic theory behind this way of reading texts actually derives from a medieval commonplace: besides the **literal meaning**, every biblical text (and at least most Christian literature) was believed to have a **spiritual meaning** as well (Beichner 1967: 33). While the literal meaning was meant to entertain, the spiritual meaning was meant to instruct by placing each text within a larger Christian universe of faith, and by clearly identifying the moral characters in the text. Augustine, one early proponent of finding spiritual meanings in texts, more simply calls any story, object, or word that refers to something earthly a **symbol** (or a sign or reference, Augustine uses these three words more or less synonymously). So, for example, while God commanding Abraham to sacrifice Isaac on Mount Moriah (Genesis 22:1–19) literally means that God did so command Abraham, for Augustine the entire story has a further spiritual meaning as well: this is a prefiguring of God the Father sacrificing his own son on what (according to tradition) is the same mountain, and hence is symbolically the sacrifice of Jesus on the Cross.

We can further divide this spiritual meaning into two different types: allegorical and moral. Speaking allegorically, the particular story or passage would refer to some other event in the past or future, thereby showing key connections to the way that God generally deals with humanity. So, to use our above example, God first demands absolute obedience of Abraham and tests him (Genesis 22:1–14), but he ultimately deals with him mercifully, providing a ram to sacrifice in place of Isaac; in the same way, according to the Bible, God has mercy on us by not having mercy on himself, sacrificing his own son so that we do not have to be sacrificed. Speaking morally, Augustine would say we should read the stories in scripture as showing us how we must live in our daily lives now as well. Just as Abraham was held to the impossibly high moral standard of absolute obedience, so we too are to be perfect in our everyday lives, and yet by God's mercy we will be spared when we fail. The central insight here is clear: certain aspects of stories gain meaning by reading them in light of other stories, past or future, while other aspects have a basic moral meaning in that they tell us how we should live our own lives.

Stories do not, and cannot, include every detail of their characters' lives. Imagine a movie that recorded literally every single activity that someone undertook during a day in real time, or a novel that tried to describe every thought that someone had. This would, doubtless, be incredibly boring! When everyday activities are included by writers and artists, then, we should wonder why. For example, if we see someone going to the bathroom in a movie, something besides the ordinary better happen while they are in there, something that tells us more about this person or their situation, or it just is not effective (or interesting) storytelling. So when we see someone eating in a story or even in a painting or other work of art, we should ask, "Why is the artist showing us such mundane details?" The Medieval theory that every text has spiritual senses points us to an interesting way to understand the inclusion of the mundane in modern day storytelling: in the enactment of such everyday practices, the artist can make interesting and meaningful reference to other stories that imbue this story with deeper and more nuanced meaning than would otherwise be possible (eating as a symbol). In addition, the artist can more effectively teach us something about good and bad characters than explicit instruction could accomplish (eating as a moral practice).

Food symbolism in stories

A quick example will help us fill out this theory and make it clearer, so let us turn to a pop culture artifact of an earlier age in which food is clearly being used both symbolically and as a moral marker: Augustine's *Confessions*. Augustine was one of the most famous men of his day in fourth- and fifth-century Rome. A brilliant rhetorician and orator who converted in midlife to Christianity and soon became a Bishop in Africa, Augustine's autobiography, the *Confessions*, was one of the most popular and famous works of both his own time and of the later Middle Ages. In it, Augustine reminisces at length about a seemingly harmless adolescent prank he committed with his friends at the age of sixteen, then spends page after page lamenting how horribly sinful and lost he was at this time. The story itself is quite simple and brief:

> In a garden nearby to our vineyard there was a pear tree, loaded with fruit that was desirable neither in appearance nor in taste. Late one night—to which hour, according to our pestilential custom, we had kept up our street games—a group of very bad youngsters set out to shake down and rob this tree. We took great loads of fruit from it, not for our own eating, but rather to throw it to the pigs; even if we did eat a little of it, we did this to do what pleased us for the reason that it was forbidden.
>
> (Augustine 1960: 70)

This is a seemingly harmless prank, especially since Augustine has hinted in the same chapter that he was committing much greater thefts, getting drunk every night, and possibly even having affairs with married women! So why does Augustine make such a big deal about this particular bit of food-related fun?

One clear reason that Augustine includes this story is for the symbolic value of this particular crime and the deeper meaning it infuses into the story. Any biblically literate person reading a story about someone eating forbidden fruit in a garden should immediately think of Adam and Eve in the Garden of Eden, chowing down on the fruit of knowledge and learning way more than they ever wanted to know about the "evil" part of the Tree of Knowledge of Good and

Evil. Augustine's act of eating of the pear tree is hence an imitation of this original act of sin and pride, which makes his act symbolic of any other human sin as well. This first sin, according to the theology of original sin that Augustine helped create, is not only a single sinful act, but is the one act in which all of humanity corporately fell together. In mimicking this original sin, therefore, Augustine is symbolically committing The Sin, not just any sinful act, and the discussion that follows is meant to apply to all sin. Let us note here three major aspects of Augustine's symbolic use of food: first, symbols deepen and nuance our reading of his story, making it about much more than just a single youthful indiscretion; second, symbols can refer to more than one story or reality at the same time; third, symbols work so well because they are so compact. We will look at each of these in turn below.

One of Augustine's central purposes in writing his autobiography is pastoral: to guide every reader along the same path of salvation that he has now followed. This sin of stealing pears is not only so innocent that it can relate to any adolescent's experience of stealing road signs or trespassing with friends, it also symbolizes *any* sin by referring to the original prideful eating of fruit in God's garden. Augustine's use of the food symbol in this case both universalizes his story and nuances it. It is universal because each of us can put ourselves into his shoes and think of times when we have done something just like this, something that seemed so innocent and yet we knew was wrong even as we did it. It is nuanced, though, because just by referencing this earlier story, Augustine adds multiple shades of meaning to his action: this is no longer just some innocent childhood prank, this is symbolic of Sin itself in all of its messiness, ugliness, and painfulness. As his discussion continues, it becomes clear that his questions about why he stole these pears are really questions about why we *ever* do *anything* that we know is wrong, and why we hurt others by doing things that do not help us, but instead do great damage to our selves. These are deep questions, and they do not really seem to fit the crime if we are just thinking of a single theft of some rotten pears … but if we are thinking of any and all human sin, then we can understand why Augustine is so worried about our tangle of confused motivations. By using food as a symbol, therefore, Augustine makes this act an Everyact that we all might do and have done, and deepens the story, making it about much more than just its literal meaning would suggest.

To take the second aspect, in eating a forbidden fruit, Augustine references the original sin of Adam and Eve, as we have noted, but then he also adds the particular detail that he and his friends throw the pears *to pigs*. In the context of other references made throughout the *Confessions*, it is clear that he is here using the theft of pears to refer to Jesus's parable of the Prodigal Son (Luke 15:11–32). In this popular parable, Jesus tells of a younger son who rejects his father, runs away to a far country where he wastes all of his money on profligate living, then becomes desperately impoverished as the country falls under a famine and is forced to take a job tending pigs. Jesus says that the prodigal longed to eat of the food of the pigs, but no one offered him any. In the same way, Augustine longs for the fruit and steals it, but rather than eating of it, he throws it mindlessly to the pigs

(Augustine 1960: 72). Augustine, we can see, is not only like Adam and Eve in their first sin; he is likewise the Prodigal Son, rejecting his father and wasting himself in sinful, empty living. In fact, Augustine suggests that he is even worse, for while the Prodigal must throw to the pigs the physical food which he knows he genuinely needs for sustenance, Augustine is like a man who does not know he is spiritually starving and ignorantly throws away the soul-saving food of God's word!

Augustine uses each reference as a way of adding further nuance to his account: if he is only Adam and Eve, then he is only lost and fallen. But if he is also the Prodigal Son, then maybe he too will come to his senses and humbly return to his father, begging to be just a slave in his father's household again (and if God is that father, then he will certainly accept Augustine back). By using the pear theft to symbolize *both* original sin and the Prodigal Son, Augustine provides us with a deeper understanding of what he has done, and of where he is going in his story (ultimately toward salvation and forgiveness, like the Prodigal Son). When readers are familiar with the entire range of referential narratives, many pop-culture texts, such as Augustine's, suddenly open up to reveal multiple layers of meaning otherwise easily missed.

Finally, and to take our third point above, it is significant that Augustine's story is quite brief. A small amount of technical language will help us here: the thing that a symbol refers *to* is called the "**referent**." In this case, Augustine's theft from the pear tree symbolically refers to (at least) two earlier referents: the story of Adam and Eve and the story of the Prodigal Son. So using this language, we can make our point quite clearly: symbols are useful, powerful, and effective because the brevity of the symbol is matched with the breadth of the referent. It takes only two sentences for Augustine to write of his theft and the subsequent disposal of the pears, but to dissect this reference fully would require pages upon pages of text.

The moral meaning of food

So far we have used Augustine's eating of the pears as a symbol that refers allegorically to other texts and stories, a symbol that both universalizes and provides nuance to his account of his midnight snack. Clearly, though, Augustine's story has not only an allegorical symbolism, but also a moral symbolism as well. That is to say, what Augustine eats (or doesn't eat), whom he eats with, when he eats, and how he eats, is a symbol that refers to deeper truths about his moral character. Looking carefully at this second level of spiritual readings can provide both a fascinating and an important layer of meaning to any pop-cultural text, and it is always important if we want to explore the religious implications of a text to know who is good and who is bad (or in what way people are good or bad; very few are simply one or the other).

But how are we supposed to figure out whether people are good or bad by analyzing when, how, with whom, and what they eat? Medieval moral theology provides us with an interesting way to interpret when people are eating correctly, or how they are going wrong, in its discussion of the Capital Vice of **Gluttony**. As medieval ethicists interpreted the vice, there are five ways to go wrong with regards to eating; we can remember these handily by using the mnemonic FRESH, standing for Fastidiously, Ravenously, Excessively, Sumptuously, and Hastily (Konyndyk DeYoung 2009: 141ff). To eat too daintily or fastidiously is to be too picky; in other words, one way of being gluttonous may be to eat *too little*. Ravenous eaters are the opposite, bolting down their food in an orgy of swallowing, both hands full of food waiting its turn to enter their all-consuming maws. The excessive eater is the one we normally think of when we picture gluttony, the overweight person who simply eats far too much, while the sumptuous eater is our other picture of gluttony, the person who covers his or her plate with nothing but rich, fatty, and/or sweet foods. Finally, the hasty eater is the person who eats *too soon*, and so generally eats alone, before everyone else sits down to the meal (Konyndyk DeYoung 2009: 141ff).

According to Augustine, the proper way to eat is to enjoy our food, but to enjoy it as a means to something else: the sustenance of our body, the good of the community, and the glory of God (Konyndyk DeYoung 2009: 150). Augustine does not eat alone ... but look at his companions! Rather than eating a civilized, cooked meal in community, he devours, or even carelessly throws away after only one bite, raw fruit with a bunch of so-called friends. Likewise, rather than eating at an appropriate time, they raid the garden at night, and then throw out the pears that fail to live up to their fastidious desires. Augustine does not eat for the good of his body, nor for the good of his community, since he joins others in sin and steals from a neighbor. Nor does Augustine eat for the glory of God, since he rejects God's law and willfully sins against him in the theft. Augustine steals and eats the pears only because he thinks that it will be fun for him to do so. His eating is an entirely self-centered and deeply disordered act.

To summarize, food, including how it is obtained, how it is consumed, what it is, and with whom it is eaten, is often used in movies, books, stories, and art generally for two purposes: first, as a symbol that imbues the artifact with more meaning by referring to some other story, act, or artifact; and second, as an indication of the character of the person or people eating. Often, of course, the first of these purposes is being used to accomplish the second, as when Augustine's symbolic reference to the original sin and to the Prodigal Son show us where he is morally, but this is not always the case. So far we have drawn four theoretical conclusions from Augustine's symbolic use of food in the story of the great pear robbery: first, symbols can add weight and depth to a story by giving it a more universal application and a more nuanced meaning; second, one story or one detail can symbolize different things, and this can either increase or decrease the power of the symbol; third, symbols get much of their power from the sparseness of the symbol and the richness of the referent; fourth, symbols frequently operate to morally define a character.

As we turn to analyze the *Lord of the Rings* and other cultural artifacts below, we will see that modern day artists, much like Augustine, frequently rely on their text having allegorical and moral meanings, in addition to the literal meaning that is on the surface. By referring to other texts, they deepen what they can say in a brief space and in a more interesting way, while providing subtle shades of meaning that it would take too much time to write out in detail. By depicting how people eat, likewise, they can characterize someone without having to describe each vice and virtue explicitly. It may sometimes be helpful to begin a work by describing someone as self-centered, anxious to fit in with the crowd and struggling with self-worth, and arrogantly unconcerned with anyone else's rights, but it is sometimes far more powerful to demonstrate each of these characteristics, as Augustine does in his brief vignette about eating pears. Food and other common objects are especially powerful symbols for these purposes precisely because of their universality: everyone must eat, and so how and what you eat defines the sort of human being (or hobbit) that you are.

Case study: Lord of the Lembas

Apples and rings: symbols and stories

In a scene that neatly parallels Augustine's story of the great pear robbery, *The Fellowship of the Ring* (the first movie in director Peter Jackson's *Lord of the Rings* [*LOTR*] trilogy) shows Merry and Pippin, two apparently adolescent and decidedly mischievous hobbit friends, steal and set off some fireworks at Bilbo's birthday party. As the movie opens, we learn that Bilbo, an old hobbit, is about to throw a large birthday party for himself, and that Gandalf, a wizard and an old friend, is going to attend and set off fireworks. After Gandalf selects from his wagon some relatively innocent fireworks, Merry and Pippin sneak up and steal the largest firework they can find, which turns out to be a large and rather dangerous dragon. Merry hands the firework to Pippin, who sneaks it off, and as Merry backs around the corner trying to look innocent, we see him take a large and conspicuous bite out of a bright, shiny apple, another Adam who has given in to temptation.

This scene uses the apple and the reference to the Garden of Eden lightly, as it is often used in contemporary culture. There is no hint here that Merry is sunk in the depths of irreparable sin, desperately in need of grace and mercy, as Augustine's parallel usage is meant to show. Indeed, Merry is a good hobbit, and he is far more of a mischievous imp than a depraved sinner in the *LOTR* films. Clearly the meaning of symbols can alter over time, and taking a bite of an apple is now largely a symbol for unimportant, even "innocent" sins, if such an oxymoron makes any sense, perhaps because our culture takes sin of all sorts less seriously than many of the ancients did. The movies do, however, retain much of Tolkien's own Catholic and intensely serious view of sin in the symbolism of the Ring of Power, which acts as a substitute for Adam and Eve's fruit in these stories, symbolizing the destructive pursuit of corrupting power. Just like the forbidden fruit, the Ring is inherently attractive and tempting because it appeals to the pride, desire for power, and selfishness of all those who come into contact with it, whether they ultimately surrender to this temptation or not. Even more, the Ring has the same effects as the "original" fruit, giving knowledge and enhanced vision of a sort (Genesis 3:7), but only at a great and terrible price for the bearer, for all its added knowledge is ultimately skewed such that the bearer sees only the evil of the world, never its full reality.

The movies demonstrate this parallel of the Ring and the Fruit in multiple scenes, especially in others' reactions to the Ring. Gandalf, Galadriel (a powerful and good Elf queen), and Aragorn (a noble and great king) show their wisdom in refusing even to touch the Ring, though all feel its powerful pull and struggle against the temptation to seize this great power. Boromir, apparently a good and noble man, is too proud, as even his brother recognizes, and so proves unable to resist, trying to seize the Ring by force when Frodo will not give it to him. Though Boromir intends to do good with the ring and save his city, he cannot see the very pride that makes him desire the Ring would inevitably lead to his downfall. Most powerfully of all, when old Bilbo sees the Ring again in Rivendell, he becomes a veritable demon for a moment, his image twisted and distorted as if reflected in an evil fun house mirror. In each case, the person involved becomes aware soon afterward that they were acting almost under an external compulsion, but only *because* of their own interior weakness.

In the world that Tolkien has created, there are forces beyond those in our own world, forces that we might deem magical or mysterious. Whenever Frodo is near the Black Riders (evil servants of Sauron, the dark lord, who crafted the Ring and is desperately searching for it), he feels an overwhelming desire to put the Ring on his finger, even after learning that doing so makes him *more* visible to the servants of Sauron, though it makes him invisible to others. As the Black Riders approach, donning the Ring warps Frodo's perception (and the viewer's) with a tunnel effect, mirroring the shape of the Ring itself; distances become distorted, Frodo becomes pale and disoriented, his eyes staring but unfocused, and he hears nothing clearly but only as through a tunnel and with a vague ringing. When he gives in and puts on the Ring, the same disorientation becomes worse: the world becomes a rushing wind that blows even colors past him, and while he can see anything evil more clearly, the rest of the world fades into darkness and shadow. The Ring conceals Frodo from the living and the good, but also conceals the living and the good from him. Conversely, while the Ring helps him to see the evil beings more clearly (the Black Riders and Sauron especially), it equally distorts his vision by making it appear that evil is the only reality, and it nakedly reveals Frodo to their gaze: and so that which conceals may also reveal, while even a revealing can also be a concealing.

The same pattern is evident in the temptation of the forbidden fruit in Genesis, both its temptation and its distorting power and revelation. For Adam and Eve, the temptation is to a powerful knowledge that would make them more like God, but the knowledge actually gained from the forbidden fruit is a distorted knowledge. While Adam and Eve learn certain truths about reality (e.g. they are naked), it is not so much *what* they learn as *how* they now perceive this reality that is altered. They already knew that they were naked in their innocence, but in their guilt, this becomes an unbearable shame (Genesis 3:10; 21). The Ring, in a parallel fashion, changes the perception of its bearer. The third film in the trilogy, *Return of the King*, powerfully demonstrates a similarly sobering change in perception through a repeated line at the beginning and end of the film that neatly references the universal experience of eating: "we even forgot the taste of bread."

As the film opens, Jackson gives us a quick rehearsal of what the Ring is and how it was found by a hobbit-like creature called Gollum long ago. Gollum's friend actually found it, but Gollum is quickly corrupted by its seduction and kills his friend to steal the Ring. Under its baleful influence, Gollum ceases to see anything but his own desires: the Ring is "precious" *to him*, and he will kill anyone to possess it. But no one possesses the Ring any more than one can truly possess sin—we do not possess our sin, it possesses us. As opposed to food, which we consume and make part of ourselves, the Ring consumes its bearer and makes it part of itself, a pitiful ring-wraith.

Warped and distorted by the Ring, Gollum becomes more and more like a hollow caricature of a hobbit, nothing more than skin stretched over bones; or as Bilbo puts it when describing how the Ring has affected him after bearing it for long years, he feels "stretched, like butter spread over too much bread." Rather than eating the cooked food of community, Gollum begins to catch fish with his bare hands and to eat them raw; the camera spares us nothing here, dwelling almost lovingly on Gollum's few blackened teeth as they tear into the still living fish's back, juice squirting out from between his chewing teeth. Even his name, as Ralph Wood points out in *The Gospel According to Tolkien*, is derived from his voracious appetite: Gollum is a nickname given him because of the repetitive swallowing noise he makes (Wood 2003: 56). Like the Ring that has come to possess him, Gollum is now nothing but a voracious appetite. He desires no good, not even his own; his desires now revolve endlessly around the gold Ring that he endlessly revolves his fingers around, stroking it and speaking to it, calling it "My Precious." Gollum's voiceover as the film begins is addressed to his Precious, and it is a powerful device for characterizing the extent of Gollum's corruption and loss: "And we forgot the taste of bread, the sound of trees, the softness of the wind. We even forgot our own name."

The power of the Ring is strong. Even Frodo, who is praised for his humility and courage in resisting the Ring for so long, is eventually warped by it. He becomes jealous of the Ring, unwilling to allow Sam, his most faithful and dear friend, to touch or even to speak of touching it. As they make their way up Mount Doom to destroy the ring in *The Return of the King*, we get the full sense of Frodo's loss of self when he eerily echoes Gollum's earlier voiceover. As Sam tries to cheer Frodo with thoughts of strawberries and cream, Frodo confesses in a weak and fading voice, "I can't recall the taste of food." Frodo is becoming like Gollum, unable to participate in the civilized community of love that bread represents, unable even to remember why such a community is attractive. We will look more at the symbolism of bread shortly, but to see why it is a symbol of civilization, consider that first the wheat must be raised by settled farmers, then ground and turned into flour. The yeast, too, the leavening agent, must be preserved in a starter that must be occasionally fed with more flour and water, making it difficult or impossible to transfer far. Finally, the whole product must be carefully cooked in an oven, not just warmed over a fire. Bread, in short, is only possible in a settled culture that works at food preparation; it cannot easily be found on the ground or cooked over a campfire.

Consumed by the circle of the Ring, Frodo has begun to be shut up within himself and his own endless desires, and can no longer even remember the taste or desire for simple, civilized food. At the end, of course, Frodo will try to make the Ring his own, giving in to the lust for power, and will only be saved by a mysterious mercy and providential grace. Even so, just as with Adam and Eve, there is no simple road back after the fruit has been taken. For Frodo, nothing in Middle Earth can any longer give him rest, for he lives in a constant ache and itch for the lost Ring of power and in pain from the wounds that he has received. In Tolkien's Christian view, even the most wonderful stories, so far as they are limited to the unredeemed earth, must be ultimately filled with a sense of loss, and Frodo's is no different.

The Ring of Power is a symbol of the Forbidden Fruit, allegorically referencing the Fall of Humanity and eating, and so connecting this desire for corrupting power and control with the desire that all human beings feel. Through this connection it also, of course, is making various important moral points concerning both our own moral lives and the moral character of each person who interacts with this terrible temptation.

Symbols and multiple referents

Bread is the food of the hearth and of community, the food that must be prepared, and it is also the Christian symbol of the Bread of Life, Jesus, broken on the cross (John 6:35). The most obvious symbol of the Eucharist in *LOTR*, however, is not plain bread, but the wondrous Elvish bread, Lembas. This brings us back to our second point about symbols: they can frequently reference more than one referent, and this can either add or detract from the use of the symbol. Lembas, Tolkien tells us, is a light, airy bread made only by certain elves from a plant that they brought from the land where the Valar, the divine beings in charge of earth, dwell. While incredibly light, it gives great sustenance, and more, as its eaters rely on it alone (Tolkien 1977: 247, 251; Tolkien 1994: 360–361; Wood 2003: 55). The connections to Catholic Eucharistic wafers are obvious: though light and airy, they are believed to give spiritual life and strength to the believer. The movie makes the connection even clearer by designing the lembas like a wafer that is split into four pie quarters (much as many Eucharistic wafers are today in Catholic and Episcopal churches). As Sam breaks it and shares it with Frodo, we watch them eat a Communion-like meal together, symbolizing their close relationship. As Frodo begins to break down under the Ring, we watch his fellowship with Sam suffer, but Sam's own deep humility and trust in his master saves their relationship and ultimately saves their mission. Just as Sam forgives all of Frodo's insults and continues to come back and support him and *speak* and *eat* with him, so is Frodo never deprived of community the way that Gollum was and is (Flieger 1983: 52–54). Though Gollum is now with Frodo and Sam all of the time, and even begins to waver and to trust Frodo again, he is never truly able to enter their communion, and this is signified by his inability to partake of their food. Gollum refuses to eat a cooked and prepared rabbit, and when he tries to eat Sam's and Frodo's lembas, he chokes. What he eats, and what he cannot eat, both defines and demonstrates his evil, isolated, and warped character.

All of this certainly can be understood without seeing the connection between lembas and the Eucharist. Gollum has become so bestial that he no longer wears clothing or eats prepared food, which clearly disgusts Sam especially, and he has become so evil that he cannot partake of Elvish food or touch Elvish clothing or ropes. None of this needs the reference to the Last Supper and Christ's sacrifice to make sense or to help define Gollum's character in distinction to Frodo's and Sam's. While true, this misses the deeper and more nuanced meaning imparted to the text when we catch Tolkien's further symbolism. After all, it is mere Western bias to consider going without clothing or eating food raw as "uncivilized" or "evil"; much of the world still does both regularly and is not obviously either less civilized or more evil than those who wear more clothing and eat cooked fast food daily. When we see the deeper connections between lembas and Eucharistic wafers, then we can understand fully the depth of Gollum's depravity and corruption and the horror of Frodo's real danger in bearing the ring. Gollum is not just unable to share in Elvish food, he is unable to partake in the basic ritual of religious community, a ritual that, as understood by Tolkien, unites one mystically with God.

While the Eucharist is the clearest referent for lembas, other interesting referents are the manna God sends the Israelites in the wilderness (Exodus 16:31) and the "daily bread" Jesus instructs his disciples to pray for (Matthew 6:11). Food becomes a symbol of Sam's hope as he and Frodo finally approach Mordor, the land of evil where they must destroy the Ring. In a touching scene, we find Sam counting all of the food they have left, and making sure that they have enough for the return trip as well! Never, until near the very end, does Sam give up hope that there will be a return journey, and even then he does not finally lose hope. Just as there was always enough manna for each day in Israel's journey through the wilderness, but never enough to gather up and store for later (Exodus 16:19–20), so there always seems to be just enough lembas for what must be done. In the character of Sam, we watch as he must slowly give up his self-sufficiency and begin to trust that there will always be his daily bread. Here the multiple referents for the lembas deepen the symbol, emphasizing its communal aspects and its spiritual strength, but equally drawing upon its connection to faith in God's providential care.

A little goes a long way: the potency of symbols

Symbols, as we noted with the work of Augustine, get much of their power from the sparseness of the reference and the richness of the referent. Precisely because symbols are so short and so powerful, artists must be extremely careful how they use them. To drop in too many references too fast gives the appearance of depth and sophistication, but really tends to just muddy the waters. Television shows are frequently guilty of this, in part, perhaps, because they are written serially (as the show is filmed) and by committees, so there may not actually *be* any set meaning that they are trying to convey. It is easy to drop in symbols because they are so small, but their weight is great and (to mix metaphors) they carry a lot of baggage!

We have already seen several examples of this power in *LOTR*, including the Ring, lembas, and Merry's apple. A different example would be the symbol of feasts in general. Hobbits are famous eaters, eating many meals a day and seemingly always eating! On the extended edition DVDs, Bilbo notes the common remark that "Hobbits' only real passion is for food," and goes on to refute this by describing their love for things that endure, for a simple life of peace and quiet and for all things that grow. In the opening scene of Bilbo's birthday party in the first film, we see an immense celebration filled with joy, laughter, dancing, and, most of all, eating and drinking. Here no one is left out, no one must scrounge for food, and everyone is invited, no matter their faults. Bilbo's party, and the hobbits' generous approach to food in general, is a picture of the Banquet of Heaven, as could be all beautifully shared meals. A later image with an added layer is the feast in Rohan (an allied horse kingdom), shared and enjoyed by human beings, hobbits, elves, and dwarves, all together.

Just like the banquet that Jesus uses to picture heaven (Luke 14:13, 23), everyone in the community is invited, and old hurts and old pains dissolve in the glory of this shared meal. The ability to partake in the meal is a demonstration of the basic humanity and goodness of all those who partake, just as the hobbits' love of food and good tobacco, while used for comic relief at times, especially with Pippin and Merry, is a clear demonstration of their ability to appreciate the goodness of creation (Wood 2003: 23–25). In dark contrast, the evil characters of *LOTR* demonstrate in their eating their deep malignity toward all beauty and goodness, as we will discuss in the next section.

To review, texts, including pop culture artifacts like *LOTR*, often have not only a literal, but also a spiritual meaning in which particular symbols are used to reference other texts, stories, or realities. Such symbols as the Ring of Power, feasts, and lembas, operate by giving both added depth and nuance to the text, often reference multiple different texts or realities, and are so powerful precisely because they are so small. Feasts fit all three of these characteristics of allegory that we have noted so far: they add depth and nuance to the scene by referencing other great feasts, such as the Banquet of Heaven, but they also reference many other things, such as the idea of plenty or of harvest, as well as great religious festivals in different cultures, and they do all of this even though the actual feast scene might be quite brief. What people feast on, how they feast, and whom they feast with, also tells us a great deal about the character of those doing the feasting!

You are what, and how, you eat: food and characterization

We have already seen several ways that Tolkien and Jackson use eating to demonstrate the essential character of various people in *LOTR*: Gollum is unable to eat civilized food or eat in a civilized manner, while Frodo and Sam share good food unselfishly, and other hobbits, elves, and humans feast in wild and pleasant abandon. In a similar vein, the Orcs, the evil warriors of Sauron and Saruman (an evil wizard), drink a dark, blood-like substance similar to wine in color but thicker, and they eat both hobbits and other Orcs, as we see with Saruman's foot soldiers after they capture Merry and Pippin in the second film. Rather than demonstrating community in their feasts, the banquets of the Orcs are bloody, violent, and competitive affairs in which you'd better watch your back or you might become the next entrée. Notice that with both the eating and the wine, the feasting of evil characters is a distortion of proper feasting. The liquor of the humans, hobbits, and elves that gives refreshment and energy becomes a vile, bloody substance that burns and gives a manic, destructive force to the drinker, while the generous table of the hobbits or of Rohan becomes the scrounging gluttony of Orcs feeding on each other. (For more on Tolkien's Augustinian view of evil as a distortion of good things (cf. Wood 57–61). Another example of this is the Orcs themselves, whom Tolkien describes as being elves that were twisted and tortured through the power of Sauron; Tolkien, *The Silmarillion*, 1977, 50.)

The most powerful example of using eating and food to make a moral point comes from a character who was clearly good at one point, but has become warped by fear and pride: the Steward of Gondor. Gondor is the last remaining great kingdom of human beings, but its last king died centuries before and the city is now run by a line of Stewards. While they originally ruled in the name of the absent king until one should reappear, there is little doubt that the current Steward has no intention of ever surrendering rule again, as he should to Aragorn, the proper king. The main city of the realm, Minas Tirith, comes quickly under attack as the third movie of the trilogy opens, and the Steward is both too proud and too afraid, both overly confident in his own abilities, and overly fearful that the city will soon fall. In his fear, and having already lost his older son, Boromir, we see the Steward send Faramir, his wiser and kinder younger son, on a suicide mission to reclaim a nearby city, apparently as an irrational punishment for surviving while the favored older son died.

Even as Faramir leaves the hall, the Steward sits down to a huge, sumptuous feast, overflowing with a whole chicken, a plate of vegetables and of cheese, fried foods and sliced meats, and a large jug of wine. Though others, including Pippin, stand nearby, the Steward, the one who is to *serve* the king, sits down to this kingly meal alone, now served by others. Fastidiously pulling up his sleeves, the Steward begins to daintily pick from the massive piles before him with his fingers, piling his plate high with delicacies. As he eats, both hands are constantly full of food, ambidextrously filling his ravenous mouth even as he continues to talk. As Faramir and the soldiers of Gondor ride to their deaths on this suicide mission, we watch and hear the Steward crunch down on a tomato, the squirting juice reminiscent both of the blood of his men as they fall and of Gollum's earlier eating of the fish. Mercilessly, Jackson juxtaposes brutal scenes of war with the Steward's oddly fastidious and yet bestial eating, all the while showing us Pippin's disgusted reaction as he tries to sing for him of the fading of all good things. Clearly the Steward lives as he eats: gluttonously.

Just as he fastidiously chooses his food, so he snobbishly rejects one son in favor of the more warlike one, then ravenously chews up men's lives and spits them out in his thoughtless conduct of war. From the time that Faramir rides out, the Steward has a thin rivulet of red juice running down his chin, and dripping from his mouth; the camera intimately studies his oddly choosy yet ravenous fingers and mouth as they dance among the sumptuous feast, tearing meat and dripping blood and juice, yet keeping his mouth permanently full, even overflowing. Dressed in his sumptuous finery, the Steward sits in a city that is under siege and starving, yet he feasts alone and bestially. In the same way, the Steward is clothed in all of his pride and selfishness, ignoring the good of his city and sending his ill-loved younger son to his death. The wastefulness of his eating symbolizes the wastefulness of his life, his uneven love for his sons, and even the death that he will soon suffer as he throws himself on a burning pyre to avoid having to struggle against the evil that is coming. A powerful and potentially very good man, the Steward has become twisted by his fear and pride till he is no longer truly a steward or a man. His eating demonstrates more powerfully than any description could that he has become an animal.

A similar scene in Paul Thomas Anderson's *There Will be Blood* (2007) demonstrates both the frequency and the power of this method of using food and eating to show the character's true nature. *There Will be Blood* is a disturbing study of an oilman named Daniel Plainview who becomes so consumed by avarice that he carelessly destroys people and communities, including his own adopted son. At the strike that has made him rich, a dynamic and charismatic preacher and his church control a key plot of ground Daniel needs to install a pipeline, and the young preacher shames Daniel in a forced baptism before he finally allows the dig. As the final scene of the film begins, Daniel is visited in his large and noticeably empty mansion by the young preacher, Eli, just as he sits down to eat. Eli pours Daniel a drink, but Daniel refuses even this small touch of community, drinking ravenously from his own bottle and eating alone. The young supplicant offers him the chance to drill on a new piece of property owned by a man named Bandy, and it is clear that Eli desperately needs the money such drilling would bring. While the young man speaks, Daniel chews loudly, picking bones out of his mouth and gnawing on tough, gristly meat. Daniel agrees to Eli's proposition, but only if Eli will freely confess that God is a superstition and that he, Eli, is a false prophet, thus shaming Eli as he earlier shamed Daniel. Having metaphorically devoured the young man and gnawed on him like a piece of beef, Daniel coldly informs him that the property in question has already been emptied of oil, thus pulling him out again like a piece of hard gristle and throwing him away. Daniel's unshaven face and maniacal eyes gleam with a chilling and feverish hate as he informs Eli that he has already drained all of the oil from the area because he owns everything around it: "I drink your water. I drink it up. Every day I drink the blood of lamb from Bandy's tract." As saliva drips from his mouth, Daniel rages that he drinks up Eli's milkshake, then screams, "I told you I would eat you! I told you I would eat you!" and brutally beats Eli to death with a bowling pin.

As he eats, so Daniel lives: brutally, rapaciously, gnawing away at everything until, finally, as he declares in the last line of the film, there is nothing left to consume: "I'm finished!" In this stunningly ironic and disturbing scene, we get references to sacrifices and to the Eucharist (the "blood of lamb") and then finally to the crucifixion itself, where Jesus declares "It is finished," just before he dies (John 19:30). I leave it to my readers to decipher this scene more fully, remembering the ways in which allegorical symbols add nuance to a scene, refer to multiple referents, and gain power through their brevity, as well as how the moral symbol of eating can demonstrate the moral character of a person.

Conclusion

Often details regarding food and eating are included in movies, books, songs, and artwork, and in stories more generally, because of the symbolic and moral value of food metaphors: they quickly, insightfully, and powerfully refer to other instances of eating and food in other contexts (the allegorical meaning of the text) and so add depth of meaning and significance to a story, and they illustrate the character of the person(s) involved in an immediate and visceral way (the moral meaning of the text). Contemporary pop culture makes frequent use of such symbols, and informed viewers can understand all aspects of the artifact more fully if they are aware of these deeper levels of meaning. Of course, understanding and appreciating such symbols requires not only an awareness that such symbols can be used, but also a familiarity with the cultural heritage of Western society, including and especially the Bible. Such a familiarity cannot be achieved either quickly or easily, but its possession is worthwhile and carries with it great rewards, both in the ability to more fully appreciate pop culture today, as several of these essays show, and in the beauty and worth of the heritage itself.

Summary

- Texts may have both a literal meaning and a spiritual meaning, the latter consisting of allegorical symbols that refer to other texts or realities and moral symbols that demonstrate the character of the person involved.
- Symbols add depth and nuance to art by turning simple, everyday scenes into powerful tools for conveying layers of meaning and characterization.
- Symbols often work by referencing more than one referent.
- Symbols gain power through their brevity.
- Common elements, such as food, not only convey the personality of characters, they can also convey their moral character, as when we see characters eating gluttonously or graciously.

Glossary terms

Allegory – a medieval term for the way in which a single story or text can reference further texts and realities.

Gluttony – a term for the vice of eating in a disordered manner, which may include eating fastidiously, ravenously, excessively, sumptuously, or too hastily (FRESH).

Literal meaning – the obvious sense of the text in its immediate context.

Reference – a symbol or artifact in a text that refers to something else.

Referent – a previous event, story, or artifact that is referred to by something else.

Spiritual meaning – a medieval term for the various further symbolic meanings that a text can have, including its allegorical, moral, or anagogical meanings (see Further reading).

Symbol – as Augustine used the term (in Latin, *signum*, or sign), something, whether a word or a story or a thing, that refers to or is a sign of something else.

Points for discussion

- What other common elements appear in artwork that can be used as symbols and tools for characterization the way that food is used? Consider, for example, the clothing of the characters in *LOTR*, or the use of color in different scenes.
- Why do we so immediately understand that someone who eats alone and in a bestial manner is expressing an evil character? Is this just our own cultural bias, or is there some deep truth about human nature and food expressed here?
- Why are so many food references religious? Does this say something about food and human nature, or just about Western culture and Christianity?
- How should we understand the consumption of alcohol and especially wine in *LOTR* and other works of art? What might wine and similar drinks reference, what further nuance might they give a scene, and how does their consumption help to characterize the people in the film?
- Why does Anderson suddenly have Daniel use so many food images as he goes insane in *There Will be Blood*? What point is he trying to get across about Daniel Plainview and about his relationship with his young nemesis, who serves as a mirror image of himself?

Further reading

Beichner, Paul E. (1967) "The Allegorical Interpretation of Medieval Literature," *PMLA* 82:1 (March): 33–38.

A brief and clear literary discussion of how medieval authors used allegorical tropes in literature, and how these were interpreted as well.

Bower, Anne L. (2004) "Watching Food: The Production of Food, Film, and Values," in Anne L. Bower (ed.) *Reel Food*, New York: Routledge.

A well-written and enjoyable collection of essays that focus solely on the use of food in films. Essays explore how food is used to create or evoke culture, gender, and meaning in movies from the 1930s through the present.

Ferry, Jane F. (2003) *Food in Film: A Culinary Performance of Communication*, New York: Routledge.

Ferry provides a wonderful anthropological analysis of food as communication, exploring ways in which communication can be like eating (gossiping as cannibalism, for example) and eating can be a way of communicating (for example, when food is a socio-economic status symbol).

Fitzgerald, Allan D. (ed.) (1999) *Augustine through the Ages: an Encyclopedia*, Cambridge: Wm. B. Eerdmans.

The premier scholarly resource for understanding Augustine. As relates to this essay, see especially the definitions offered of *Confessiones* and Sacraments.

Isaacs, Neil D. and Zimbardo, Rose A. (eds) (1968) *Tolkien and the Critics: Essays on J. R. R. Tolkien's* The Lord of the Rings, Notre Dame: University of Notre Dame Press.

A useful collection of essays on a wide range of topics related to Tolkien, several of which have informed my own thought about what Tolkien is up to with food. For more on the complex moral universe of *LOTR* as seen in Tolkien's view of evil and corruption, see especially the essays by Meyer Spacks and C.S. Lewis.

Bibliography

Augustine (1960) *The Confessions of Saint Augustine*, ed. John K. Ryan, New York: Image Books.

Beichner, Paul E. (1967) "The Allegorical Interpretation of Medieval Literature," *PMLA* 82:1 (March): 33–38.

Bower, Anne L. (2004) "Watching Food: The Production of Food, Film, and Values," in Anne L. Bower (ed.) *Reel Food*, New York: Routledge.

Ferry, Jane F. (2003) *Food in Film: A Culinary Performance of Communication*, New York: Routledge.

Kass, Leon R. (1994) *The Hungry Soul: Eating and the Perfecting of Our Nature*, New York: The Free Press.

Konyndyk DeYoung, Rebecca (2009) *Glittering Vices: A New Look at the Seven Deadly Sins and their Remedies*, Grand Rapids, MI: Brazos Press.

Tolkien, J.R.R. (1994) *The Lord of the Rings*, New York: Houghton Mifflin Company.

——(1977) *The Silmarillion*, New York: Ballantine Books.

Wood, Ralph (2003) *The Gospel According to Tolkien: Visions of the Kingdom in Middle-earth*, London: Westminster John Knox Press.

12 Cursing then and now

Jeremiah's Scroll and the Boston Red Sox Jersey (can the Bible shed light on pop culture practices?)

Terry Ray Clark

Introduction

Can understanding the ancient world that lies behind the biblical texts shed light on modern day popular cultural practices? How is sinking a scroll in an enemy's river in 6th century BCE Babylon similar to burying a baseball jersey in the foundation of an opponent's stadium in modern day America? This essay is an exercise of theory and method in the area of Bible and Popular Culture. It compares and contrasts two examples of ritual cursing, one ancient and one modern. Technical concepts and practices of ancient cursing rituals will be examined as they shed light on the biblical material of Jer 51:59–64. These will then be used to better understand a particular instance of cursing in the context of the baseball rivalry between the Boston Red Sox and the New York Yankees. The goal of this essay is to demonstrate the usefulness of studying popular religious culture in light of ancient religious beliefs and practices. But, conversely, this study also suggests that the ancient world might occasionally be approached with less bias if examined through the lens of popular culture.

At the outset, I would like to make a few disclaimers. First, the use of the term "ritual curse" might seem repetitive to those who are already aware that cursing sometimes involves more than simply uttering expletives. Here, by way of contrast, I want to direct special attention to the fact that sometimes the verbal act of cursing was, in the ancient world, just like today, accompanied by so-called performative behaviors, that is, actions that are more than just instructive or symbolic, but which are also ritually or magically effective (cf. Hillers 1995). In other words, they accomplish something; they change the world in some circumstantial way. Even in the absence of any significant non-verbal behaviors, the verbal aspect of the curse often involves "pronouncements where the uttering of the sentence is not a description of an action, but [is] itself the doing of an action, or part of the doing of an action" (Hillers 1995: 758, following Austin 1962). This has variously been referred to as a "performative utterance" or a "speech act" (Austin 1962). Much like a judge or jury pronouncing that an accused person is either innocent or guilty, a speech act is more than just speech. It actually changes the real life situation or status of someone.

Second, there are many pitfalls inherent in uncritically comparing ancient practices with modern ones. However, one of the purposes of the present volume is to explore questions of theory and method in the emerging and rapidly growing field of Religion and Popular Culture. A subset of this field, namely, Bible and Popular Culture, recognizes that some things found in the ancient world, in this case ancient beliefs and practices reflected in the biblical texts, persist and continue to have relevance for our understanding of modern society. Conversely, it might also be the case that some aspects of the ancient world might be better understood when viewed in light of modern day phenomena.

Third, I readily admit that I am not an expert on the subject of baseball. I am not concerned here with the debate over whether baseball or any other sport or form of sports fandom should qualify as a modern day religious practice. There may be material here of some relevance for that subject, but I leave its pursuit to other scholars of religion and culture with a different agenda.

Now, to set the context for this essay: in the fall of 2007, a construction worker, who happened to be a Boston Red Sox fan, was employed to lay concrete for one day at the site of the new Yankee stadium. In an attempt to reverse what was believed by many fans to be a long-standing curse on the Red Sox organization, he buried a Boston player jersey in the foundation of a corridor near the visiting team's locker room. By doing this, he hoped to doom the Sox's arch-rivals. His intention was to (secretly) sink a curse deeply enough beneath the enemy team's home field, that it could not be circumvented or revoked. By injecting the foreign object into the very marrow of the enemy's home turf, he hoped to initiate the growth of a cancer that, because of its hidden nature, would never be discovered or removed.

Theory and method

A curse in the past

My immediate reaction to hearing about this modern day curse was to reflect upon a story about an ancient cursing ritual supposedly performed on behalf of the **prophet** Jeremiah in the Hebrew Bible/Old Testament (Jer 51:59–64). The biblical text reads as follows in the NRSV translation:

> **Jeremiah 51:59–64:** 59The word that the prophet Jeremiah commanded Seraiah, son of Neriah son of Mahseiah, when he went with King Zedekiah of Judah to Babylon, in the fourth year of his reign. Seraiah was the quartermaster. 60Jeremiah wrote in a scroll all the disasters that would come on Babylon, all these words that are written concerning Babylon. 61And Jeremiah said to Seraiah: "When you come to Babylon, see that you read all these words, 62and say, 'O LORD, you yourself threatened to destroy this place so that neither human beings nor animals shall live in it, and it shall be desolate forever.' 63When you finish reading this scroll, tie a stone to it, and throw it into the middle of the Euphrates, 64and say, 'Thus shall Babylon sink, to rise no more, because of the disasters that I am bringing on her.'" Thus far are the words of Jeremiah.

This unit of text is classified as an expanded "colophon" for a collection of oracles against Babylon that immediately precedes it in Jer 50:1–51:58 (Lundbom 2004: 502). A colophon is an end-piece or concluding notation for a larger work that gives some kind of important information about what precedes it, such as biographical information about the author, or details about the date, publication, and/or purpose of the composition (cf. "Colophon" in the *Oxford English Dictionary*). In this case, the colophon narrates how the oracles of judgment against Babylon might function collectively as a curse, which is put into effect when the scroll containing Yahweh's judgments is deposited in the Land of Babylon. Copied onto a single scroll, the judgments would be actualized when the scroll was sunk in the Euphrates River, a body of water that flows through the land of Babylon. The impression this colophon gives is that it is not enough for Jeremiah merely to receive, record, and even recite Yahweh's promises of disaster against Babylon from his location in the land of Judah. In an effort to further guarantee their fulfillment, someone must recite and deposit a physical copy of them in the vicinity of those upon whom they are to take effect. What we appear to have then, in the colophon, is a command from the prophet to a certain scribe named Seraiah to perform an act of **sympathetic magic** using the written and previously revealed words of Yahweh in conjunction with words of Jeremiah and the words and actions of Seraiah. Apparently, Seraiah serves here as a valid representative and effective extension of the prophet's unique power in this cursing ritual, much like the prophets in ancient Israel served as effective representatives of their god, Yahweh.

In this regard, Seraiah is not only to read aloud all the scroll's oracles of judgment once he arrives in Babylon, but he is also to remind Yahweh, on the basis of those judgments that Yahweh has previously revealed to the prophet, that the deity is obligated to fulfill these promises, and truly make Babylon "desolate forever" (v. 62). The final act is to sink the scroll and recite a "**simile curse**": as the scroll descends, "thus shall Babylon sink, to rise no more" (v. 64) (on simile curses, cf. Hillers 1983: 181–185). A fascinating aspect of this simile (i.e. as the stone sinks, so shall Babylon) is the concluding phrase: "because of the disasters that I am bringing on her [i.e. Babylon]." Who exactly is the referent for the first person personal pronoun "I"?

Given the literary context and the absence of the so-called prophetic **messenger formula** ("Thus says Yahweh"), one might conclude that the one "bringing" the disaster is: a) Seraiah, the one who performs the cursing ritual; b) Jeremiah, through the agency of Seraiah; or c) Yahweh, through the mediation of both the prophet and his scribe. Lundbom claims that this final statement by Seraiah should be understood as "Yahweh speaking in the first person," but I am suspicious that such an interpretation oversimplifies the more complex nature of ancient Near Eastern curse rituals (Lundbom 2004: 505). Lundbom himself admits that the lack of the messenger formula makes the matter ambiguous, but that the "pronouncement, nevertheless, is a curse" (2004: 509). This highlights, I believe, the fact that the scroll does not merely "[announce] all the evil that would come eventually to Babylon," according to Lundbom (2004: 509), but rather that the act of sinking the scroll will also help to effect the divine judgments.

While some scholars are loath to consider this incident as constituting any form of magic, the issue is worthy of further consideration. One finds some similarity here with another incident found in Jer 36, concerning a scroll of disaster oracles against Judah, which the prophet had dictated to his scribe Baruch. When that scroll is read aloud for the Judean king Jehoiakim, the king responds by cutting off the columns of the scroll, one by one, and throwing them into the fire. Such a response raises questions about whether this is simply a sign of Jehoiakim's disagreement with the scroll's message, a sign of disrespect for the prophet, or an attempt to circumvent the fulfillment of the disaster prophecies by destroying the physical form in which the words are manifest. Yahweh's response to this affront by the king is to command the prophet to replace the burned scroll and utter a new oracle of disaster, which this time includes the deity's promise to fulfill his prior words. He will indeed bring upon the king, his servants, and the inhabitants of Jerusalem and Judah "all the calamities that I declared against them but they would not hear" (v. 27). Holladay refers to this incident as "the king's blasphemous destruction of the words of Yahweh," but ultimately he seems more concerned with the way Jehoiakim's response disrespects Yahweh, rather than with considering the possibility that it actually serves as an attempt, via sympathetic magic, to undo the curse that the words themselves might contain (Holladay 1989: 260).

Treating this incident, as I am suggesting here, as a form of sympathetic magic, would not be inconsistent with more widespread practices of cursing in the ancient Near East. However, it does stand in opposition to the longstanding tendency for many in the field of biblical studies to treat Israelite religion as something unique and therefore significantly different from its larger cultural environment. In some ways, of course, Israelite religion is unique, but it did not arise in a vacuum, no matter how badly some would like to think so. Ancient Israel was not utterly or uniquely "pure" in comparison to their neighbors. Thus, it is not simply on the basis of evidence that some dispute the idea that Israel ever practiced anything as "abhorrent" or "pagan" as to be labeled magic. Israelite religion is often treated as more pure than all its ancient rivals because of a desire, conscious or unconscious, by the inheritors of these traditions to consider their own religion better than all rivals. Such a perspective is driven more by ideology than evidence. The contrasting challenge of the academy should be, in all cases, to demonstrate its claims, rather than simply state them (and restate them *ad nauseum*).

Israel's neighbors in ancient Mesopotamia provide an important means of comparison. In ancient Mesopotamia, magic is not clearly distinguished from religion. It is "homogeneously integrated into it" (Farber 1995: 1895). What exactly is magic in the ancient Near East? Farber defines it as "the whole area of religious behavior which tries to influence man's success, well-being, health, and wealth by using methods based neither on rational experience nor solely on private or public worship of a deity" (1995: 1896). Farber notes that under the rubric of magic should also be included attempts to "[enhance] ... the effect" of medicinal practices or conduct private rituals to ward off evil (1995: 1896). In ancient

Canaan and Israel, we find a similar phenomenon, in which magic "is charted within the continuum of religious practice; there is no rigid boundary between the two." Magic is simply the "[attempt] to control, if not force, the divinity, or at least the world of nature" to do one's bidding (De Tarragon 1995: 2075).

De Tarragon includes within this category the practice of invoking a deity's name in order to accomplish one's own will. An interesting example of this can be found in the story of the prophet Elisha cursing in Yahweh's name a large band of young boys who had come out to mock him in 2 Kgs 2:23–24. After uttering the curse, two she-bears come out of the forest to maul 42 of the mockers; end of story. The reader is left to draw his or her own conclusions as to why the curse is effective, but the implication seems to be that Yahweh's name can be invoked by certain, special individuals to accomplish their own will. A true "Man of God" can wield or benefit from divine power with a simple verbal summoning formula.[1]

Sympathetic magic in the ancient world "is inspired by the rules of similarity" (De Tarragon 1995: 2076). The simile curse of Jer 51 provides an excellent example, whereby the sinking of a scroll is intended to symbolize the sinking of one's enemy. Such an act should be understood as more than simply "a natural extension of the preached word," or merely demonstrative of the wishes of the one attempting a curse (cf. Lundbom 2004: 508, following Zimmerli 1995: 427–428). Zimmerli (1995: 509) considers the sinking of the scroll as merely a symbolic act, and not an example of sympathetic magic, even though he still considers the pronouncement to be a curse.

But this is not merely a symbolic action designed to demonstrate one's wishes or teach an audience the appropriate ideological perspective on Babylon. Performed "in conjunction with the curse's utterance," the accompanying ritual is better understood as intentionally effective. Here, as elsewhere in the ancient Near East, "the [so-called symbolic] object was manipulated in some way so as to establish a connection between the object and the target of the curse" (Kitz 2007: 625). Usually, this connection was established by the spoken words of the curse itself, although this could be implicitly or explicitly communicated. In the case of Jer 51, the scroll plays a dual role: not only does it contain the words of Yahweh's curses against Babylon, in written form, but it also becomes the physical point of connection with Babylon in an implied simile. The words, the scroll, and Babylon are all intended to sink together. Verbal curses, in this sense, should be understood as more than just explicated wishes. They are "performative utterances" which may also be conjoined with other forms of performative or ritual action.

The ritual in Jer 51 also contains another magical aspect. The burying of the scroll in the Land of Babylon highlights the implicit desire for greater proximity to the object of the curse in order to increase the likelihood of the curse's effectiveness. If this were not so, the prophet could simply have buried the scroll himself in Judean soil or sunk it in a more conveniently located body of water, such as the Jordan River. Burying the foreign object in Babylon is apparently a key component for the intended effectiveness of the ritual. Likewise, I would argue, is the decision to bury it in a river, which would greatly decrease the possibility that the Babylonians would be able to locate or exhume the cursed object, and then either destroy it or remove it from the region. Having already experienced the burning of one of his scrolls by King Jehoiakim, Jeremiah takes care when cursing Babylon to circumvent the same thing happening again. In light of this, I would also argue that Seraiah's cursing ritual was probably designed to take place in private rather than public, although the text of Jer 51 is unclear on this point. A private cursing ritual would be more likely to go undetected by the Babylonians, allowing the scroll to avoid detection and retrieval, and also allowing both the scroll and the parties responsible for depositing it to avoid harm from the local authorities.

Case study

A curse in the present

Shifting now to the present day context, let us examine the details surrounding the Red Sox Jersey incident. First, we need to contextualize the event. In 2004, the Boston Red Sox defeated the New York Yankees in a best of 7 series in the pennant race after trailing 3 games to 0. They went on to sweep the St. Louis Cardinals 4 games to 0 and capture the World Series for the first time since 1918. This should, for all practical purposes, have signaled the end of Boston's championship drought, and any curse the team was believed to have suffered for the better part of a century. Nevertheless, three years later, a Red Sox fan attempted to curse Boston's historical nemesis—the Yankees—in order to reverse what was believed to have been an earlier curse on the Red Sox that occurred in 1918 when Boston, in an ill-fated move, sold Babe Ruth to the Yankees. This event led to what was eventually dubbed the "Curse of the Bambino," because it was interpreted by many Boston fans as the reason for the Sox's 85 year dry spell. (For more on this curse and the history of its propagation, cf. Shaughnessy 2004 and Caterine 2004.)

Apparently, even though the 2004 World Series victory was believed to have broken the curse, for one Red Sox fan, this was not enough. In a modern day form of the ancient simile curse, Gino Castignoli, the New York City construction worker, sought to reverse the "Curse of the Bambino." He did this by burying the jersey of David Ortiz, a slugger known by fans as "Big Papi," in the new Yankee stadium. Castignoli has been quoted as saying, "When I stuck it in, I said, 'The Yankees are done for the next 30 years.' I only put a 30-year curse because I'm 46 and in 30 years I'll be dead, and I won't care if the Yankees win then" (Olshan *et al.* 2008). It is unclear whether this number might also have been chosen for symbolic reasons, because Ortiz's jersey number is 34. However, I have found no report thus far that suggests this was intended to be part of the curse's simile.

It was reported that Castignoli had originally refused to work on this particular job site because of his great hatred of the Yankees (Olshan *et al.* 2008). However, he was able to reconcile himself to entering the "unholy land" of the enemy for a single day after hatching his plot to plant a curse. As in the case of Jeremiah's curse, and perhaps also Elisha's, opportunity and proximity play an important role in ritual magic. In an ESPN interview (2008), Castignoli explained his rationale. He accused the Yankees of being "the bullies of the American League … the bullies of all baseball," in reference to the amount of money the Yankees have spent to become such a dominant team (Castignoli 2008). In the same interview, he refers to supporting the Yankees as "rooting for big business," and calls himself a "hero [for] Red Sox Nation." His acceptance of the one-day job for the express purpose of planting the curse was, in his words, "My mission for the Red Sox Nation" (Castignoli 2008). The so-called underdog's recourse to fighting with the weapon of magic is apparently an acceptable practice whenever one has the perception of being bullied by a greater foe (although we might debate the clarity of this perception in the case of the prophet Elisha previously discussed).

Another important element of Castignoli's simile curse is David Ortiz's similarities to Babe Ruth. Not only did Big Papi become an effective slugger for Boston, but his acquisition by the Sox was considered by Castignoli the inverse of Boston's loss of the Babe in the early 20th century. The Yankees pompously passed on the opportunity to acquire Ortiz in 2003, because, in Castignoli's estimation, they believed they had enough power hitting without him (Olshan *et al.* 2008). Castignoli hatched his plot to make sure the Yankees "acquired" Ortiz anyway, in the form of the slugger's cursed jersey. Witnesses helped to foil the plot when Castignoli, who wore the Ortiz jersey to work, took it off, planted it in the cement, and "documented" the event on his cell phone camera (Olshan *et al.* 2008).

Reaction to this incident has been as fascinating as the attempted curse itself, and also revelatory of the way many in our society feel about the efficacy of modern magic, which in this case bears fascinating similarity to ancient beliefs and practices. Initially, the Yankees responded to the report of the curse with skepticism, laughing it off, at least publicly. However, once evidence of the incident was forthcoming, they changed their tune. Mayor Bloomberg called it an "outrage," and claimed that he would like to "go in there and pitch for the Yankees and beat the Red Sox with a perfect game. That would be a way to end the curse" (Olshan *et al.* 2008). It seems the curse quickly acquired validity for him. Yankee owner Hank Steinbrenner was quoted as saying, "I hope his [Castignoli's] coworkers kick the s— out of him" (Zimmerman 2008). Another former Red Sox player, Johnny Damon, who signed with the Yankees in 2005, downplayed his fear of a buried jersey, but added that he "would worry if you took a body and put it under there," which raises another set of questions about our society's taboos surrounding burial practices which we do not have time to explore in this context (Olshan *et al.* 2008).

By and large, Yankee fans were not amused. Liza Oviedo was quoted as saying, "That shirt is cursed. They should dig it out and have a bonfire with it," which seems to suggest that it should be burned, not unlike what Jehoiakim did with Jeremiah's scroll (Olshan *et al.* 2008). Christopher Rogers suggested burying all Red Sox jerseys "under two tons of concrete … because that's what we [the Yankees] do. We bury them [the Red Sox]" (Olshan *et al.* 2008). Alice McGillion, a spokeswoman for the Yankees, expressed appreciation to the New York Post for revealing the location of the jersey's burial because it would allow the Yankees to "put an extra layer of concrete over it to make sure it stays buried" (Olshan *et al.* 2008). Self-proclaimed Long Island Wiccan priestess Bonnie Thompson responded with some sympathetic magic of her own. She supposedly "cast a spell" that included the performative act of "lay[ing] a Red Sox jersey on the ground and beat[ing] it with a broom," while reciting the words, "I cast out all negative energies from the Red Sox jinx. Their buried T-shirt has no effect here." She did this clothed in a black dress and a Yankees ball cap (Olshan *et al.* 2008).

Coworkers of Castignoli were troubled that they may have unwittingly participated in "sinking [their beloved] franchise" (Doyle *et al.* 2008). Tim Wiles, director of the National Baseball Hall of Fame and Museum in Cooperstown, believes this attempt to curse an opponent is "unprecedented" (Doyle *et al.* 2008). Perhaps in some of its details, this is the case, but not in light of ancient Near Eastern simile curses. In fact, baseball has already seen something similar. According to Mickey Bradley, co-author of the 2007 book *Haunted Baseball*, another construction worker and Yankees fan claims to have buried "an unknown good-luck charm in a water main trench" beneath the former Yankee stadium in 1920 (Bradley and Gordon 2007). Bradley was quoted as saying that "prior" to this date, the Yankees "never won a World Series" (Bradley and Gordon 2007). Apparently, blessings as well as curses can be effectively buried.

Peter J. Nash, author of the book *Boston's Royal Rooters* (2005), a history of Red Sox fans, claims that Castignoli's curse "just takes the rivalry to a whole new level" (Doyle *et al.* 2008). Referring to the Sox's victory over New York in 2004, he claims that "there is a [new] curse in effect already. Maybe the Red Sox T-shirt is like the icing on the cake, a nice little F-you from Boston" (Doyle *et al.* 2008). What Nash fails to realize is that this represents a significant aspect of cursing, as well as **imprecatory prayers**, throughout history. For many, it is not enough simply to turn back the ill effects of the enemy's magic. Reversing a curse often involves an attempt to create a boomerang effect, placing the curse back upon the party that initiated it (cf. the Balaam oracles in the Hebrew Bible, Numbers 22–24), or replacing it with a new curse of one's own. In effect, warding off a curse is not always simply about protecting oneself. It can also be about revenge, and this appears to have been Castignoli's intention all along—to make the Yankees suffer for a significant period of time, much like the Red Sox have suffered. Only then will real justice be accomplished in such a way that the universe is placed not in a state of balance or parity, but that it instead favors the home team. For many, the conception and goal of religious harmony is not that *everyone* occasionally wins, but that the *home team* wins.

Ultimately, in the case of the Red Sox jersey, the Yankees decided not to take any chances. They exhumed the shirt at the expense of approximately $50,000. Construction workers spent nearly half a day drilling a two foot deep by four foot wide hole "before finding the dilapidated yet 'magical' Ortiz jersey," which, skeptical reporter Bill Burt was quick to point out, "wasn't even authentic" (Burt 2008). Regardless, it was authentic enough for the Yankees organization. As Burt went on to comment, "Curses ... are really nonsense. That is, unless you believe in them. Or, your baseball team believes in them" (Burt 2008).

Comparing and contrasting past and present

What tentative conclusions may we draw from these two examples about the nature of ritual cursing, and what is the significance for the Study of Bible and Popular Culture? Scholars like Anne Marie Kitz have typically defined curses as "maledictions [that] solicit a deity or deities to do harm to a person, place or thing. Since curses are wishes, they are, therefore, petitionary prayers to the deities" (Kitz 2007: 616). But I would add that, much like other forms of magic, they are also sometimes more than simply *requests* for divine assistance. They are attempts to compel sacred forces to act on behalf of one's wishes. Whether found in the context of the bible or popular culture, they constitute a form of negative magic. They also contain what Kitz describes as an "inherent reflective nature. To petition a deity to injure another is to seek a blessing for oneself" (Kitz 2007: 616).

The most glaring contrast between the two cases examined here is the fact that no explicit reference is made to supernatural forces or entities in the context of the Red Sox jersey curse. Castignoli considered himself, as did numerous Yankee fans, capable of effecting a curse on the basis of three things: his own authorization, a readily available and appropriate ritual object, and the opportunity via proximity to the enemy to effectively deposit it. While there is significant ambiguity in the Jeremiah text concerning the issues of agency and authority to effect a curse on behalf of the prophet and/or God, this seems to be less of a concern in the modern day situation. This might suggest that at least some modern Americans are religiously different in significant ways from some ancient Near Easterners. Instead of attempting to compel a deity to bring disaster on one's enemy, some moderns perhaps feel themselves equipped with the power to destroy their rivals with magical means.

In both cases examined here, we find a number of similarities, including the non-arbitrary use of symbolic objects (a scroll and a jersey), which are designed to embody the curse and establish an important point of connection between the ritual object and the target of its action. In this regard, the direction, placement, and/or location are critical to the curse's effectiveness (in the land or river of Babylon; in a stadium). Burying the curse deeply, so as to make it irretrievable is likewise important, because the curse can potentially be revoked by exhumation and destruction of the more than just symbolic object. Thus, preventing the enemy from undermining the curse is an important consideration. These examples suggest that belief in the effectiveness of curses persists across great cultural and temporal distances. And finally, these examples also raise important questions about who in a given context has the authority to curse. In ancient Israel, some forms of cursing may have been considered the explicit reserve of a specialized class of divinely designated individuals, such as prophets, and perhaps by extension, their scribes, because it was their unique relationship with the gods as the guarantors of blessing and curse that allowed their curses to be effective. However, even then as now, proximity to the enemy's land and access to certain symbolic and potentially magical objects are as important as the skill to write, read, and/or deposit the objects properly. Thus, the issues of agency, authority, and opportunity must be considered.

Conclusion

In conclusion, when analyzing both the ancient as well as modern day context, we should consider the possibility that instead of encountering a dichotomy of magic *vs.* religion, or the simple choice between magic *or* religion, we may instead conclude that magic *is* religion. As Hillers has suggested, "magical thought … is more pervasive in the Old Testament than has previously been recognized" (Hillers 1983: 185), but the same may be said of the modern day context. Religion and culture are not easily distinguished as separate domains in the past or the present. Such an insight should guide us as we endeavor to compare and contrast ancient and modern phenomena in the evolving field of Bible and Popular Culture. With appropriate qualifications, some human behaviors and values may persist over great periods of time, geographic spaces, and cultures. As we proceed in this field of study, it would behoove us to do so with great caution, but also great enthusiasm. Much is at stake, but also, much stands to be gained. The ancients may have something to teach us about ourselves, and the moderns may have something to teach us about the ancients.

Summary

- In spite of being separated by great distances in culture, time, and geography, cursing rituals in the ancient Near East resemble modern day cursing rituals in some important ways.
- Cursing is a form of performative utterance often accompanied by non-verbal symbolic and ritual acts believed to be helpful for making the curse effective.
- In both ancient and modern day contexts, the line between certain religious practices and the practice of magic is very thin.
- Some ancient religious practices can shed light on modern day religious behavior, and vice-versa.

Glossary terms

Imprecatory prayer – any attempt to see harm done to another person by verbally invoking the intervention of a higher power.

Messenger formula – a verbal formula often accompanying prophetic speech, which designates certain human utterances as the literal voice of a higher power (usually a deity) speaking through the human mouth.

Prophet – someone who acts as a spokesperson or mouthpiece for a deity, either revealing the deity's will for the present or predicting the future as a result of receiving divinely-granted insight. In addition, prophets sometimes advocate for the desires or needs of humans by speaking to the gods on their behalf.

Simile curse – a complex type of performative utterance in which harm is done to another party through the combination of a spoken formula and a symbolic action that mimics in some way the damage to be accomplished.

Sympathetic magic – an attempt to manipulate some person, place, or event by performing ritual activity with some likeness or imitation of the person, place or event.

Points for discussion

- Can you think of other modern day religious beliefs and behaviors that have their origin in an ancient culture? Have the beliefs and behaviors changed significantly over time? Why or why not?
- Do you agree that religion and magic are very closely related, or perhaps even inseparable, in both the ancient and modern worlds? Why or why not?
- What are some other ways in which the Bible and Pop Culture are tied together in our society? What other biblical influences (characters, motifs, teachings, practices, etc.) do you notice in your environment? Why do you think this is the case?

Note

1 For a humorous, yet enlightening cartoon interpretation of this story, cf. Extreme Bible Stories, Episode 1: "Don't Dis Elisha," Online. Available HTTP: www.seanet.com/~billr/xbs/.

Further reading

Fretheim, Terence E. (2002) *Jeremiah*, Smyth & Helwys Bible Commentary, Macon, GA: Smyth & Helwys Publishing.

A good one-volume commentary by a seasoned biblical scholar, with a user-friendly format that includes a variety of interpretive approaches and a CD-Rom for portability.

Hillers, Delbert R. (1964) *Treaty Curses and the Old Testament Prophets*, Rome: Pontifical Biblical Institute.

A classic work on treaty curses by one of the foremost biblical scholars of covenants and treaties in ancient Israel.

Brichto, Herbert C. (1963) *The Problem of "Curse" in the Hebrew Bible*, SBL Monograph, 13, Philadelphia: Society of Biblical Literature.

Another classic work on curses in the Hebrew Bible, with special emphasis on semantic issues.

Blank, Sheldon H. (1950–51) "The Curse, Blasphemy, the Spell, and the Oath," *Hebrew Union College Annual*, 23: 73–95.

Examination of the similarities and differences between these various terms, and their meaning and function in the Hebrew Bible.

Fensham, F. Charles (1962) "Malediction and Benediction in Ancient Near Eastern Vassal-Treaties and the Old Testament," *Zeitschrift für die Alttestamentliche Wissenschaft*, 74 (1): 1–9.

Comparative analysis of blessings and curses in the Hebrew Bible in light of their occurrences in ancient Near Eastern treaty contexts.

Morrise, Mark J. (1993) "Simile Curses in the Ancient Near East, Old Testament, and Book of Mormon," *Journal of Book of Mormon Studies*, 2 (1): 124–138. Online. Available HTTP: http://maxwellinstitute.byu.edu/publications/jbms/?vol=2& num=1&id=23.

A more recent analysis of simile curses in the Hebrew Bible and the Book of Mormon.

Jeansonne, John (25 May 2008) "THE HOT TOPIC: Curses! Can't bury the past," *Newsday.com*. Online. Available HTTP: http://newsday.com/sports/baseball/ny-sphot255702045may25,0,3664299.story (accessed 21 January 2009).

A popular response to curses in the modern day context.

Bibliography

Austin, J.L. (1962) *How to Do Things with Words*, 2nd edn, ed. J.O. Urmson and Marina Sbisa, Cambridge: Harvard University Press.

Bradley, Mickey and Gordon, Dan (2007) *Haunted Baseball: Ghosts, Curses, Legends, and Eerie Events*, reprint edn, Guilford, CT: Lyons Press.

Burt, Bill (16 April 2008) "Ortiz Curse Fiasco Reflects Poorly on Yankees," *Eagle-Tribune Online*. Online. Available HTTP: www.eagletribune.com/pusports/local_story_107003201.html (accessed 29 September 2009).

Caterine, Darryl V. (2004) "Curses and Catharsis in Red Sox Nation: Baseball and Ritual Violence in American Culture," *Journal of Religion and Popular Culture*, 8. Online. Available HTTP: www.usask.ca/relst/jrpc/art8-redsox.html (accessed 31 January 2011).

De Tarragon, Jean-Michel (2001) "Witchcraft, Magic, and Divination in Canaan and Ancient Israel," in Jack M. Sasson (ed.) *Civilizations of the Ancient Near East*, Vol. 3 of 4, Peabody, MA: Hendrickson, 2071–2082.

Doyle, John, Bennet, Chuck, and Olshan, Jeremy (11 April 2008) "High 'jinx' Hits Yankees," *New York Post*. Online. Available HTTP: www.nypost.com/p/news/regional/high_jinx_hits_yankees_k1d2aGMGy7jS6Xkx7yPsgO (accessed 31 January 2011).

ESPN.Com (13, April 2008) "Construction Worker Tells His Side of 'Jerseygate.'" Online. Available HTTP: http://espn.go.com/video/clip?id=3345159& categoryid=2521705 (accessed 29 September 2009).

Farber, Walter (2001) "Witchcraft, Magic, and Divination in Ancient Mesopotamia," in Jack M. Sasson (ed.) *Civilizations of the Ancient Near East*, Vol. 3 of 4, Peabody, MA: Hendrickson, 1895–1910.

Hillers, Delbert R. (1983) "The Effective Simile in Biblical Literature," *Journal of the American Oriental Society* 103 (1): 181–185.

——(1995) "Some Performative Utterances in the Bible," in David P. Wright, David Noel Freedman, and Avi Hurvitz (eds) *Pomegranates and Golden Bells: Studies in Biblical, Jewish, and Near Eastern Ritual, Law, and Literature in Honor of Jacob Milgrom*, Winona Lake, IN: Eisenbrauns, 757–766.

Holladay, William L. (1989) *Jeremiah 2*, Hermeneia, Minneapolis: Fortress, 1989.

Kitz, Anne Marie (2007) "Curses and Cursing in the Ancient Near East," *Religion Compass* 1 (6): 615–627.

Lundbom, Jack R. (2004) *Jeremiah 37-52*, Anchor Bible Commentary, 21C, New York: Doubleday.

Nash, Peter J. (2005) *Boston's Royal Rooters*, Charleston, SC: Arcadia.

Olshan, Jeremy, Nicholas, Jason, and Bennet, Chuck (12 April 2008) "'Under'miner a Bx. Traitor," *New York Post*. Online. Available HTTP: www.nypost.com/p/news/regional/under_miner_bx_traitor_yK6HNCL6hqyt0fYZoymoUP (accessed 29 September 2009).

Shaughnessy, Dan (2004) *The Curse of the Bambino*, New York: Penguin.
Weiner, E.S.C. and Simpson, J.A. (1991) *The Compact Oxford English Dictionary*, new edn, New York: Oxford University Press, 1991.
Zimmerli, Walther (1995) "From Prophetic Word to Prophetic Book," in Robert P. Gordon (ed.) *"The Place is too small for us": The Israelite Prophets in Recent Scholarship*, Sources for Biblical and Theological Study 5, Winona Lake, IN: Eisenbrauns, 419–442.
Zimmerman, Caroline (13 April 2008) "Yanks Exhume Sox Jersey at New Stadium," *NEWSER*. Online. Available HTTP: www.newser.com/story/24357/yanks-exhume-sox-jersey-at-new-stadium.html (accessed 29 September 2009).

13 Postmodern prophecy

Bob Dylan and the practices of self-subversion

Mark W. Flory

Introduction to postmodern prophecy

In the movie *Masked and Anonymous* (dir. Larry Charles 2003), Bob Dylan stars as Jack Fate, the son of a dying dictator, sentenced to prison for betraying his father. Fate is released from prison so that he can star in a benefit concert for victims of the revolution, a concert organized by Uncle Sweetheart (John Goodman), a snake-oil salesman, and Nina, a harried but hopeful promoter. The dialogue of the movie resembles a Dylan song, with its abundance of allusions, its weighty themes (death, violence, freedom, meaning, truth), its intentional obscurity, and its apocalyptic tone and events. All of this seems to mean a great deal, but again and again, when a character gives a speech that appears to give a meaning to the chaos, Jack Fate dismisses or undermines it in one terse statement. For example, Jack meets the wonderfully weird character called Animal Wrangler (Woody Harrelson), whose devotion to animals and dislike of humans has become a very elaborate conspiracy theory. At the end of Wrangler's long, rambling speech, Jack turns to walk away with Uncle Sweetheart, who asks him what Wrangler was talking about. Jack shrugs, "Guy's into animals, I guess." In the same way, the entire movie seems to be about weighty matters, and the audience feels compelled to come up with a coherent interpretation, only to find that the allusions do not allude to anything, the symbols are not symbols of anything, and whatever meaning we find may easily be replaced by another. Significantly, the audience's failure to find meaning in the movie reflects—indeed, it is an extension of—the failure to find meaning of the characters in the movie. Whereas a conventional, coherent plot would provide us with meanings and explanations of events, *Masked and Anonymous* reflects layers and layers of competing meanings, bordering on madness, enticing the audience to enter into the process of meaning-making itself.

Postmodern art and philosophy provide many such examples of the attempt to give a form to openness, to express freedom in a work without thereby limiting the freedom. To this end, postmodernists have utilized a host of techniques that serve to invite interpretation, only to subvert the very possibility of **interpretive closure**, thereby placing the burden of interpretation on the audience, undermining the traditional relationship of active artist and passive audience.

This combination of prophetic voice (or what I will refer to as the "prophetic stance"; see below) and postmodern techniques of subversion produces what I call "postmodern prophecy." Not all postmodern art and philosophy is prophetic, even if it is subversive. However, I will argue that the tradition of prophecy is continued within postmodernism, that it is identifiable as prophetic and yet post-modern. As an example of this postmodern prophecy, I will examine the life, works, and performance style of Bob Dylan. Bob Dylan's work invites (even demands) interpretation while thwarting all attempts at achieving finality or interpretive closure. Dylan's corpus, by its resistance to interpretive closure, by its intentional evasion of such closure, calls us to become active participants in the creative act rather than passive consumers of artistic commodities. The structure of this call is clearly prophetic. Just as the ancient prophets called the people of Israel to account for their actions before God, thereby placing them before their ultimate responsibility, so postmodern prophecy calls us today to face our responsibility for making meaning, albeit in the changed conditions of postmodernism.

Theory and method

Prophetic stance

In this section, I will argue that while the conditions of postmodernity significantly differ from those conditions that gave rise to Hebrew prophecy, the structural similarities between the Hebrew prophets and certain postmodern artists (in particular, Bob Dylan) justify the nomenclature "postmodern prophecy." At the same time, I hope to show the particularly postmodern nature of such prophecy, arising as it does in the changed conditions of postmodernity.

The phrase "postmodern prophecy" may seem paradoxical, or even self-negating. However, I do not intend to cultivate paradox for the sake of paradox, a tendency too often charged to postmodernists, and too often correctly. To show how prophecy can be postmodern, and yet prophetic, we need to define the structure and purpose of ancient Hebrew prophecy. As we shall see, while the historical, religious, and ideological conditions of ancient prophecy differed from those of postmodernism, the structure and purpose of prophecy remains constant. I will use the term "prophetic stance" to characterize this common element between Hebrew and postmodern prophecy. This is *not* to suggest that other similarities between Hebrew and postmodern prophecy either do or do not exist. To examine these issues thoroughly would require a much longer article. Rather, I will only attempt to show that the structural similarity between the two traditions of prophecy justifies us in calling the postmodern tradition "prophecy." In the following section, I will address the significant ways in which postmodernism calls forth techniques and types of prophecy that are uniquely postmodern. Clearly, not all postmodern art or theory is prophetic, but we will examine some of the ways in which some postmodern work also assumes the prophetic stance.

Scholarly literature on Hebrew prophecy often refers to an element called "prophetic voice." This voice, however, is much more than just the voice of the prophet. It also includes the social position of the prophet, the mediatory nature of the prophetic vocation (i.e. that the message is not the prophet's own), the performative nature of the prophetic act, and the prophet's attempt to place his or her audience in a position of responsibility for making meaning (interpretation). Because this is a much more complex structure than the term "prophetic voice" suggests, I will here call it "prophetic stance."

The prophet stands, first, as a mediator between God's message and the people. The message is not the prophet's own, but God's. The prophet is often reluctant to bring the message to the people. In fact, the trope (literary commonplace) of the "reluctant sage" aptly describes many of the prophets (Sawyer 1993: 9). The most famous examples, perhaps, are Moses' reluctance to prophesy because of a claimed speech impediment, and Jonah's attempt to flee God, which results in his being thrown overboard at sea and swallowed by a whale. This initial reluctance, however, contrasts sharply with the prophet's subsequent passion and engagement, a feature that David Petersen terms "maximalism" (Petersen 1987: 9). This maximalism reveals itself in both the person and the performance of the prophet.

Scholars of Israelite prophecy often call this quality of the prophet "charisma." However, this term is inadequate for three reasons. First, "charisma" is a Greek term meaning "gifts," and refers especially to spiritual gifts. While some prophets may indeed have possessed some of these gifts (such as speaking in tongues, divination, telepathy, etc.), they were certainly not a primary characteristic of the prophetic vocation. In addition, such gifts are much more characteristic of other religious traditions, such as mysticism. Third, as Abraham Heschel observed, it is "not the fact of having been affected, but the fact of his having received a power to affect others" that most characterizes the prophetic vocation (Heschel 1969: 21). Still, the prophet stands before the people not simply as a messenger, but as a person possessed:

> There an ecstatic man shouted his wild threats among the people; there his speech often was a strange stammering, a marvelous gibberish. And we see how he conducted himself! He collapsed in bitter pain, weeping and wailing about the coming disaster (Ezek. 21:11); he beat his breast and clapped his hands; he wobbled like a drunk; he stood there naked or with a yoke around his neck or madly swinging a sword in his hand (Ezek. 5:1–17; 21:13–22)!
>
> (Gunkel 1987: 25)

The message that causes such contortions in the prophet contains nothing less than the justice and mercy of God. While it is probably true, as Abraham Heschel insists, that the God of the prophets was not the transcendent, immovable God of the Greek philosophers, but a God of concern for humankind and *pathos* toward God's creation, nevertheless, the relationship of the prophet to God was largely one of submission. The prophetic message originates not from the prophet, but from God. In addition, the message refers to a future judgment that likewise imposes a responsibility upon the prophet, and through the prophet, upon the people. In this way, the prophetic role and the prophetic message are open-ended both in source and in goal.

Despite this the prophet roots the prophetic message in the history and traditions of Israel. The prophet's retelling of the salvation history (providence) that led the Israelite nation out of bondage in Egypt and through the wilderness to the Promised Land emphasizes the faithfulness of God to His people, and by contrast, the infidelity of the people to God. Thus, the retelling of the history of the nation sets the stage for the prophet's foretelling of judgment. The prophetic stance is not primarily one of divination (prediction); rather, the prophet's foretelling of judgment works in tandem with the retelling of the salvational events of the past to place the prophet's audience within this divine, providential story. The prophet thereby places the burden upon his audience either to return to God, or to face the consequences.

The prophet calls upon many rhetorical techniques and performance styles (as we noted above) in order to place his audience within this providential history. Through implicating his audience in the story of Israel in this way, the prophet also implicates them in the divine desire for and mission of justice and mercy. This divine mission calls the people to enact in their social and political life the divine ideals of social equity, freedom of the prisoners, and care for the needy and sick. The prophet calls, on behalf of God, the people back to their covenantal relationship and commitment to justice and mercy.

While this is not a comprehensive picture of Israelite prophecy by any means, it is sufficient for present purposes, namely to provide a baseline against which to compare postmodern prophecy. This will enable us both to see in what regard postmodern prophecy is authentically prophetic, and in what ways it is distinctly postmodern.

Prophecy in postmodernism

Having established the structure and purpose of the prophetic stance of the Hebrew prophets, it remains to be seen whether such a structure and purpose persists in the changed conditions of postmodernism, and whether in these conditions it remains prophecy. Certainly, the differences between the social and spiritual conditions of ancient Israel and postmodernity are notable. Postmodernity, in general, rejects the worldview of ancient Israel, with its transcendent deity, monarchical political structures, patriarchal (male-dominated) social systems, slavery, and superstition. However, it is possible that the structure and purpose of the prophetic stance of the Hebrew prophets continues to inform postmodern prophecy, despite these differences.

While very many books and articles on postmodernism begin by rehearsing the difficulty of defining the nature of postmodernism itself, they generally agree on certain important characteristics. As with our defining of the structure of prophecy in the previous section, in order to validate the idea of "postmodern prophecy," we do not require any greater proof of the validity of our terminology than this. It will be enough for the present project if we can show that the general structure of prophecy continues within the conditions of postmodernism.

As we have seen, the role of the prophet is to stand as mediator between God and the people. Postmodern prophecy continues this mediatory role, but within the immanent (this-worldly) conditions of modernism. The modernist rejection of metaphysical absolutes (God, the Good, the One, Truth, Justice, etc.) means that the postmodern prophet can no longer claim divine sanction for his message. So, the question arises: what does the postmodern prophet mediate between? What is the source of authority for the postmodern prophetic message? As I suggested above, the source (God) and goal (the future judgment) of traditional Israelite prophecy remain open. The same can be said of postmodern prophecy.

However, whereas the openness of traditional prophecy resides in the fact of the prophet's appeal to God and to a yet-to-be-determined future, postmodern prophecy remains open by continually disturbing the conventional relationships of author, text, and audience. Piling up reference upon reference to all variety of other texts (multireferentiality); subverting the authorial function by means of pseudonyms and false frames; utilizing aphorisms (short sayings or sections arranged in a seemingly random way), fragments, pastiche; and ignoring traditional canons, genres, and boundaries—in all these ways, postmodern literature attempts to embody or give voice to otherness, to freedom, to the absence of determinate meaning. As we will see in the next section, Bob Dylan utilizes all of these techniques throughout his career and canon.

Like ancient prophecy, the goal of such literary and performative techniques is to place the burden of responsibility for interpretation on the reader. In both the ancient and the postmodern traditions of prophecy, the audience is implicated in the message itself, and called upon to participate in the creation of meaning. In this way, both kinds of prophecy, in their different contexts and different ways, disallow the easy assimilation or consumption of the prophetic message; the meaning of the prophetic message occurs in the response of the people to that message. In this way, both traditions of prophecy give a literary form to freedom.

At the same time, the Israelite prophets rooted their message in the history of Israel, calling the nation to repentance and restoration, as well as to justice and mercy. We can certainly find many examples of postmodern prophecy that similarly root themselves in the past, and emphasize social justice issues. As Fredric Jameson has noted, the mining of history is a common approach of postmodern artists (Jameson 1999: 368), and certainly postmodern philosophers have engaged philosophical history deeply.

Arguably, the single most common feature of postmodern art and theory is its strongly ethical impetus. Most of the literary techniques borrowed or developed by postmodern artists and philosophers serve the ethical concern for the other. And, as with the Israelite prophets, many postmodernists are maximalists in this regard. For example, Luis Buñuel's film, *That Obscure Object of Desire* (dir. Buñuel 1977) places a dysfunctional love story within the context of the wave of terrorist attacks in Europe in the 1970s. And, while we might be tempted to conclude that Buñuel is making a comment on the nature of love or passion by juxtaposing it with the terroristic passion, he utterly undermines any such simple correlations by the end of his movie. Still, while we find it difficult to say exactly what Buñuel's "message" is, we are impressed that there *is* a message. We could say, we have a passion for meaning; and it is this passion—creative and destructive—that Buñuel gives a visual form to.

In these ways, and many more, postmodern prophecy continues the tradition of prophecy within the context of postmodernism. Now we will examine the life and work of Bob Dylan, as an example of postmodern prophecy.

Case study

Bob Dylan: postmodern prophet

> "No, listen: If I wasn't Bob Dylan, I'd probably think that Bob Dylan has a lot of answers myself."
>
> (Rosenbaum's interview with Dylan in 1978, in Cott 2006: 233)

Many commentators have noted the similarities between Dylan's work and ancient Hebrew prophecy (Di Lauro 2005; Rogovoy 2009). However, the literature of "Dylanology" (as writing on Dylan has come to be known, unfortunately) displays a lack of consensus about the nature of these similarities. Commentaries on and reviews of Dylan's work frequently lament the difficulty, if not impossibility, of a consistent analysis of Dylan's work, or even of individual songs (see, e.g. Gray 2000: 154; Smith 2005: 57; Rogovoy 2009: 237). For many interpreters, this difficulty apparently causes a great deal of anxiety, since if Dylan's works are so opaque, it may be that Dylan is serving only his own "private agendas" (Smith 2005: 9), or worse, no agenda at all (see Ricks 2004: 34). But of course, it is assumed, a private or "secret" agenda is no agenda at all, and it is hard to see how Dylan's agenda can be secret if, at the same time, Dylan's songs compel us to conclude that "there must be some agenda" associated with it (see Smith 2005: 32).

In response to this anxiety, Dylanologists often commit the **genetic fallacy** in order to get some kind of interpretive "handle" on Dylan. (The term "handle" comes from Ricks 2004: 1–6; for other examples of a developmental interpretation of Dylan's work, see Bell 2000; Smith 2005: 67–68; Marqusee 2003: 119, 281.) However, where one commentator remarks that "it's always a mistake to treat Dylan's lyrics as part of an autobiographical roman à clef" (Marqusee 2003: 114), another just as confidently asserts that even when Dylan's lyrics leave Dylan the artist out of account, Dylan the artist—his biography—still accompanies the text (Gray 2000: 140). Such biographical, developmental interpretations commit a number of errors: they attempt to explain Dylan's work by reducing it to a pre-conceived pattern ("stages," or "phases," and other intuitively applicable, but inaccurate, terms); they mistake the story of a text's production with an analysis of the text; and they view this development as teleological. This kind of reductive interpretation gives us the illusion of having a "handle" on Dylan, without having actually to engage Dylan at all.

This characteristic of Dylan's work—that, as Michael Gray says vis à vis "Visions of Johanna," it is "hard to say what the song is 'about' and yet it impresses us as saying a good deal" (Gray 2000: 154)—reveals itself in individual songs, in

Dylan's canon as a whole, and in the relationship between Dylan's art and his life (see Lebold 2007: 60). This dual enticement to and defiance of interpretation, as I have argued, is a chief characteristic of postmodern art, and we find it in every aspect of Dylan's art and life.

For example, the stylistic diversity of Dylan's work challenges the accepted canons of aesthetics and interpretation, thereby undermining any attempt to categorize (and thereby, to evade responsibility for interpreting) his work. Dylan has never let himself be hemmed in by any preconceived genre or style limitations. This is not to say that he eschews given traditions of genre or style; rather, he utilizes a very broad palette of styles, even in the body of a single song. Dylan's songs are at once multi-referential (see Marqusee 2003: 140–141), and self-referential (in reference to "Like a Rolling Stone, see Marqusee 2003: 165; Bell 2000: 114). As Paul Davies says, Dylan's "performance is the axis of so many media which critical orthodoxy used to segregate" (Davies 1990: 162). For example, Christophe Lebold provides a wonderful elaboration of "It's All Over Now, Baby Blue," revealing the use of invective, narration, aphorism, inversions and subversions, what he calls "open structure" (Lebold 2007: 60–61), and many other techniques to entice the audience to interpret the song and to subvert such interpretations at the same time.

In part, we can explain Dylan's seemingly cavalier attitude toward recognized aesthetic boundaries as evidence of his roots in the folk and blues traditions. These traditions, like the prophetic tradition, are not closed canons, but develop by a complex combination of sharing, teaching, borrowing, and outright stealing. Of course, the irony of such a "tradition" is that in upholding continuing creativity, it encourages a kind of syncretism that brings in elements that are not consistent with previous practice. Thus, the tradition of such folk traditions is self-subversive: the "weirdness" (Greil Marcus' wonderful term for the strain of radical eccentricity and defiance of conventions within the American folk and blues traditions) that it can contain is seemingly boundless (see Marcus 1997).

Within each of these developing canons—prophecy and Dylan's corpus—the diversity of genres combines with a diversity of performance styles. As I mentioned above, the prophets of old spoke, cried out, whispered, orated, cajoled, pontificated, judged, called to account, *performed*. In the same way, we seriously misuse Dylan's work if we merely read it, rather than hear it (or better, see and hear it) performed. As Janet Gezari says, to read Dylan rightly, one would have "to whine, cajole, seduce, admire, thank, despise, disdain, put down, put up with, exhort, and much much more" (Gezari 2001: 481). In this sense, a song (or at least, a Dylan song) is, as Christophe Lebold writes, a "hyper-literary object" (Lebold 2007: 60). Lebold warns us against separating the lyrics from the music, separating these from the performances, or separating any or all of these from Dylan's serial creation of literary and actual personae (Lebold 2007: 60).

Indeed, we might say that Dylan's literary and oratorical virtuosity is but the manifestation of a more encompassing aspect of his craft and person, namely his "chameleon-like" propensity and ability to assume various guises and personae (Rogovoy 2009: 224). This perspectivism has as its most obvious form the periodic and very public reinventions of himself and his art. For example, in his early years (the early to mid-1960s), Dylan created a persona by using pseudonyms, by creating a working-class and itinerant biography, by the channeling of Woody Guthrie, and by his apparent advocacy of progressive politics. This persona gave many people within the folk and protest movements the illusion that Dylan was "theirs." Dylan's inhabitation of this persona, however, was always riven with disparate elements, influences, and anomalies. Thus, it is problematic to view his move to electric rock, rock dandyism, and introspective lyrics as either a betrayal (as it was viewed at the time, the famous cry of "Judas!" from an audience member at the famed "Royal Albert Hall" performance in 1966 being the most memorable and succinct statement of this feeling) or a progression. Each of Dylan's serial personae has its own integrity. He does not merely superficially or inauthentically believe in "anything," but engages each thing at a deep level, living through it fully before moving on. In this sense, Marqusee is correct when he says that Dylan's "refusal to believe in anything for very long goes hand in hand with a willingness to believe, momentarily, in almost anything" (Marqusee 2003: 328). This should not be taken to mean that Dylan is unserious, flighty, or fickle; rather, Dylan's serial assumption of personae (in song and in life) is integral to his overall program of subversion.

Dylan's work and life display a kind of perspectivism in which every perspective is valid, from its side. The artist assumes each perspective in turn, and lives through it, adheres to its limits, examines its possibilities, not merely expeditiously (for kicks, or for the systematic derangement of the senses, or for money and fame), but purposefully. As Lebold says, Dylan's personae provide entertainment value, but they also have "real metaphysical and moral purposes" (Lebold 2007: 68). Such perspectivism is both dalliance (artistic "play") and serious; it subverts the common notion of and distinction between play and seriousness. In this way, the openness to different perspectives becomes the very "message" of the work. Perspectivism and openness are no mere techniques; they are the very working out of the message itself. Such perspectivism serves Dylan as a means of indirection, of disturbing any simple correlations between the life of the artist and the work of art. As Dylan himself has said, "the songs are the star of the show, not me" (Hilburn, in Cott 2006: 431).

Therefore, Dylan's work as a whole (his lyrics, music, voice, performances, and persona) produce a constant and ongoing self-subversion. As Lebold puts it, "Dylan attains an elusive and protean identity," a "palimpsest of identities" (Lebold 2007: 66). Unfortunately, Lebold does not draw the full implications of his own insight. If Dylan is truly engaged in "the permanent constructing and deconstructing of himself" (Lebold 2007: 63), then there is by definition no permanence, no identity. Or, perhaps, identity is nothing more or less than the constant play with identities.

Like the prophets of old, Dylan removes himself in order to let his words and music confront his audience. In this confrontation, the audience members are not passive recipients of a pre-digested message; Dylan directly assaults the consumerist model of popular culture. In the process, he puts the burden of freedom on his audience members—on each individual audience member. However, since freedom is nothing if not free, how each person assumes this task cannot be predetermined. In this way, Dylan acts as a prophet within and to postmodernity, reminding us of the covenant with "weirdness" that is our heritage, and of the challenges of transformation that that heritage entails.

Summary

- Postmodern prophecy continues the tradition of ancient Israelite prophecy within the conditions of the postmodern.
- Whereas Israelite prophecy assumed a transcendent God and a providential history that would culminate in a future judgment, postmodern prophecy disavows this religious and historical context.
- Nevertheless, postmodern artistic techniques of subversion often serve a similar purpose: to place the burden of responsibility on the audience, to prevent the audience from evading that responsibility.
- In this way, ancient and postmodern prophecy both attempt to engage the audience in the act of creation.

Glossary terms

Genetic fallacy – the attempt to explain the work of an artist by reference to the artist's biography and development, or by reference to the genesis of the work itself. The genetic fallacy is often viewed as an evasion of the responsibility for meaning that a text imposes on the reader. Thus, it is the favorite refuge of uncreative critics.

Interpretive closure – the attempt to find a complete, satisfactory, or final explanation of a text. Postmodern texts in particular deliberately attempt to undermine such an attempt.

Points for discussion

- Some forms of postmodern prophecy eliminate the transcendent referent, God, common in ancient forms of prophecy. How can ancient prophecy, which assumes this and other supernatural beings and events, be translated into contemporary concepts and practices, given modern culture's suspicion of the supernatural?
- If openness, indeterminateness, and self-subversion characterize (postmodern) prophecy, how can we even speak of prophecy as a tradition? How can prophecy have the kind of continuity that a tradition, presumably, must have? How can we assess whether Dylan and his work fit within such a tradition?

Further reading, viewing, and listening

Dylan, Bob (2004) *Chronicles, Vol. 1*, New York: Simon and Schuster.
Hajdu, D. (2001) *Positively 4th Street*, New York: Farrar, Straus, and Giroux.

Marcus, G. (1997) *Invisible Republic: Bob Dylan's Basement Tapes*, New York: Henry Holt.

Marcus, G. (2006) *Like a Rolling Stone: Bob Dylan at the Crossroads*, New York: Public Affairs.

Wilentz, S. (2010) *Bob Dylan in America*, New York: Doubleday.

I'm Not There (2007) dir. Todd Haynes, New York: Killer Films.

Masked and Anonymous (2003) dir. Larry Charles, London: BBC Films.

Bibliography

Bell, R.H. (2000) "Double Dylan," *Popular Music and Society*, 24 (2), Summer, 109–126.

Cott, J. (2006) *Bob Dylan: The Essential Interviews*, New York: Wenner Books.

Davies, Paul (1990) "'There's no success like failure': From Rags to Riches in the Lyrics of Bob Dylan," in *The Yearbook of English Studies* 20, Literature in the Modern Media: Radio, Film, and Television Special Number, London: Modern Humanities Research Association, 162–181.

Di Lauro, F. (2005) "Living in the End Times: the Prophetic Language of Bob Dylan," in *The Buddha of Suburbia: Proceedings of the Eighth Australian and International Religion, Literature and the Arts Conference 2004*, Sydney Studies in Religion [Electronic], online. Available HTTP: http://hdl.handle.net/2123/1253 (accessed 6 January 2011).

Gezari, J. (2001) "Bob Dylan and the Tone behind the Language," *Southwest Review* 86:4: 480–499.

Gray, M. (2000) *Song and Dance Man III: The Art of Bob Dylan*, New York: Continuum.

Gunkel, H. (1987) "The Prophets as Writers and Poets," in Petersen, D.L. (ed.) *Prophecy in Israel*, Philadelphia, PA: Fortress Press, 22–73.

Heschel, A. (1969) *The Prophets, Vol. 1*, New York: Harper & Row.

Jameson, F. (1999) *Postmodernism, or The Cultural Logic of Late Capitalism*, Durham: Duke University Press.

Lebold, C. (2007) "A Face like a Mask and a Voice that Croaks: An Integrated Poetics of Bob Dylan's Voice, Personae, and Lyrics," *Oral Tradition*, 22 (1): 57–70.

Marcus, G. (1997) *Invisible Republic: Bob Dylan's Basement Tapes*, New York: Henry Holt.

——(2006) *Like a Rolling Stone: Bob Dylan at the Crossroads*, New York: Public Affairs.

Marqusee, M. (2003) *Wicked Messenger: Bob Dylan and the 1960s*, New York: Seven Stories Press.

Petersen, D.L. (ed.) (1987) *Prophecy in Israel*, Philadelphia, PA: Fortress Press.

Ricks, C. (2004) *Dylan's Visions of Sin*, New York: HarperCollins.

Rogovoy, Seth (2009) *Bob Dylan: Prophet, Mystic, Poet*, New York: Scribner.

Sawyer, John F.A. (1993) *Prophecy and the Biblical Prophets*, Oxford: Oxford University Press.

Smith, L.D. (2005) *Writing Dylan: The Songs of a Lonesome Traveler*, Westport, CT and London: Praeger Publishers.

Index

THE BIBLE
AND
AMERICAN CULTURE